REHEARSALS OF DISCOMPOSURE

REHEARSALS OF DISCOMPOSURE

*Alienation and Reconciliation in
Modern Literature: Franz Kafka,
Ignazio Silone, D. H. Lawrence,
T. S. Eliot*

by Nathan A. Scott, Jr.

KING'S CROWN PRESS

Columbia University, New York

COPYRIGHT © 1952 BY NATHAN A. SCOTT, JR.

First printing 1952
Second printing 1958

*King's Crown Press is a subsidiary imprint of
Columbia University Press established for the
purpose of making certain scholarly material
available at minimum cost. Toward that end, the
publishers have adopted every reasonable economy
except such as would interfere with a legible format.
The work is presented substantially as submitted by
the author, without the usual editorial and
typographical attention of Columbia University
Press.*

PUBLISHED IN GREAT BRITAIN BY JOHN LEHMANN, LTD.

MANUFACTURED IN THE UNITED STATES OF AMERICA

For the three to whom my debt is immeasurable—

MY MOTHER AND FATHER

AND MY WIFE CHARLOTTE

The times of spiritual history in which anthropological thought has so far found its depth of experience have been those very times in which a feeling of strict and inescapable solitude took possession of man; and it was the most solitary man in whom the thought became fruitful. In the ice of solitude man becomes most inexorably a question to himself, and just because the question pitilessly summons and draws into play his most secret life he becomes an experience to himself.

—Martin Buber, *Between Man and Man*

art becomes exile too,
A secret and a code studied in secret,
Declaring the agony of modern life.
The child will learn of life from these great
    men.
He will participate in their solitude,
And maybe in the end, on such a night
As this, return to the starting-point, his name,
Showing himself as such among his friends.

—Delmore Schwartz, *Shenandoah*

PREFACE

THIS IMPERFECT and fearfully taken excursus is the result of a fairly continuous, if too frequently desultory, reading in theology and literature over the past several years, which issued finally in the desire to set down in some systematic fashion a personal experience of certain contemporary interrelations between the two subject matters. The result is a kind of "ambiguity" of which Mr. Empson might, conceivably, not approve, for this essay belongs to a *genre* which, being based on analyses of literature yet not being *criticism* in the strict sense, has on occasion been an object of disapproval in contemporary criticism. And yet we continue to feel the necessity of dealing, through literature, with certain subjects which are larger than and extend beyond the order of purely aesthetic questions which is, presumably, the domain of literary criticism. There are, in other words, other things to be done and said in relation to imaginative literature than the correction of taste and the performance of those acts of discrimination among the formal elements of literary works of art which go to make up the critic's function, as it is now usually understood; and if this type of work cannot lay claim to the fullest significance for *aesthetic* discussion, it may yet have an *existential* validity. That is to say, it may have a certain rightness that derives from the legitimacy of our seeking a deeper understanding of our world and of ourselves through a careful reading of the representative literature of our time. And let me rush on to say that we are enabled to do this because literature is not merely "significant form." It is, of course, that too, among other things, but it is also something more: it is, fundamentally, a response to experience. But I do not, of course, want at this point to invoke the old

distinction between form and content, whose inutility we have
long since come to acknowledge. We have come to recognize, for
example, that there is a dimension of form, if for a moment it
may be abstracted out of its organic relation to content, which is
itself a response to experience. But when an important work of
literary art is considered as an integral, self-subsisting organic
structure, it is, I think, apprehended, first and last, as a response
to experience that is expressive of a coherent, if not systematically
articulated, vision of human life. And it is in the light of this
basic presupposition that I have tried to characterize certain
contemporary writers (about whom, I should say, with the exception of Silone, a good deal has been written before) in their relation to the spiritual problem which is the subject of this book.

I should like to define my *genre* by way of saying that these
pages constitute an essay in philosophical anthropology, but I
fear that that old and dignified term no longer conveys very
much to modern readers, and even those few who have some notion as to its true meaning might want to cavil about the appropriateness of its application to an essay dealing with poets and
novelists. It is not strange, of course, that this term should have
lost its meaning for our contemporaries and that the term "anthropology," which once designated that aspect of philosophic
inquiry concerned with "the doctrine of man," is now affixed to
investigations of primitive society, for modern philosophy, as
every sophomore can realize after taking "Phil. I," has only rarely
yielded synoptic studies of the nature of man. Its focus has rather
been on logic and epistemology, and the language of an Augustine or a Pascal or an Unamuno has fallen with disconcerting and
enigmatic effect upon the ears of our modern schoolmen.

I recall having luncheon one day many months ago with two
friends—one, a young academic, a professional philosopher, and
the other, an executive in a prominent New York social-welfare

agency. We had been talking about suicide, just after a prominent public man had taken his life, when my second friend suddenly asked the first what contemporary philosophy had to say on
this dark and obscure facet of human experience. My philoso-
pher-friend was so obviously taken aback at this naive query from
an uninstructed layman that his innate good manners almost
failed to conceal his amusement at the question. He did make
a half-hearted attempt to recall Durkheim's work on the subject
and referred his questioner to the textbooks of Freudian psychology and the Paris existentialists, but finally admitted that
such a question had, of course, not been a subject of serious philosophic discussion in recent times. And he was clearly con-
founded by another's failing to recognize the incongruity between such a problem—which at most would be the concern only
of an actuarial statistician—and the real business of philosophy.
Thus did this brilliant young logician provide a striking instance
of a whole state of mind among modern academic intellectuals,
for modern philosophy has generally sought to evade the ultimate
precariousness of the human situation through the exploration of
the endless complexities of phenomenal existences as they make
their impact upon the human consciousness in the purely logical
and epistemological question. And the result has been that the
urgency of the human predicament, as it reveals itself in the
existential terms of contingency and anxiety, guilt and suffering,
love and despair, isolation and death, has been ignored. This conspiratorial silence over the human tragedy which has been the
main earmark of the academic tradition was, of course, broken
by Kierkegaard and Nietzsche, Bergson and Max Scheler,
Chestov and Unamuno, and, in our time, has been shattered not
only by Heidegger and Sartre in secular terms but also by those
men in whom the Christian tradition has authentically maintained itself—by Berdyaev and Barth, Przywara and Maritain,

Tillich and Niebuhr. But these figures have, on the whole, been
forced to live on the periphery of our official intellectual life and
are perhaps only now beginning to exert a decisive influence on a
nascent *Zeitgeist*, the large outlines of which are yet not too
clearly distinguishable.

The conveyance of self-knowledge has, then, been a task which
has been pre-empted by the modern artist, of whose spiritual
visage, in the realm of literature, I have taken here Kafka, Silone,
Lawrence, and Eliot as outstanding prototypes, for they compose
our human scene in dark colors and sombre tones in accordance
with a deep sensibility to what Mallarmé, over the tomb of Verlaine, spoke of as the *"triste honneur de l'isolement"* ("the sad
honor of isolation"). On the occasion of this tribute to Verlaine,
Mallarmé declared: *"La solitude, le froid, l'inélégance et la
pénurie. . .d'ordinaire composent le sort qu'encourt l'enfant avec
son ingénue audace marchant en l'existence selon sa divinité."*
("Solitude, cold, homeliness and poverty usually compose the
fate which the child undergoes with his ingenuous boldness
walking in life according to his divinity.") [1] And this sentence
might well be taken as a definitive expression of the conclusion
to which the modern writer, in his exploration of the human condition, has been led. He has discovered that self-recognition is a
point at which one arrives only by the acceptance of a tragic sense
of life, by the acceptance of existence as separation, as isolation
and estrangement—and this vision has related to him the soul's
anguish over its finitude and contingency.

This renewal of concern about the nature of man which has
taken place, outside the confines of academic philosophy, among
poets and novelists has been accompanied and, in large measure,
prompted by the crisis of modern civilization, in relation to which
all things of the spirit in these past years have taken their form.
But these writers have not merely been journalists giving prosaic

reports on social and political dislocation, for their experience
of the insecurities of the modern world has been deepened into
an experience of a more perennial and a more ultimate dimension
of human insecurity from which there is no escape. They have
tended increasingly to spell this basic intuition out in terms of a
metaphysic of alienation or estrangement, and it is with certain
representative statements on this theme of spiritual isolation that
I am concerned in this essay, for I believe them to contain insights into the nature of man which must be taken up into any
philosophical anthropology that is to be relevant for our period.

I am greatly indebted to many of my former teachers on the
faculties of Union Theological Seminary and Columbia University for the warm encouragement and patient guidance which they
so generously gave to me at many crucial points during the period
when this study was being written. For their kindness I shall
always remain grateful. A portion of the manuscript has been
saved from many stylistic faults by the searching eye turned upon
it by my colleague, Professor Virginia W. Callahan of the Clas-
sics Department of Howard University. And my wife, Charlotte
Hanley Scott, was in this, as in all things, the loyal partner and
very "heart of grace" without whom that which was begun might
never have been completed.

N. A. S., Jr.

Howard University
December, 1951

ACKNOWLEDGMENTS

THE AUTHOR is indebted to the following publishers and authors for permission to quote copyrighted material from their publications: Mrs. Dorothy S. Norman (Franz Kafka, "Letter to My Father," A *Franz Kafka Miscellany: Pre-Fascist Exile*, published by Twice A Year Press); Vanguard Press, Inc. (Paul Goodman, *Kafka's Prayer*; Franz Kafka, *Metamorphosis*); Schocken Books, Inc. (Max Brod, *Franz Kafka: a Biography*; Franz Kafka, *The Great Wall of China, Parables*); Alfred A. Knopf, Inc. (Franz Kafka, *The Trial*); Harper and Brothers (Ignazio Silone, *The Seed Beneath the Snow, Bread and Wine, And He Hid Himself*; Amos Wilder, *The Spiritual Aspects of the New Poetry*); Harcourt, Brace and Co. (T. S. Eliot, *Collected Poems: 1909–1935, Murder in the Cathedral, The Family Reunion, Four Quartets, The Idea of a Christian Society, Selected Essays: 1917–1932*; Denis de Rougemont, *Love in the Western World*); Random House (W. H. Auden, *Collected Poetry*; Ignazio Silone, *Fontamara*); R. P. Blackmur (*The Double Agent: Essays in Craft and Elucidation*); Macmillan and Co. (Martin Buber, *Between Man and Man*); Columbia University Press (William York Tindall, *D. H. Lawrence and Susan His Cow*); Oxford University Press (F. O. Matthiessen, *The Achievement of T. S. Eliot*); University of North Carolina Press (Cleanth Brooks, *Modern Poetry and the Tradition*); Allen and Unwin Ltd. (Jacob Burckhardt, *The Civilization of the Renaissance in Italy*; D. G. James *Scepticism and Poetry*); S.P.C.K. House (Brother George Every, *Christian Discrimination*); Chatto and Windus (H. J. C. Grierson, *The Background of English Literature*); W. W. Norton and Co. (Irwin Edman, *Arts and the Man*); Farrar, Straus and Young, Inc.

(Harry Slochower, *No Voice Is Wholly Lost*); Sheed and Ward (Wallace Fowlie, *Jacob's Night: The Religious Renascence in France*; Sister Mary James Power, *Poets at Prayer*; Jacques Maritain, *The Twilight of Civilization*); Charles Scribner's Sons (Henry P. Van Dusen, ed., *The Christian Answer*; Reinhold Niebuhr, *Discerning the Signs of the Times*; Louise Bogan, *The Sleeping Fury*); Princeton University Press (Sören Kierkegaard, *Fear and Trembling*; Joseph Bennett, *Baudelaire: a Criticism*); Yale University Press (Herbert Tauber, *Franz Kafka: an Interpretation of His Works*); D. S. Savage (*The Personal Principle: Studies in Modern Poetry*); John Middleton Murry (*Adam and Eve: an Essay Toward a New and Better Society*); Faber and Faber Ltd. (Herbert Read, *Art and Society*); Rinehart and Co., Inc. (Erich Fromm, *Escape from Freedom*); T. and T. Clark (Martin Buber, *I and Thou*); Henry Holt and Co. (Henri Bergson, *The Two Sources of Morality and Religion*); the Viking Press (Max Lerner, *Ideas for the Ice Age*; *The Portable D. H. Lawrence*, ed. by Diana Trilling; *The Letters of D. H. Lawrence*, ed. by Aldous Huxley; D. H. Lawrence, *Aaron's Rod, Studies in Classic American Literature, Fantasia of the Unconscious, Psychoanalysis and the Unconscious, Sons and Lovers, The Rainbow, Women in Love*; Malcolm Cowley, *Exile's Return*); Cambridge University Press (J. S. Whale, *Christian Doctrine*); John Lehmann Ltd. (David Gascoyne, *Poems 1937–1942*); Leonard Unger and Louis L. Martz (Louis L. Martz, "The Wheel and the Point: Aspects of Imagery and Theme in Eliot's Later Poetry," *T. S. Eliot: a Selected Critique*, ed. by Leonard Unger); New Directions (Delmore Schwartz, *Shenandoah*; Franz Kafka, "The Judgment," trans. by Rosa M. Beuscher); Jonathan Cape (Stephen Spender, *The Destructive Element*; John Middleton Murry, *Son of Woman*); H. T. Mason, Centaur Books (D. H. Lawrence, *Reflections on the Death of a Porcupine*); Eliseo Vivas ("Kafka's Distorted Mask," *The Kenyon Review*, Vol. X, No. 1, Winter, 1948); and Philip Rahv ("The Hero as Lonely Man," *The Kenyon Review*, Vol. I, No. 1, Winter, 1939).

The author is further indebted to the editors of the following periodicals for permission to quote material which is fully listed in the bibliography and notes: *Accent, Focus One, Focus Two, Focus Three, The Kenyon Review*, and *The Sewanee Review*.

CONTENTS

INTRODUCTION 1

FRANZ KAFKA: THE SENSE OF COSMIC EXILE 11

IGNAZIO SILONE: NOVELIST OF THE REVOLUTIONARY
SENSIBILITY 66

D. H. LAWRENCE: CHARTIST OF THE *Via Mystica* 112

T. S. ELIOT: A CONTEMPORARY SYNTHESIS 178

CONCLUSION 246

NOTES 263

SELECTED BIBLIOGRAPHY 273

INDEX 289

INTRODUCTION

I am no part of a whole, I am not integrated, not included.—Sören Kierkegaard

The terror of which I write is not of Germany, but of the soul.—Edgar Allan Poe

Naked and alone we came into exile. In her dark womb we did not know our mother's face; from the prison of her flesh have we come into the unspeakable and incommunicable prison of this earth. Which of us has known his brother? Which of us has looked into his father's heart? . . . Which of us is not forever a stranger and alone?—Thomas Wolfe

THESE WORDS from Kierkegaard, Poe, and Thomas Wolfe mark the clue and the lineament of one of the most compelling traditions of sensibility in contemporary literature—one which is perhaps best identified by the terms *isolation, estrangement, alienation,* and one which has engaged some of the most interesting and sensitive talents in our recent literary history. Even the most cursory catalogue of representative monuments of recent expression—which might include Kafka's *The Castle,* Graham Greene's *Brighton Rock,* Djuna Barnes's *Nightwood,* Sartre's *No Exit,* and W. H. Auden's *The Age of Anxiety*—immediately reveals, beyond all differences of style and *genre,* an underlying unity of temperament and experience which is consistently organized into a description of the contemporary tragedy in terms of dereliction and estrangement and exile, not in terms of an alienation within a stable world, but in a world where "things fall apart," where "the centre" does not "hold" (the phrase is W. B. Yeats's), where man's deepest tension is not social or economic but an *angoisse métaphysique.*

These writers write not out of the innocence of the child who is amazed that the world is as evil as it is but out of a deeply tragic perception of the dissonance and incoherence in contemporary life. They are children of an age whose moral physiognomy has been shaped by "wars and rumors of wars," by demonic hierarchies of power and wickedness in high places, and of an age which has had to deal with such catastrophe in the face of the disintegration of its traditional faiths. They are men who have been nourished by Pascal and Kierkegaard, by Baudelaire and Spengler and Freud, rather than by the great exponents of Liberalism. And finally, they are men for whom faith is largely a dilemma rather than an unquestioned principle of orthodoxy.

I propose, within the compass of this essay, to examine certain representative statements of three dimensions of this sensibility, in which various definitions are given of what it means to live *apart* in the modern world. On one level, it seems to me, the experience is of an isolation that is _absolute_ and expresses itself in terms of what Harry Slochower has called a sense of "cosmic exile," the seriousness of which frequently hovers precariously on the verge of nihilism. This is the dimension of Kafka and Sartre, of William Faulkner and Robert Penn Warren. On another level, the estrangement is _relational,_ and gains expression in an agonizing sense of isolation from the modern community; and this is the realm of Ignazio Silone and André Malraux, of George Orwell and Rex Warner, of Hemingway and Dos Passos. A third level is somewhat less amenable to swift characterization: here the experience is of what might be called the structural discontinuities between persons, which are the result of man's finitude. It is the *ontological* solitude of man which gives rise to melancholy, the fact that I am I and you are you, and we are *ontologically* discrete factors between whom there is finally void and separateness. It is the experience out of which came the line from one of Mallarmé's most famous poems, *"We were two: I maintain it."* This is, of course, an awareness that runs perennially through the history of literature, but the special feeling of the contemporary mind about this matter is something that is peculiarly its own, for, where life itself is looked upon as a hospital, this permanent aspect of man's condition is felt to be heightened and intensified by the pervasive illness of our age. This, it seems to me, is the standpoint occupied by such figures, in other ways so diverse, as D. H. Lawrence, Proust, Rilke, and Thomas Wolfe. Now, of course, it must be granted that in the work of practically all these writers these three types of emphasis are interwoven, but, nevertheless, in the work of each a central thematic configuration is apparent which we are, I think, justified in stressing.

So then Kafka, Silone, and Lawrence will be our subjects, the work of each being organized in terms of these respective frames of reference, which are, I say again, by no means altogether adequate enclosures of these men but which are yet provisionally and partially valid contextual schemes in so far as they emphasize their typicality. And finally, the essay concludes with an analysis of the work of T. S. Eliot, whose centrality in the present situation has now to be argued not at all and who, in the period of his development extending from *Prufrock* through *The Hollow Men*, formulated an unusually comprehensive statement of the contemporary experience of estrangement and isolation in all its various aspects, but who, in his later phase, extending from *Ash Wednesday* through *The Cocktail Party*, has organized what is unquestionably the most controversial and what is, in my view, the most complete strategy of reconciliation in recent literature.

The interesting and provocative studies by many recent critics
of the relation between tradition and the individual talent suggest the importance of placing this body of literature in the
perspective of spiritual history. And when this is done, it may
be seen that the contemporary literature of estrangement is
not primarily a descendant of that strain of melancholy running throughout the nineteenth century which includes Leopardi, Vigny, Leconte de Lisle, Matthew Arnold, and Lord
Tennyson—a melancholy which is the expression of a profoundly felt alienation from nature brought about by the
mechanistic interpretation of the universe by a scientific materialism—although this special form of disconsolateness does,
to some extent, survive among writers of the twentieth century,
especially among the poets, and is clearly embodied in Yeats,
for example, whose work reveals the extent to which the cleavage
between the artist's sensibility and the theoretical knowledge
of his age continues to be a factor with which we must reckon.
Nor is the sensibility, of which this body of writing is an expression, essentially a descendant of that romantic medieval nostalgia which extends back into the end of the eighteenth century
and which received forceful expression in the nineteenth century in the work of Sir Walter Scott and Victor Hugo. It belongs rather to that tradition in modern literature which begins
with Poe and his influence on Baudelaire, Rimbaud, and *les
symbolistes*, and which receives contemporary formulation, in
prose and poetry, in the work of a group of highly significant
writers, some of whom I have already mentioned.

As Edmund Wilson has reminded us in his celebrated essay
"Axel and Rimbaud," the characteristic proclivity of the Symbolists toward the private joke, the obscure innuendo rather than
the plain statement, and the intensely personal point of view
announced a fundamental dislocation of the modern writer
from his civilization which has ever since been the basic datum

of a main segment of modern literature. And neither the categories of Bohemianism nor of Vigny's "ivory tower," which have been variously used by students of the history of thought to comprehend this phenomenon, lead us to the crux of the problem here, for both principles of explanation suggest, by implication at least, that it is the eccentricity of the modern writer's ego or the deliberate preciosity of his way of life which has been the cause of his isolation—when, really, these have been merely symptomatic not of the modern writer's psychic abnormalities but of a state of tragic disorganization and breakdown within the structure of modern civilization. The fact is, as Henry James was telling us here in America many years ago, that the basic impulses of modern industrial society have been toward a way of life and a hierarchy of values which have robbed the life of the spirit, the life of the mind, of its traditional dignity and usefulness to the community. The tyrannizing of Sinclair Lewis's Main Street and Zenith over men of sensibility in our time may, of course, by now have been remarked upon *ad nauseam*, and yet it remains one of the fundamental explanations of the fact that a Valéry and a Kafka and a Lawrence, to mention representative cases, have not borne the same relationship to the modern community as did the Greek tragedians to Periclean Athens or as did Shakespeare and Jonson to Elizabethan England. Our business, our industry, our economics, have been so absolutized, have been made so autonomous, have been so radically divorced from the spiritually creative forces of modern culture that the man who *imagines* and has *visions* has come to be looked upon as freakish and effeminate and superfluous to the major operations of our common life. This whole process of atomization within the modern community has been comprehended by religious critics of culture as of one and the same piece with the more general problem of modern secularism. They—and I have in mind such critics as Niebuhr, Maritain, V. A. Demant, and Berdyaev—suggest that our declivity proceeds from the disintegration of the medieval *corpus Christianum* and the rise of those new enthusiasms for the autonomous, self-sufficient, "reasonable" individual, which are subsumed under the term *Renaissance*. They point to the absence of a unitive spiritual force in our recent cultural history as being the basic reason for the cleft between the practical reason and the imagination in modern times. And I think the logic involved in this kind of analysis has a good deal of force, but however one takes the strictures of a Maritain or a Berdyaev, the fact remains of the isolation and estrangement from modern society that have been felt by the main body of modern artists. The broad majority of men acknowledges, without especial regret, and the creative minority, with profound grief, that the system of our common life has rarely valued very highly the works of the mind or of the spirit. Thus Baudelaire's *L'Étranger* and those restless cosmopolites who inhabit the bleak international world of Henry James, Conrad's Lord Jim and Kafka's "isolatoes," Gide's Michel and Auden's Airman, Camus's Meursault and many of the heroes of modern literature live in a solitude that is at once an extension of their creators' condition—and, more tellingly, a dismal portrait of *la condition humaine* in its ultimate contemporary aspect.

And here we approach the nub of the matter. On the one hand, the modern writer has known himself, as an artist, as a man of sensibility, to be at odds with the whole polity of modern society; he has felt himself to be an alien, a stranger, "no part of a whole . . . not integrated, not included"—not included because the presuppositions of his society in no fundamental way validated his existence as a bearer of culture, even when he belonged to a W.P.A. writers' project or a national academy. He has known himself to be, in the words of Tiutchev,

living in "an hour of wordless longing . . . without home, orphaned, alone." This dimension of his alienation has, of course,
been given classic formulation by Thomas Mann in his great
story *Tonio Kröger* and must certainly in part be explanatory
of the phenomenon with which we have by now become familiar
—the search for a country, that has driven Rimbaud, Henry
James, Eliot, Mann, and Auden from one continent to another.

But, on the other hand, the men of profoundest vision have
been, more and more, inhabiting their solitude as artists-in-exile
so creatively as to apprehend their alienation as not merely
a matter of aesthetic perspective but as the real condition of
contemporary man in the broad inarticulate mass. In the years
between the wars, our generation, as Professor George Sabine
has said,[1] having inherited not the world of John Dewey but
that of Nietzsche, the artist's "estrangement" has become no
longer a phenomenon unique but rather something shared. The
writers who seem to bring most to us today are those who recognize this fact and who, when they write of their own lostness,
so universalize their individual experience as to project a fundamental and radical criticism of contemporary history, thus using their own ambivalence as a platform from which to achieve
a new synthesis with the human enterprise. Those who have
failed to achieve this transcension (to use the terms of the
Kierkegaardian schematization) from the aesthetic to the ethical
and finally to the metaphysical or the religious are those who
no longer seem to have anything of compelling significance to
say to us.

This is, I think, why such a man as Sherwood Anderson, who,
in the twentieth century, was one of the first to organize and
formulate this tradition of modern sensibility for the American
writer, no longer seems to belong significantly to the texture of
contemporary experience. His story is a familiar one. We know

of his abdication in middle age from his respectable, commercial existence as the manager of a paint factory in Elyria, Ohio, in order to devote himself with singlemindedness to the practice of literature and truth in spiritual exile from the American community. And we know those too intense, too sincere stories of loneliness which kept somehow coming from his nervous pen for the twenty years that remained until his death in 1941, all of which seem to be dramatizing little more than the moment of his expressed valediction to Philistia. Indeed Anderson, it seems, never left off asking us to believe in his private sensibility, in the pathos of his own loneliness, in his personal tragedy. And this particular kind of failure of the moral imagination is, of course, characteristic not only of Anderson but of a minor tradition in modern writing.

If the contemporary writer is to recover his poise, so limited a vision is not enough. If his conception of what it means to live *apart* in the modern world is to comprehend human existence as having a more ultimate dimension than that of pathos, he must get beyond the mere preoccupation with the somersaults of his own ego, for the reinstatement of a genuinely tragic acceptance of life (which was, of course, the beginning of moral responsibility for the Greeks as well as for the Christians) must rest at last not alone on a sense of one's individual isolation but on a sense of membership in a community of men who are estranged—who are estranged from the best in their cultural traditions, from themselves, and finally from that immanent *logos* within the human heart which is Love and in the power of which man's alienation can alone be transcended. When our ambivalence is thus finally comprehended not from the standpoint of the defections of bourgeois society but rather from the standpoint of a certain tragic defect in the human faculty, it becomes possible for our poets and novelists to achieve some sense of man as Man, and thereby to give us a presentiment of abiding values beyond the aeon's despair, to reproduce the aeon's declivity not only in profile but also in depth.

The conviction that informs the following pages is that those writers who have succeeded in achieving this kind of vantage point over their purely individual isolation as artists, through the recognition that theirs is only a special aspect of the collectivity of man's lostness today, are those who are contributing not simply to a contemporary "literature of estrangement" but to the new "literature of criticism." I am aware of the disfavor into which Matthew Arnold's phrase concerning the purpose of literature as being the "criticism of life" has recently fallen; its current dismissal was plainly put by F. O. Matthiessen, when he said: ". . . indeed, no one lately has taken that phrase very seriously." [2] And yet it would appear that for those who have constant dealings with literature the continuing relevance of Arnold's dictum (which may, to be sure, have to be detached from the actual critical practice which Arnold's methods fostered) is established by one of the central doctrines of the very school of contemporary critical opinion to which the late Mr. Matthiessen belonged and which derives largely from the ideas of T. S. Eliot, for their emphasis upon the fundamental importance of the writer's "sense of his age" seems to me to be essentially equivalent to the truth that is contained in Arnold's phrase. At any rate, it is in this sense that I use the term "criticism" in the above context. I have in mind those writers who belong to the general tradition of modern sensibility which I have been describing, but who have gotten sufficiently beyond their private ambivalence to get a sense of their age and thereby to produce a "criticism" of contemporary experience. Such a dialectical movement involves, beyond "estrangement," a strategy of "reconciliation," and such a movement, though perhaps not immediately apparent, is, nevertheless, characteristic finally, I think, of the writers to the analysis of whose work the

main body of this essay is to be devoted: Franz Kafka, Ignazio
Silone, D. H. Lawrence, and T. S. Eliot. And for this reason,
then, if one tried to establish a relation between the type of sensibility of which these men are diversely representative and the
main tradition of Western philosophical anthropology, it would
have to be said that they live somewhere on the boundary line
between Absolute Idealism and the extreme solipsism of, let
us say, a Stirner. They acknowledge, with Hegel and Royce and
Hocking, the existence of a great republic of consciousness,
though not affirming with them the inseparability of the single ego. But, on the other hand, they are insistent in their affirmation of the alienation of the modern soul, though yet not
contending that the *république des esprits* by which the soul
is confronted but from which it is estranged is merely a system
of image-sequences, reflecting the several moods of the isolated
ego. Their stress, to be sure, is more nominative than voca-
tive, but one feels a constant straining effort toward re-alignment
of the self in its proper field of personal and social relations and
re-establishment of communication with the ongoing movement of life. They are, then, if placed on the map of current
movements, "Existential poets," in the sense that they are
concerned with "our real existence in all its concreteness, in
all its accidental elements, in its freedom and responsibility,
in its failure, and in its separation from its true and essential being." [3] In their view man's present life is fundamentally problematic, and so their characters do not, as
it were, speak of themselves in the third person but rather,
finding themselves strangers and alone in a world in which
an original contract with life has been ruptured, live "in the
world as in an open field," [4] wrestling constantly with their
questionable personal existences in the effort to attain the essential "relation."

FRANZ KAFKA: THE SENSE OF COSMIC EXILE

Who, in the dark, has cast the harbor-chain?
This is no journey to a land we know.
The autumn night receives us, hoarse with rain;
Storm flakes with roaring foam the way we go.

Sodden with summer, stupid with its loves,
The country which we leave, and now this bare
Circle of ocean which the heaven proves
Deep as its height, and barren with despair . . .

Bend to the chart, in the extinguished night
Mariners! Make way slowly; stay from sleep;
That we may have short respite from such light.

And learn, with joy, the gulf, the vast, the deep.
—Louise Bogan, "Putting to Sea"

THE FIRST ANOMALY that the critic experiences on coming to
Franz Kafka is contained in the fact that of all novelists of the
present century we are today probably finding him most absorb-
ing and most relevant—and yet a somewhat irritating subject for
the critical essay. Among his peers, there are, for instance, those
vast and wonderful notebooks for experimentation of Joyce's;
there are the delightfully baffling complications of Proust's
world of bourgeois ennui; and there is even the quiet sanity of
E. M. Forster of which Lionel Trilling has made us again aware:
with all this and much more those who enjoy contriving statements of analysis and appreciation of the work of modern
writers may spend many pleasant and exhilarating days, jotting
down notes for some such commentary as this. The intelligence

may be excited and strenuous demands frequently exerted upon the imagination, and yet we are happily not *engaged*, our total selves are not grasped and held suspended in an eschatological atmosphere, our wills are not brought into play. The order of human existence as such is not challenged, and consequently our experience rarely includes elements of pain but more generally only various types of pleasure. But not so with this curious, enigmatic writer whose genius so teasingly eludes the critical alembic, whose grammar is so far beyond the circumference of "modern" thought, and whose experience seems yet so consonant with the contemporary. We would evade him if we could—just as we would evade those confrontations with our distress to which we are sometimes led by the psychoanalyst or the Christian preacher who is shrewd enough to penetrate our barriers of self-defense. But through such evasion we cannot receive the clarification that lies beyond the initial embarrassment of self-awareness, and so its delusive comforts must be refused. We must, then, come to terms with Kafka. But not alone for this personal, existential reason, for the critical task has to do with the clarification of critical perspective, and this is being made increasingly urgent by a constantly growing complex of dogmatism that has been poisoning the wells of discourse about Kafka in recent years and making plain talk about his "meaning" increasingly more difficult.

There are, of course, reasons for this. And the chief reason for the intensity and the animus that have characterized discussion about Kafka in recent years has been that there are in his work metaphysical overtones of a kind that appear in perhaps only a handful of novels written in this century and that are of a type particularly offensive to the secular imagination. For Kafka is, first and last, preoccupied with that dimension of our world's meaning which cannot be fully comprehended in terms of purely empirical categories and to which we can establish a meaningful relation only by transcending the conventional immediacies of social and biological existence. This is the initial stumbling-block for the contemporary plain reader and critic, for, ever since Balzac, with a certain few notable exceptions, the modern novelist has been concerned to produce a vast and complicated document, in T. S. Eliot's phrase, "of the noises that human beings currently make in their daily simple needs of communication." [1] So much has this been the case that very frequently both critic and plain reader have come to expect their novels to be vehicles of "reportage," and when the novelist departs from the convention he irritates his readers into dogmatic invective and abuse. Certainly this has been true in the case of Kafka, whose aim was never merely to present a segment of human life but rather to urge us through a process of discovery—of ourselves and of a relation in which we stand to forces which run "counter to the familiar systole and diastole of the human heart and its history." [2]

But coupled with this initial difficulty is still another, probably of the same general piece. Baudelaire once remarked, by way of explaining his conception of poetry: "In the written word, there is always a gap completed by the imagination of the hearer." And, of course, it is through our completion of this gap that literature, in its own magical way, enlarges our awareness of the world's dimensions. But because of the defection, already mentioned, which has characterized the general history of the modern novel, this function has been chiefly performed by poetry—and by those novels whose texture has been more akin to poetry than to prose. And I think that it would be fair to say that where the novelist has been aware of this dilemma his work has assumed a problematic aspect, in the sense that it has been the happy or unhappy result of an effort aimed at a fusion of Naturalism (which has been, on the whole, the tradition of the modern novel) and Symbolism (which has been chiefly a characteristic tendency of modern poetry). Indeed, it is in terms of this ambivalence of attitude that we must understand the work of Joyce and Proust and Kafka—and among living writers, of Djuna Barnes and Elizabeth Bowen, of Henry Green and William Sansom, of Graham Greene and Robert Penn Warren.

But to define the tradition of formalistic inventiveness and experimentation to which Kafka belongs is not altogether to get at the root of the second difficulty concerning which I have hinted above. For the other thing which makes Kafka's uniqueness so difficult for the contemporary reader to grasp is that in contrast to Joyce and Gertrude Stein, for example, who used the methods of Symbolism to express an essentially naturalistic attitude, Kafka used the methods of traditional Naturalism to express a metaphysical orientation of a profoundly anti-naturalistic bent. And this is a chief element in the distinctive role he occupies in the major *avant-garde* literature of the twentieth century. He at once pointed a new way to the resolution of the basic formal problem of modern literature—which, as Edmund Wilson pointed out some years ago, has been: how to bring Naturalism to terms with Symbolism—and he introduced into the modern novel as a central preoccupation the religious dimension of human experience.

But perhaps our discriminations are too nice, for both aspects of Kafka's work which I have mentioned as constituting difficulties for his readers today seem finally to relate to a certain mode of apprehending the world which is today out of fashion. Indeed the quickest measure of its unpopularity is provided by the really perverse, or—if this be unfair—excessively temperamental reading of Kafka which many recent critics have given us, especially those of the American school. Critical reaction of this kind is, of course, understandable to an extent, for Kafka, being a metaphysical or religious writer not in a marginal but in a substantive sense, is dealing with matters of ultimate concern to which we instinctively respond temperamentally. And furthermore, one of the intrinsic ambiguities of his work consists in the fact that, symbolism being of the very texture of his writing, it is possible for it to be correlated with apparent cogency to many different systems of understanding or levels of experience, though such correlations should be made simultaneously, with emphasis on that level of experience which is most central to the *corpus* as a whole. And the failure of much recent Kafka-criticism to arrive at an estimate in such broad terms is, I think, not only a failure of intelligence but of the moral imagination as well.

For many the simplest mode of dismissal of a religious orientation of personality has come to be the argument that it is a symptom of disease, of personal illness, and hence without seriousness. This kind of logic has been recently much applied to Kafka, a striking instance being Paul Goodman's study *Kafka's Prayer*, which is distinguished for little more than its unreadability and the Talmudic thoroughness with which it grinds the Freudian axe. Goodman takes the entire canon as being basically a record of neurotic obsession and seeks to get at Kafka's "truth" in terms of such categories as "masochism," "blissful orgasm," "sadistic-anal ritual," "castration," "sociopsychic structure," and "celestial witchery." He admits the theological aspect of Kafka's interests, but proceeds to define religious thought as "the self-awareness of the self, partly known, as part of the id and in relation to the superego that gives it power and duty and that it guesses at." "Religious thought," he says, "expresses not the socio-psychological events but the metapsychology in which the events are organized." It is "the exploration . . . of the form of one's happiness." [3] Religious thought, in other words, is merely self-consciousness: to be self-conscious is to be religious. So Kafka's work being autobiographical and therefore "religious," Goodman's "method is to look for the soul in the religious ideas." [4] That is to say, treating the whole body of work as a prolonged confession of neurosis (neurosis, of course, being merely a particular type of self-awareness and therefore a particular type of *religious* experience), he proceeds to define the neurosis, the assumption being that to have done this is to have defined the significance of the work itself. Thus does Goodman take his fantastically unsound premises as a mandate for the application of the psychoanalytic category to a literary and philosophical problem. The following passage is a fair illustration of the kind of oracular mysticism in which he finally ends that is surely far more obscurantist than anything that the "mystical interpreters" against whom he so much inveighs (Max Brod and Herbert Tauber and the critics who have taken their work seriously) have produced:

. . . the kind of superego, or the stage of the superego, that is important for Kafka's religious thought is not mostly the late-introjected superego of the fifth or sixth year, introjected after the complete formation of the ego as the "heir of the Oedipus complex," but especially the early superego, first to third year, that accompanies the first formation of the ego. This earlier introjection (so Melanie Klein after Abraham) protects the tender soul from its own savage, cannibalistic destruction of the persons and objects of the world, that would make impossible the formation of any ego at all. Conversely, as the heir of the cannibalism, the early superego is more pitiless and savage toward the ego than is the paternal superego, whose internal energy is eros or jealousy (and whose projected appearance is the fearful threat of castration rather than total incorporation). Likewise the early superego is implacable, for there is no means in the ego, no means of identification, to satisfy that which limits and defines the resources and nature of the ego altogether.

This last point is expressed in a beautiful piece of reasoning by Melanie Klein: the destruction was wrought by the child at a time when it was omnipotent, before there was a distinction between impulse and reality; therefore the destruction was infinite; but the desire for restitution to the devoured objects belongs to the period when his resources are only finite, and therefore he cannot make good. Does not this hopelessness precisely define the underlying structure of some of Kafka's nightmares, e.g. *The Burrow?* [5]

Goodman takes great pains to belabor his contention that Kafka's "theology" is most fully contained in the *Aphorisms* and that the longer stories and the three novels are largely thematic elaborations of certain basic motifs that are to be found in his epigrams and proverbs. Of course, by "theology" he means merely the systematic revelation of self-consciousness; hence, he says, after an exegesis of this material, he finds:

1. An ego closed against the instincts, narcissistically binding their energy,
2. but so aware of itself that it does not misjudge, rationalize, or condemn the things of the world, but can contemplate them as they are.
3. This ego controls the beginnings of motion and prevents a spontaneous reaction to vital stimuli, except the one spontaneous reaction of self-analysis.
4. At the same time, since its action is so conscious and checked from rationalizing interference, the rest of the soul freely answers to any unconscious power: self-awareness has neutralized conventional timidities and demands, introjections, superstitions.
5. Fearful of whatever will rob it of clarity and "life," the ego is anesthetic and modest in its requirements,
6. yet it senses that it is only a part of the soul, its "life" is not life itself, so it strains itself to its limits in order to live.
7. Finally, its isolation from its instincts is maintained by a re-

pressed childish destructiveness, turned on itself as a threat to devour unless consciousness is maintained.[6]

Goodman clearly takes his stand, then, with those (Harry Slochower, Edwin Berry Burgum, Charles Neider, and others) who see in Kafka's work merely an interesting case history of mental disease and consequent spiritual debility, a "successful communication of psychotic content"[7] or a novel expression of "the negative, repressive form of the sex act."[8] This form of psychological reductionism need not be seriously considered on its own terms, in spite of the conspicuous place it occupies on the map of present-day Kafka-criticism, for, though it may produce interesting psychoanalytic biography, its solecistic determination to expose a personality behind the work of art hardly fulfills the function of sober criticism which focuses always on the living unity of the artist and his work. Moreover, the facile assumption that the delineation of the psychological origins of metaphysical and religious experience—of which Kafka's work is primarily an aesthetic statement—is determinative of its validity or invalidity is never warranted.

Still another method of analysis that has been much applied to Kafka involves a similar disruption of the living unity between the artist and his work, but here the critic errs not in the direction of exclusive concentration upon biography but rather in the direction of exclusive preoccupation with the writer's ideas, as if here were merely a discarnate mind operating upon experience but never being itself crucially molded by it. This would seem to be an almost characteristic tendency of those who are concerned to define the integrity of Kafka's work in religious terms and who, in doing so, often sunder, quite as much as their naturalistic opponents, that natural Gestalt which is the real and given unity between the human creator and the created work of art.

An extreme example of this second kind of failure is to be found in the reading of Kafka given us by the American critic John Kelly. Mr. Kelly, in his fascinating essay,[9] draws some shrewdly observed and highly interesting parallels between Kafka and that Continental movement of neo-Calvinism which derives from the legacy of Kierkegaard and which is variously known as Theological Existentialism and the Theology of Crisis. And, indeed, the structure of Kafka's thought does appear to bear at several points certain remarkable similarities to that of Kierkegaard and Karl Barth and Emil Brunner, but so completely does Mr. Kelly ignore the biographical and the social context that the brilliance of his argument strikes us, not altogether unreasonably, as a *tour de force*, and one is left with the impression that Kafka was essentially a theologian whose intelligence was perhaps not sufficiently rigorous to enable him to construct a dogmatic theology but who yet had a gift for casting his theological ideas in fictional form. Now it is true that theology enters Kafka's poetic economy, but it is not true that that economy can be exhaustively construed merely in terms of a series of theological propositions: there is, to be sure, a theological structure as a constant background of reference, but "the poetic economy" is a pattern of nervously pulsating themes or situations.* And it is on this latter that the critic's main job bears.

Less frequent is the rather gauche conclusion that Kafka's work is merely an expression of social decadence—although a dogged advocacy of this point of view is to be found in Edwin Berry Burgum's essay in which he declares:

. . . though his writing was mostly done before the first World War,

* Readers familiar with Philip Wheelwright's essay, "Eliot's Philosophical Themes" (*T. S. Eliot: a Study of His Writings by Several Hands*, ed. by B. Rajan), may recall a similar statement of his about Eliot, upon which the structure of the sentence above is very closely based.

his attempt to escape a dominating father left him afraid of the responsibilities of freedom in a way symbolic of the later passage of German society from the tyranny of the Empire to the Weimar Republic . . . His own diseased personality symbolized the disease at the heart of German society. The progress of his personal deterioration paralleled the degeneration of the society that produced him.[10]

And yet if Kafka were merely a "symbolic prototype of the German personality" in a particular moment of its declivity following 1918, he would be simply an historical illustration for students of social and cultural history, and our inordinate interest in his work today would be only a curious instance of cultural anachronism. But the very heat with which one feels that Burgum's essay was composed suggests that this is not the case.

The more frequent insistence coming from those who are determined to compress Kafka's work within social perspectives is that, whatever his achievement, it must be considered as belonging in the category to which we consign "social criticism." And it would seem that there is some warrant for such a view, but surely none at all for the impatient dismissal of other possible readings of Kafka which frequently issues from critics of this persuasion. The real justification, of course, for calling attention to his preoccupation with modern phenomena of social dislocation arises from the fact that for Kafka the ultimate religious problem of the disparateness between man and God first emerges as the general problem of the individual's relation to the social matrix. He writes, for example, in *Notes from the Year 1920*:

He was once part of a monumental group. Round some elevated figure or other in the centre were ranged in carefully thought-out order symbolical images of the military caste, the arts, the sciences, the handicrafts. He was one of those many figures. Now the group is long since dispersed, or at least he has left it and makes his way through life alone. He no longer has even his old vocation, indeed he has actually forgotten what he once represented. Probably it is this very forgetting that gives rise to a certain melancholy, uncertainty, unrest, a certain longing for vanished ages, darkening the present. And yet this longing is an essential element in human effort, perhaps indeed human effort itself.[11]

Nowhere in modern literature can we find a more moving statement of the pathos of contemporary man's attempt to get into touch again with a communal unity that in fact no longer exists. Or again, the constantly recurring image of the immeasurably complex and altogether irrational hierarchy of officials that we get in the later novels seems to exteriorize the individual's sense of bafflement before the endless elaborations of social confusion in the modern world. But Kafka's particularization of the human problem does not terminate with observations such as these, for his delineation of the social crisis is given only as "a concrete visualization of the individual's sense of the wider issues of existence." [12] Kafka moves, in other words, "along a broad way which embraces the cosmic as well as the human relationship." [13] Or, as Max Lerner has succinctly put it, in one of his too rare ventures into criticism: "He goes beyond the problems of man facing his society to the problem of man facing himself and the unknown and inaccessible within him . . . . for Kafka social constructions and even social reconstruction are not enough. His protagonists are seeking always not a compact with man but a compact with God." [14]

Many recent commentators, however, have preferred to ignore this patently metaphysical or religious dimension of Kafka's work and to concentrate on that aspect of his vision which is suggested by the term "social criticism," thus failing to see the broader frame of reference against which the "social criticism" must be measured. Julian Symons, the English critic, for instance, reluctantly admits the possibility of Kafka's work having religious implications but refuses to discuss them, saying that, of course, "the point for us is a social one [one wonders why the point for us must be only a social one]: the way in which Kafka's maladjustment to his time is reflected in his work, and colours it, and refracts back so that Kafka's work mirrors the time and ourselves . . ." [15] Or Stephen Spender, who is almost always illuminating in his comments on literature, in *The Destructive Element* speaks only of Kafka's "social vision." * And the most able of American students of Kafka, Charles Neider, avows that "even if Kafka did write about the divine and so on, it does not follow that his books do not possess a secular and more fruitful meaning." [16] This "secular and more fruitful meaning" Mr. Neider proceeds to define in terms of Kafka's relation to the category of "cabalism," a concept which apparently designates for Mr. Neider those social and cultural myths which, in functioning beyond the time of their legitimacy, cease to have any foundation in reason. In his view, in other words, Kafka's writing represents a continuous satire on the various social and religious cabalisms of modern life.

Philip Rahv, in writing on Kafka some years ago, remarked: "The difficulty of understanding him is on a different plane . . . from the difficulties encountered in reading writers like Henry James, Proust or Joyce. Whereas the obscurities of the latter inhere in the elaborate stylization of their material and in their complex structural designs, in Kafka's case the mystification is entirely one of meaning," because, as Mr. Rahv suggests further on in his essay, his "narratives are speculations

* One feels, however, that in the sixteen years that have elapsed since the first appearance of this book Mr. Spender's development has been such as would impel him now to make a somewhat different assessment of Kafka.

translated into the language of the imagination." [17] Now this intrinsic ambiguity in Kafka's work does explain in part, I suppose, the inadequacy of many present-day estimates of his achievement—but not altogether, for the failure of the critical intelligence here is often related, one feels, to a failure of the moral imagination as well. And I mean by this simply that Kafka's "meaning," even when dimly glimpsed, is seen to be of a kind that runs counter to certain characteristic contemporary prejudices which, for the sake of brevity, may be subsumed under the term "naturalism." Hence, the various attempts to terminate the scope of his vision at the level of psychology or sociology or when this cannot be managed, his dismissal as "an explorer of great courage" but one who seems to be "getting from somewhere that I have never been, to somewhere else that I should not want to go anyway." [18] Or when the religious factor in his thought is acknowledged, it is immediately dismissed as "essentially magical and animistic" [19] and merely another aspect of the more general "failure of nerve" in the twentieth century. And in the case of Paul Goodman, it is contended that when Kafka leads us to think he is preoccupied with man's relation to God and something like Kierkegaard's "teleological suspension of the ethical," he is really brooding over the interrelations between the various aspects of his subconscious. It would seem, in other words, that the majority of the critics who have taken the trouble to write about him— or, for that matter, about Eliot or Auden or Greene or any of the other contemporary writers whose "nerve" has failed them —have been almost constitutionally unable to understand a religious construction of experience as meaningful and have consequently felt obliged to labor at translations of it into "secular and more fruitful meanings."

The most crucial issue, then, in the whole "Kafka problem"

concerns not so much the formal, technical aspect of his art —for, indeed, his manner is unmistakable in its classic Flaubertian realism—but rather what it is that he is saying about the human situation. Most recent critical estimates of Kafka have sought to prove that there is discoverable in his work no probing of the human problem on the religious level but only some kind of vaguely fictionalized sociology—or, the theological concern is admitted as being present, but this is taken as a sign of neurosis. The implication is, of course, however it may be drawn, that a theological orientation is an impossibility for sane and sober modern men. All questions, to be sure, would seem to have been settled, at least inadvertently in Kafka's case, for neither the frivolous nor the insane evoke the kind of high and sustained interest that Kafka has held for some years now among readers of modern literature. And the very violence of the naturalist critics' invective against the "mystical" interpreters of his work would seem to suggest that the possibility of his substantive quality being theological or religious is perhaps not quite so phantasmal for them as they insist.

At any rate, it appears to me futile to try to say anything at all to the point about Kafka unless we reach certain "agreements" or "understandings" with him at the outset. The first of these is simply that *religious* experience is as valid an appropriation of reality, in its own way, as *scientific* experience or *social* experience and is at least as autonomous and irreducible as are these other types; that man's awareness of being related to God is as irreducible to his sense of being related to a social environment as is that experience irreducible to chemical or biological terms; and that, in principle, no one of these *types* of experience is any more or less amenable to imaginative statement than any other. And the second "understanding" is based upon the first: it is simply that, *religious* experience having an irreducibly integral and meaningful quality of its own, there can be no justification for regarding it as an inevitable con- comitant or expression of neurosis. These would seem to be the presuppositions the explicit formulation of which the current critical quarrels about Kafka make necessary for a broad and generous reading of his work.

One of the few possibly valid aspects of Paul Goodman's study of Kafka is the title that he gives his book, for he implies that that single line in the *Meditations*—"Writing as a form of prayer"—was Kafka's way of saying that for him the practice of his art had a therapeutic value, which is true. Max Brod, Kafka's lifelong friend and biographer, to whom we shall for- ever be indebted for his pioneering interpretations, has made it clear that Kafka was not writing for the diversion or instruc- tion of an audience but, rather, out of certain deep inner necessities. "It was the medium through which he exteriorized his dilemmas and thus to a certain extent obtained a control over them." [20] Thus we are obliged at the very outset to examine this personal context or psychic background of Kafka's art.

And here there is immediately thrust upon our attention the most constant fact of Kafka's life—his relationship with his father. "My writing," says Kafka in his long "Letter to My Father," which, for some reason, Max Brod, as his executor, continues to refuse to publish in its entirety, "was about you, in it I only poured out the grief I could not sigh at your breast. It was a purposely drawn-out parting from you, except that you had forced it on me, while I determined its direction." Indeed, as Dr. Brod tells us, Kafka at one time considered collecting all of his work under the title *The Attempt to Escape from Father*.[21] What was the nature of this relationship which was the source of so much pain and anxiety for Kafka throughout his life? To answer this question we must see him in the environment of the Kafka family.*

Franz Kafka, born on the third day of July, 1883, in Prague, was the first of six children to come of the union of Hermann and Julie Kafka. Two younger brothers, Heinrich and George, died in infancy, and between the eldest of Franz's three sisters and himself there was a gap of six years. So, though late in life he achieved an intimate relationship with his youngest sister, in his childhood and youth he had no close relations with the other children in the family. His childhood, as Dr. Brod suggests, "by all accounts, must have been indescribably lonely." Kafka himself dwells on these early years in his diary and refers to their emptiness and vacancy as "earth-weight."

As a boy he attended only German schools—"first the German elementary school in the Fleischmarkt, and then the German grammar school in the Old Town Square"—and was indeed reared as a German. It was only in the latter years that he began to examine and cultivate his connections with Judaism.

The duality between his maternal and paternal backgrounds is an interesting one and is basic to much of the tension that Franz was to experience in relation to his family. His mother, Julie Löwy Kafka, came from an old rabbinical family highly steeped in Talmudic tradition. They were scholars and mystics who found it difficult to manage the exigencies of practical existence—people of high intelligence and delicate sensibilities. The mother, then, appears as "the emblem of reason"—a phrase which Kafka used retrospectively in the diaries.

The paternal side of his family, however, would seem to have been characterized primarily by "a fighting capacity for living and getting the better of life, even physical strength, too." [22]

* For data of this kind we must rely on Max Brod, whose biographical reconstruction of Kafka's career remains the definitive work of its kind.

Hermann Kafka seems to have conformed to the bourgeois prototype almost to the point of caricature. In his certainty that the whole of life was contained within the pursuits of business and the perfunctory but regular attendance on the rites of orthodox Judaism, and in his distrust for and contempt of the life of the spirit, his was an inordinate arrogance and complacency. And quite early his son's tendency was the source of irritation and displeasure to him, for Franz's most enduring proclivity was towards the way of life represented for him by his mother's people. But he could never bring himself finally to dismiss the pragmatic wisdom, the robust hardiness and solidity which his father symbolized: these qualities seemed to him more in accord with the way things actually are and the way people really live in this world than those qualities of intellect and sensibility to which he naturally inclined and which were symbolized for him by his mother's people. And it is probable that his initial experience of anxiety and guilt concerning the true way for himself—the *Tao*—have their origin in his involvement in this spiritual antinomy within the family. This construction would also explain the fact that of all contemporary writers Kafka's strongest preference was for the young Thomas Mann, doubtless because the central drama in much of Mann's early work—in *Buddenbrooks*, in *Death in Venice* and *Tonio Kröger*—was precisely this conflict between the claims of the spiritual and those of the bourgeois.

The great sense of isolation which Kafka felt as a result of this fundamental contradiction between the two points of view within the family was intensified even more by his inability to find refuge from his father's tyranny in a deeply reinforcing relationship with his mother, for here too the father's power was felt. Julie Kafka, both out of prudence, I suppose, and genuine love for her husband, refrained from asserting herself against him. But, in so accommodating her position to that of her husband, "the parents formed a unity, a common front against their son, which the mother could leave only secretly even to show her love for him." [23] And so, as Dr. Brod reminds us, in the short story *The Married Couple* Kafka makes the visitor say to Mr. N's wife, who reminds him of his mother: "Whatever you may say, a mother can do wonders. She puts together again what we have wrecked. I lost her when I was a child." Evidently, in Franz's eyes, his mother was imprisoned to his father's will and against this tyranny no "reasonable" protest could avail. So it is not surprising that Kafka early decided upon the inaccessibility, the incommensurability, of his father's world—a world of austerity, of ruthlessness, of competition and success. In the "Letter to My Father" he says, "For me you developed the bewildering effect that all tyrants have whose might is founded not on reason, but on their own personality." Thus does Franz suggest what was for him the impossibility of consummating an act of pure rebellion and protest—the impossibility, indeed, of any other course except that of submission to the irrational and incomprehensible authority of his father. The submission, however, was reluctant, and in this very reluctance was contained the ambivalence of Kafka's attitude: an inability to rebel and an unwillingness to submit—nevertheless, the final surrender to the absurd parental tyranny.

Capitulation to his father is, I think, connoted by his eventual decision to pursue a legal career rather than to devote himself exclusively to literature. Significantly, the third chapter of Dr. Brod's book is entitled "To Earn One's Living or Live One's Life," which certainly suggests one major aspect of Kafka's dilemma. One suspects that he felt it necessary to seek expiation for his deviateness in an act of self-immolation that would affirm the rightness of his father's world of masculinity, material security and achievement. And so he chose, instead of living his life, to earn his living, in order to justify himself in the eyes of his father. On July 18, 1906, he obtained his doctorate in jurisprudence at the Imperial and Royal Karl-Ferdinand German University of Prague and subsequently went into the Civil Service.

"The year 1912," says Max Brod, was "a decisive one in Kafka's life." On August 13, he met in Brod's home in Prague a young woman from Berlin, whom Brod mysteriously refers to as "Fräulein F.B." The succeeding five years seem to have been a period of great suffering. Kafka was tormented by his constant vacillation between the impulse to marry the girl, thereby affirming again the normal, conventional world of his father, and the deeper instinct to escape the distractions of marriage and domesticity which, he felt, would deny him the solitude in which he could alone be creative. Nevertheless, he became engaged in the spring of 1914. The engagement was broken off that summer but was renewed in 1916. This time Franz made a desperate effort to see it through. Brod recalls this last effort:

Franz had already begun the conventional round of calls on relatives and acquaintances and even went to Hungary, to Arad, with F., to pay a visit to her sister. Franz and the conventions! It was a pitiful sight. At the same time he certainly made every effort to conform to the conventions that were held to be seemly . . . Comically enough the pair of them paid even me a formal call, on July 9, 1917 —the sight of the two, both rather embarrassed, above all Franz, wearing an unaccustomed high stiff collar, had something moving in it, and at the same time something horrible.[24]

But on Christmas day, 1917, Kafka brought the relationship to an end, insisting that his poor health (he was already a tubercular) now made it impossible. But in the "Letter" he declares to his father:

The most important obstable to marriage is the already ineradicable conviction that, in order to preserve and especially to guide a family, all the qualities I see in you are necessary—and I mean all of them, the good and the bad, just the way they are organically united in you: strength, coupled with a tendency to ridicule the other fellow, health and a certain recklessness, speaking ability combined with aloofness, self-confidence and dissatisfaction with everyone else, sophistication and tyranny, knowledge of people and a distrust of most of them. Then too, there were good traits without any drawbacks, such as industry, perseverance, presence of mind, fearlessness. Of all these qualities I had comparatively few, almost none, in fact. And yet what right had I to risk marriage, seeing, as I did, that you yourself had a hard struggle during your married life, that you even failed toward your children. Of course I did not question myself explicitly in this way, nor did I answer explicitly, otherwise common sense would have settled it by pointing to other men, who are different from you (to name one close and very different person: Uncle R.) and still got married, and at least did not break under it, which is a good deal and would have been more than enough for me.

However, I did not ask this question; I only lived it, from childhood on. The problem of marriage was not the starting point of my self-probings anyway; I had always questioned myself over every trifle; in every trifle you convinced me, by your example and by the way you brought me up, as I have tried to describe it, of my incapability. And what was true, and justified you in all trifling matters, would of course be insurmountably true of the Highest, that is, marriage.*

And so it was that Kafka's sense of debasement and inadequacy before the looming image of his father at this point and at every other point qualified his whole career. Never, it seems, could he overcome the urgency of his need for his father's approval,

---

* This letter, which Kafka wrote in the hope that it would bring about a new understanding between himself and his father, was given to his mother who was in turn to give it to Franz's father, but, perhaps wisely, she never did, returning it finally to Franz.

and because of the fundamental dissimilarity between the two personalities the approval was never forthcoming. The consequence for Kafka was an enduring anxiety and an enduring sense of guilt.

Parallels have frequently been drawn between the Kafkan and the Kierkegaardian biographies, but it would seem that they are rather more apparent than substantial. The central fact in the lives of both was, to be sure, the relationship with the father, but Kierkegaard's relationship with his father was so qualitatively different from that of Kafka's that superficial similarities pale into insignificance. It is true, as in Kafka's case, that the powerful personality of Michael Kierkegaard set the terms of his son's whole life; indeed so true is it that Professor Geismar says, "It would be rather difficult to over-emphasize the influence that Kierkegaard's father had upon the life and work of his gifted son." [25] Though the two were estranged from each other for a time during Kierkegaard's youth, when his frivolous days at the University of Copenhagen were over and he settled down to his life's work, he discovered that he and his father stood on common ground in their deep concern with problems of philosophy and religion, and there was between them the deepest community of interest. It was, indeed, from his father that Sören inherited a "keen intelligence, an unusual power in dialectics, a strong imagination, a painfully melancholy disposition, and an inability to live without an attempt to understand life in its deepest root." [26] Michael Kierkegaard, in fact (and think how remote this is from Hermann Kafka for whom "haberdashery" was, until his death, the Alpha and Omega of existence), gave up his prosperous business enterprises at the age of forty, in order that he might devote himself wholly, without distraction, to intellectual and spiritual pursuits. The difference is, in other words, that Kafka's father was a philistine through and through, and Kierkegaard's father was a man whose "metaphysical passion" was inordinate. Between Sören and his father there was a deep coherence of spirit and imagination, and between Franz and his father there was nothing but estrangement, in the presence of which Kafka felt an overwhelming sense of guilt.

Though fully recognizing the essential interiority of Kafka's experience, Max Brod cannot resist wondering why he did not seek refuge "in that distance which so many children feel obliged to put between themselves and their parents; or rather, since he did manage to put that distance between himself and his father, and in later years hardly spoke to him, why did he suffer so from this distance and coldness?" [27] This is, indeed, a question, though put from an external point of view, which we cannot escape asking, and I think we can find a fairly satisfactory answer to it. It may, of course, be frivolously dismissed in some such terms as those of Edmund Wilson, who feels that Kafka was simply "too much at home in his isolation to be able to bring himself to the point of taking the risk of trying to get out of it," that his "impotence was that of a man constitutionally lacking in vitality and walled in by a series of prisons that fitted one into the other like diminishing Chinese eggs." [28] But this kind of uncharitable denigration is in no way borne out either by Max Brod's first-hand account of Kafka's life or by a careful reading of his total work.

It appears to me that a more adequate answer can be given in terms of a distinction approximating one that Herbert Read employed some years ago. In his little essay *Form in Modern Poetry*, Mr. Read distinguishes between the personality and the character of the artist. He defines his "character" as "an enduring disposition to inhibit instinctive impulses *in accordance with a regulative* principle." [29] And he sees the artist's "personality," which he seems to take as the total structure of instinct and natural tendency, as opposed to his "character." I am not certain that I should want to make quite the same use of this distinction that Mr. Read has made, but I yet feel it to be a useful one, in so far as it reminds us of the determinative influence exerted on "personality" by that dimension of man's self-consciousness and self-transcendence that goes beyond psychological determinism.

Now, I do not think it too far-fetched to assume that had Kafka's "character" not represented a disposition of a certain kind he might perhaps have been able to manage his relationship with his father more successfully. "In him," says Brod, "there was a rare mixture of hopelessness and constructive urge." [30] The "constructive urge" is indicated by Brod's testimony that "to those who knew him closely . . . he presented quite a different picture from that of a man haunted by the 'father-image'; they had the picture of a man glowingly under the impulsion of form, the desire and power to mold things, the urge to know, interest in observing life, and the love of humanity." [31] This hardly sounds like Edmund Wilson's man of "impotence," "constitutionally lacking in vitality." It seems fair to suppose, then, that the natural force of Kafka's "personality," his "constructive urge," might have enabled him to "seek refuge in that distance which so many children feel obliged to put between themselves and their parents," but that his special "character"-structure would not allow this. And Kafka's "character" must now be defined as religious.

It is generally assumed today by critics operating upon the basis of Freudian assumptions that religious experience is merely an analogue of a particular constellation of psychological facts, that one's God, if one has a God, is merely a "projection" of something or other that originates in a psychological dilemma.

Illustrative of this point of view is Edmund Wilson's insistence, for example, that "we can hardly feel toward Kafka's father, whose aspect Kafka's God always wears, the same childish awe that Kafka did." [32] It is well to remember, however, that this attitude represents a characteristic contemporary prejudice that is not supported by the most cogent logic. For the Freudian account of the origin of religious belief, though it may have a certain validity, does not justify the kind of anti-metaphysical positivism whose popularity is, in part, due to Freud's influence: it is itself by no means an induction from the psychological evidence but rather a philosophical dogma which must be understood within the realm of metaphysical-theological discourse. If it be assumed, then—and this assumption is recognizably familiar and legitimate within the realm of such discourse—that the realities of religion are not illusory but are manifested and apprehended in their impingement upon the human scene, a new approach to Kafka's psychology becomes possible. That is to say, in regard to the question as to why Kafka failed to establish sufficient "distance" between himself and his father to manage the relationship successfully, we can say—and I think illuminatingly—continuing to use Herbert Read's distinction between "personality" and "character," that, though the natural force of Kafka's "personality" would seem to have been such as to have enabled him to deal with his personal problem, his "character" represented an enduring disposition toward a kind of religious experience that intensified his problem. Or to put the matter differently, it is more probably true than the psychoanalytic interpreters are willing to admit that Kafka's religious experience was not simply a mythical projection of his personal problem and that he did not involuntarily draw his God upon the scale of his father-image, but, instead, constructed the father-image in accordance with a deeper religious disturbance in which he encountered a deity whose visage was terrible and awful to look upon. I do not mean to say that his picture of his father was altogether illusory, for Hermann Kafka was, on any account, an uncomprehending, smug little bourgeois, with no resources of intelligence or imagination for self-criticism, whose tyrannizing over his family was unconscionable. And so sensitive a boy as Franz might have been expected to apprehend this parental authority as absurd and cruel and irrational. But Kafka's "personality," if it were what it is attested to have been by Brod and others who knew him intimately, should have enabled him to separate himself from the intractable parent; his failure to do so is perhaps to be explained in terms of his "character"-structure (the regulative principles in accordance with which he organized his experience) which persuaded him to see his father as a *model* of that transcendental authority between which and man there is no equality and in accordance with which man is judged and found guilty, even prior to the moment of action.

In other words, there was in Kafka a tendency to confuse two realms of experience, and this confusion resulted in the father-image being taken as a religious symbol, thus assuming a seriousness and a numinous quality it ought not to have had. Herbert Tauber was, I think, mindful of this when, in his interpretation of "The Judgment," he observed that the struggle therein between the father and the son amounts to "a struggle between two worlds: that of the vital existence, in which probability and reservation rule, and conscience is relegated to the position of watchdog of a drugged smugness, and that other world in which each step has an incalculable importance, because it is taken under the horizon of an absolute summons to the right road." [33] And the father, being here "the authoritative bearer of this summons," wears the "aspect of God." The son in "The Judgment" may not perhaps be appropriately regarded as a self-portrait, but certainly the father, in so far as he is the agency of a transcendent judgment upon the son's guilt, seems to be a portrait of Kafka's own parent.

So, then, Kafka's personal failure was, I think, part and parcel of an intellectual failure, for had he been able to make his way to a more appropriate symbolism for his religious experience, had he been more successful in translating his spiritual awareness into an appropriate language, his emancipation of himself from his father might, in time, have been managed. Had he, for instance, explored the resources of Christian thought more profoundly, he might have found there a body of symbolism, refined and elaborated by a long and many-faceted tradition, into which he could have translated his experience of a transcendent and incommensurable Deity, as did Augustine and Pascal and Kierkegaard theirs. But, failing this, he turned to that which was closest at hand, his father, and found in him a concrete equivalent of that which he could bring himself to call by no other name than "the Indestructible," thus lending, I say, a numinous cast to the father-image which it could hardly have assumed had a more appropriate "objective correlative" been taken from a tradition of dogma. This is, I think, what Max Brod hints at when he says:

While the psychoanalyst supposes that a man draws the picture he has of God involuntarily after his own father, the opposite possibility . . . cannot be excluded that it is just sensitive people like Kafka who have their idea of "father" enriched, enlarged, and their horizon filled by their experience of God.[34]

It should now be clear why it is that though psychological considerations are not indispensable for an appreciation of what it is that Kafka is saying about human existence they are yet of the utmost importance for an understanding of the form of his art in so far as they frequently disclose the origin of his symbols. A clear illustration of this is to be found in the long story *Metamorphosis*, the central event of which is given in the first sentence of the narrative:

As Gregor Samsa awoke one morning from a troubled dream, he found himself changed in his bed to some monstrous kind of vermin. . . . Lying on his plate-like, solid back and raising his head a bit, he saw his arched, brown belly divided by bowed corrugations, on top of which the blanket was about to slip down, since it could not hold by itself. His many legs—lamentably thin as compared with his usual size—were dangling helplessly before his eyes.

Philip Rahv has very suggestively analyzed the subjective meaning of the insect symbol here by showing that quite frequently brothers and sisters are symbolically represented in dreams as animals or insects and that, since in this story of family life one of the underlying themes is the displacement of Samsa in the family hierarchy by his sister, it should, on the psychological plane, be looked upon as, on Kafka's part, a construct of wish and guilt thoughts.[35] That is to say, Samsa, having been a successful salesman, was once the pillar of his family, but now, being helpless, his sister assumes in the eyes of his parents the role of leadership and reassuring strength that he had once occupied. "We know," says Mr. Rahv,

that in childhood an antagonism existed between Kafka and his sister, for he doubtless resented his father's affection for her at a time when he himself was being slighted. It seems to me that this allows, if we take into consideration the dream-technique of displacement and condensation, for the understanding of the story as a mixture of wish and guilt thoughts. Samsa wishes himself into the coveted and responsible position of family provider, thus lowering the father to the humiliating state of chronic dependence which in real life is his own; the guilt-compulsion, however, hastens to annul this imagined pleasure by compelling him to suffer himself the grotesque fate (transformation into an insect) which he had prepared for his sister.[36]

The story is, however, not simply "a mixture of wish and guilt thoughts," though Mr. Rahv's statement of the connection that it bears to Kafka's own situation is acute in the degree to which he reveals the origin of the symbolism. It is in fact a comment on the eventual and inevitable loss of life by him in whom conscience knows no alarm, on the sense of guilt which overwhelms the man whose life has been "measured out . . . with coffee spoons," when, in the middle of his journey, in a dark wood, having lost the straight path, he suddenly awakens for the first time to self-recognition. This is Gregor. He has hitherto sought complete dominance over the lives of those around him, self-confidently managing and ruling over his own family, distributing to each in accordance with his conception of their needs. His sister, for example, loves the violin, and Gregor has planned to disregard all objections that the family might raise and send her to the Conservatory. His attitude toward his father has been one of contempt and condescension. The spiritual premises of his life have, in other words, been pride and complacency and self-assertion. His only worries have been those of a traveling salesman: he has not measured his ego against its divine foundation, and so his has been an easy conscience. But suddenly one morning he wakes to find the foundations of his superficial existence a *débris* of crumbled illusions, himself overcome by a profound sense of estrangement from his environment and transformed into an obscenity. And in his father's eyes he is himself responsible for the metamorphosis: "In his eyes the insect is an outward expression of Gregor's malice, a revelation of his innermost, damnable being." [37] Thus does Kafka project the "crisis," "the judgment," which redounds upon the human spirit when it stands in clear and unequivocal opposition to God. The tragedy of Gregor is the tragedy of the autonomous man as he becomes insecure in his autonomy—which is, indeed, the presiding theme in the whole of Kafka's work.

There is a close affinity between *Metamorphosis* and the powerful little story "The Judgment," though the logic of the former is, I think, more close-knit and, therefore, more credible. One Sunday morning the hero, George Bendemann, a young businessman, sits in his bedroom, having just finished a letter to a boyhood friend, who, some years previously, dissatisfied with his progress at home, had gone to Russia and set himself up in a business which is now, it appears, going badly. The distant friend is now settling down to the bitter loneliness of unhappy bachelorhood in a foreign country. George reflects on the difficulty of writing to one who can only be pitied but whom one cannot help. He feels that if he advises his friend to return home he will be implying that he is a failure; and he is reluctant to inform him of his own engagement and forthcoming marriage, because he feels that to do so would only be to remind the friend of his own desolate solitude. But, nevertheless, he brings himself to announce the engagement in his letter. And then, finally, with the completed letter in his hand, he goes in to see his father. Many months have elapsed since he has entered his father's bedroom, though they see each other every day in their business offices. He finds his father sitting in a darkened room by a corner window reading a newspaper, with most of his breakfast lying before him untouched. George explains to him the difficulty he has had in deciding whether or not to inform his friend in Petersburg of his forthcoming marriage and confesses his final decision to do so. Whereupon his father cryptically replies:

"George . . . now listen. You came to me about this matter to ask my advice. That does you honor, without doubt. But it is nothing, it is worse than nothing if you do not tell me the whole truth now. I do not wish to stir up things that do not belong here. . . . But while we happen to be on this subject, on this letter, I beg of you, George, do not deceive me. It is a trifle, it is not worth one's breath, but do not deceive me. Do you really have this friend in Petersburg?"

It seems, of course, at this point that the old boy is not in full possession of his faculties: in reply to George's expression of concern for his health, he declares to his son that he really has no friend in Petersburg, and as George carries his father to his bed, he has "a terrible feeling when he noticed during the few steps to the bed that his father was playing with the watch chain on his breast. He could not put him to bed immediately because he held so tightly to this chain." And then, on getting settled in his bed, the old man cries out:

"Well do I know your friend. He would be a son after my own heart. That's why you have deceived him all these years. Why else? Do you think I did not weep for him? That's why you lock yourself up in your office; do not disturb, the chief is engaged—only so that you can write your perfidious notes to Russia. But fortunately it is not necessary to teach a father to see through his son."

He then accuses George of having profaned the memory of his mother and betrayed his friend, but declares that he, as the friend's representative, has secretly informed him. And this furiously delivered philippic culminates in the final curse: "And, therefore know you: I sentence you to death by drowning!" But here we are really stunned when George feels himself driven out of the room and out of the house, across the road to the water, into which he plunges himself; his last words are "Dear parents, I always loved you, despite everything." (Significantly, neither George Bendemann nor Gregor Samsa denies the fact of his guilt.) And at that moment "the traffic over the bridge . . . was endless."

This fantastic denouement, I say, stuns us, and we are compelled to re-examine the narrative—whereupon we discover, as if for the first time, as we did with Gregor Samsa, the complacency and pharisaism in George's attitude (as he contrasts his own security with the precariousness of his friend's existence in Petersburg), the pride he takes in the fact that his *fiancée* comes from one of the best families, his patronizing attitude toward his old father, his smug observance of the old man's deterioration, his brusque handling of him. And it is this whole empty, self-confident existence that is being qualified by the final "judgment." We at first admire George's sensitive thoughtfulness of his friend in Russia, but we soon begin to suspect that the distant friend whose life he would like to rearrange is actually his own inaccessible self, and in the first slight discomposure that George manifests in his reflections about him we sense the beginnings of a personal crisis. The friend becomes, as Herbert Tauber has put it, an "unfulfilled task, which throws self-confidently forward-marching life out of step." [38] And likewise the father's senile insanity at first appears to be merely absurd, but when he suddenly overwhelms George with the question, "Do you really have this friend in Petersburg?" the insecure foundations of George's life begin to give way, and it is George's speech that assumes the aspect of madness, while his father's assumes that of an absolute infallibility which *appears* absurd from our human side. The father proceeds to champion the friend, that deeper aspect of George's self which he would keep far distant, and out of this collision between two opposing points of view there develops the drama of a transcendent annulment of the autonomous person whose pride calls down upon itself the wrath of God, which seems like madness but which is actually inexorable Justice. Thus the absurdity of *our* condition, as with Gregor and George, is disclosed by "the gratuitous catastrophe for which we are nevertheless responsible," [39] *sub specie aeternitatis*. The very brutality of the contingencies which hover over human existence discloses the eschatological crisis in which man perpetually stands.

This crisis—which, for Kafka, is constitutive of the distinctively human situation as such—might be defined as *a depth of distress*, which attends man's suspension between the two radically dissimilar dimensions of time and eternity, a distress which inheres in the fact that man exists in a field of relationships the presiding antinomy of which is the tension between the orders of Nature and Grace. History, for Kafka, is not, as Benedetto Croce would have it, "its own mystic Dionysus, its own suffering Christ" to which "the transcendental God is a stranger" (*History as the Story of Liberty*), for man

is a free and secure citizen of the world . . . fettered to a chain which is long enough to give him the freedom of all earthly space, and yet only so long that nothing can drag him past the frontiers of the world. But simultaneously he is a free and secure citizen of Heaven as well, for he is also fettered by a similarly designed heavenly chain. So that if he heads, say, for the earth, his heavenly collar throttles him, and if he heads for Heaven, his earthly one does the same. And yet all the possibilities are his, and he feels it; more, he actually refuses to account for the deadlock by an error in the original fettering.[40]

Man lives, then, at the point of juncture between nature and spirit, and thus, being situated in ambiguity, lives in a state of crisis. And preoccupation with this problem constitutes the fundamental orientation discoverable in Kafka's work.

Kafka's vision of this dimensional incommensurability between the world and God is given its most striking allegorical statement in the long story "Investigations of a Dog," which is largely given over to the record of a dog's inquiries concerning the source from which the food for dogs comes. The conventional and universally accepted explanation in the world of dogdom—which does not, however, satisfy our dog-hero—is that this food comes out of the earth and is brought forth by mystic libations, the recitation of magic formulas, the singing of incantatory hymns and the performance of ritual dances. Our hero has observed, though, that all dogs seem to snatch their food out of the air as if it falls somehow "from above." And this contradiction offends and startles his good sense. In his attempts to wrestle with the problem he suffers alienation from the community and what Albert Camus calls "supernatural anxiety." In his quest for truth he rejects the official theology of the dog-community (the so-called "science of music"), as well as empirical science. And all his inquiries constantly bring him back to the great experience of his youth, to the day on which he encountered

a little company of dogs, or rather I did not encounter them, they appeared before me. Before that I had been running along in darkness for some time, filled with a premonition of great things . . . and now I suddenly came to a stop with the feeling that I was in the right place, and looking up saw that it was a bright day. . . . I greeted the morning with an uncertain barking, when—as if I had conjured them up—out of some place of darkness, to the accompaniment of terrible sounds such as I had never heard before, seven dogs stepped into the light. . . . They did not speak, they did not sing, they remained, all of them, silent, almost determinedly silent; but from the empty air they conjured music.[41]

This is, of course, his encounter with the transcendent, and in its negative representation by the "shameless" behavior of the dogs in walking on their hind legs, thus "blatantly making a show of their nakedness," Kafka projects an ironic image of the way the "moral code" may be shattered by the secret foundations of existence.

Continuing to press his metaphysical inquiries, our dog-hero tries asceticism as a method of penetrating the mysteries of existence. He engages in a fasting experiment, but the mystical-ascetical strategy leads finally to a dead end, for its direct and unmediated assault upon the mysteries of existence wears the aspect of "wrestling" with the divine and forcing it to reveal its secrets. But grace can be attained only by humility and prayer —not in individualistic isolation but in community with the whole of dogdom; indeed, the hero himself admits:

I do not possess that key except in common with all the others; I cannot grasp it without their help. The hardest bones, containing the richest marrow, can be conquered only by a united crunching of all the teeth of all the dogs. . . . That of course is only a figure of speech and exaggerated.[42]

But it is yet a figure which is profound in the degree to which it suggests that the truth which the dog seeks is contained in the dark obscurity of racial history and is a racial truth. Of this he is reminded by the beautiful hound who rescues him from his fasting experiment and whose primitive, elemental integrity suggests to our hero that the truth which he seeks is, in Philip Rahv's phrase, "an existential truth of dogdom." The problem, then, as finally posed, is how the inwardness and incommensurability of spirituality can be given embodiment in existence, or, rather, how the tension between the religious and the ethical may be reconciled. So this is not, as Paul Goodman would have it, merely a whimsical dog story, in the manner, say, of Albert Payson Terhune, but an intensely serious parabolic statement of an ultimate human problem.

Now, the integrality of the distinction that has been invoked, between "the religious" and "the ethical," for a consideration of Kafka's work cannot be too much insisted upon, and I should like now to give it definition in terms of its use by Kierkegaard, for the Kafkan and Kierkegaardian meanings are practically identical. Kierkegaard applies the term "ethical" to those conceptions of human life which apprehend it primarily as a task. Life lived ethically is life lived publicly and overtly, within a context of duties and obligations, through the medium of one's vocation. For Kierkegaard an ethical apprehension of life is primarily embodied in terms of *self-expression* and implies an acceptance of the normal conventions of biological and social existence as the proper and inevitable field of relationships within which the self is to gain realization. But he conceives of a religious apprehension of life as being embodied in a certain kind of dislocation from the ordinary world of duties and obligations and ethical striving—a dislocation which follows upon the realization of the fundamental qualitative discontinuity between the temporal and the divine, between man and God. Kierkegaard even suggests that when life is understood religiously, so great is the distance between the *ethical* concern (which, focusing as it does on either the desire of happiness, the *summum bonum*, or the fulfillment of duty is, whether in its eudaemonistic phase or its legalistic phase, by reason of its very nature anthropocentric) and the *religious* concern (which is theocentric in its reference) seen to be that often there appears to be a fundamental conflict between the two which necessitates a *teleological suspension of the ethical*, in order that the religious demand may be fulfilled. He graphically illustrates what he means by this concept in his lengthy exegesis of the Abraham-Isaac story in *Fear and Trembling*. Abraham's intention with respect to Isaac his son must, Kierkegaard reminds us, from the perspectives of social ethics, be considered simply murderous, but considered religiously, it has a spiritual justification that validates the suspension of the ethical demand. The category of "the religious," then, applies properly, he contends, to the awareness of the incommensurability between divine law and human law and the sense of guilt that follows upon this awareness— and it is opposed to all ethical idealism.

And yet it is Kierkegaard's most abiding conviction that somehow the apparently ineluctable chasm between these two dimensions must be overcome if real selfhood is to be attained, and that failure to do so must mean either immersion within the conventional amenities of existence, man becoming merely a function of social pressures and obligations, or, devotion to the universal and the unconditioned in isolation from the human community, and consequent loss of selfhood in an historically irrelevant mysticism. He gave a kind of poetic formulation to this conviction in his picture of the "knight of faith," who knows

that it is glorious to belong to the universal. He knows that it is beautiful and salutary to be the individual who translates himself into the universal, who edits as it were a pure and elegant edition of himself, as free from errors as possible and which everyone can read. He knows that it is refreshing to become intelligible to oneself in the universal so that he understands it and so that every individual who understands him understands through him in turn the universal, and both rejoice in the security of the universal. He knows that it is beautiful to be born as the individual who has the universal as his home. . . . But he knows also that . . . it is terrible to walk without meeting a single traveller. He knows very well where he is and how he is related to men.[43]

The "knight of faith," in other words, does not simply renounce his membership in the human community and his claim to its finite goods, in ascetic resignation, so that he may relate himself absolutely to God, since a profound adjustment to "the universal," though perhaps necessitating an initial movement of renunciation, finally drives one back into the world to a new kind of acceptance of it. Indeed, so happy is the "knight's" relationship to the temporal and the finite that those "who carry the jewel of faith are likely to be delusive, because their outward appearance bears a striking resemblance to that which both the infinite resignation and faith profoundly despise . . . to Philistinism." [44]

Thus did Kierkegaard reconcile the claims of the socio-ethical task with those of the religious demand. The precise way in which he went about achieving this synthesis is beyond the scope of our argument here, but that he did so, within the framework of Christian orthodoxy, seems to be indicated by the major conclusions of his thought and constitutes the chief difference between him and Kafka, who never really succeeded in doing so. But the point for us is that his problem is precisely that of Kafka, who, it may be apropos to note, according to Max Brod, was intimately acquainted with *Fear and Trembling* and who, though perhaps not able to make his way to a solution as satisfactory and as internally consistent as Kierkegaard's, was, nevertheless, preoccupied with an almost identical issue.

The clearest statement of this whole matter is given in *The Castle*, which is the definitive book for an understanding of Kafka's problems. K., a land-surveyor, arrives, late one evening, in the Village to which, he believes, he has been called to practice his profession. He goes to the inn by the bridge for lodging where the landlord, not being able to provide him with a room, gives him a bag of straw in the parlor on which to sleep. And K., being weary after a day's travel, immediately retires; but he is shortly awakened by a young man who says that he is the son of the Castellan and who demands that K. present his permit to pass the night in the Village, which, as he reminds him, belongs to the Castle. K. has no such permit but identifies himself as the land-surveyor whom, he says, the Count West-west is expecting. The young man telephones the Castle for a verification of K.'s story, whereupon, after some misunderstand-ings, he learns that the Castle is expecting a land-surveyor, and so, assuming K. is the one, he goes away.

On the following morning K. goes out into the village after breakfast to make his way to the Castle, the outlines of which are visible above the town. But after a time he discovers that it is by no means as near as he had supposed, that the farther he walks the farther away it appears. Finally, worn out by his exertions, he asks the inhabitants of a little cottage on the main thoroughfare to take him in and allow him to rest. He is ad-mitted and finds himself in a large kitchen in which there are two men bathing in a large wooden tub, a woman in a far corner suckling an infant with several children around her, and the old man who had admitted him. He takes a seat and re-laxes in the warm atmosphere of the large room, but is soon told by one of the men who had been bathing when he entered: "You can't stay here, sir . . . You're probably surprised at our lack of hospitality, but hospitality is not our custom here, we have no use for visitors." With this curt dismissal he is ushered out of the house.

It is now snowing outside, and as K. stands alone in the street trying to extricate his feet from the snow, he is recog-nized by a man and his wife in a neighboring cottage. They ask for whom he is waiting, and when he tells them that he is waiting for a sledge to come by on which he may get a ride back to the inn, the man tells him that there is no traffic along this road and volunteers to take him back in his own sledge. The name of his benefactor, K. discovers, is Gerstäcker.

As they approach the inn K. notices that darkness is already setting in; it had been morning when he left, and he feels that he has only been gone for an hour or two, but evening is already approaching. On entering the inn he finds two young men at the door whose names are Arthur and Jeremiah; they tell him that they are the two assistants he has been expecting, and though K. does not recognize them as his old associates, he accepts them nevertheless, and they go into the parlor for beer. While they are drinking, a Castle-Messenger named Barnabas comes in with a letter for K. from the "Chief of Department X," which informs him that his immediate superior is to be the Superintendent of the Village. K. wants to ponder the contents of the letter alone, and so he leaves his assistants and Barnabas for a few minutes to go to the room which the landlord has given him. On his return to the parlor, Barnabas tells him that the Chief of Department X, whose signature K. had not been able to decipher, is Klamm. K. then instructs Barnabas to convey his regards to Klamm and to indicate to him that he has no requests to make at the present time.

Immediately after Barnabas takes his leave K. realizes that he has forgotten to make arrangements with him for his coming at regular intervals to pick up messages for Klamm, and so he rushes out into the night and calls him back. In the course of the conversation he expresses dissatisfaction with his present lodging—and then, thinking that Barnabas is going back to the Castle, K. decides to accompany him. But instead Barnabas takes him to his home where he introduces K. to his aged and infirm parents and to his two sisters, Olga and Amalia. Olga, in making preparations for the evening meal, discovers that there is no beer in the house and decides to go to the nearby inn, which is called the Herrenhof, to secure some. K. accompanies her, thinking that perhaps there he can get a decent

night's lodging, but on their arrival he learns that this inn is
reserved exclusively for gentlemen from the Castle and that
on this particular evening Klamm is the only guest. He is over-
whelmed by the possibility of seeing and meeting this mysterious personage who, it seems, is to have so much to do with his
fate in his new situation.

Olga takes him into the barroom where he meets Frieda, an
employee of the inn, who allows him to peer through a peep-
hole at Herr Klamm. Frieda tells him that she is Klamm's mistress (and of course it occurs to K. that through Frieda he
may be able to establish contact with Klamm), but with startling swiftness she becomes enamored of K., who persuades her
that they ought to live together. Wanting to be alone with her
new lover she clears the barroom of the night's patrons, and,
anticipating the landlord's nightly tour of inspection before
closing, she hides K. behind the bar; when the landlord comes
in, he inquires for K., but Frieda assures him that K. has departed, and so he leaves. Whereupon Frieda darkens the room
and settles down with K. to a night of love on the floor behind
the bar, in the midst of cast-off bottles and garbage. On the following morning K. takes her back with him to his inn.

Thus does the novel begin. Beyond this initial indication of
its flavor and atmosphere it is not necessary to continue with
a detailed *précis* of the narrative which, suffice it to say, gathers
an increasing density with K.'s repeated and persistent attempts
to win a place for himself in the little community of the Village and to establish contact with the Castle. The Village is,
of course, existence, the world, in the background of which
stands its general foundation, the Castle, the Unconditioned,
"the unchallenged giver of all laws," [45] the *Deus absconditus*
which, says Kafka at one point in his diaries, "impels me to the
absurdity, 'I for my part would have perished long since.' I for

my part." And between the two—the Castle and the Village—
there is so great a distance that the seeking pilgrim is brought
frequently to the brink of nihilistic resignation. Yet he has a
deep and finally unshakeable conviction that there is between
them a secret connection the discovery of which will in effect
be salvific and which waits only upon a proper adjustment to
the Village.

Max Brod recalls Kafka's having once referred him to an anec-
dote recounted by Flaubert's niece in a Preface to her uncle's
correspondence. She tells of coming home with him along the
Seine one afternoon from a visit in the country to one of her
friends whom they had found surrounded by her children in
the midst of a charming home; and she says that her uncle,
in thinking back over the afternoon and the pleasant hours
they had passed in the midst of this lovely family, suddenly
exclaimed: *"Ils sont dans le vrai!"*—meaning, of course, that the
kind of sweet and wholesomely normal affirmation of life that
this family scene had connoted was itself *le vrai*, containing in
itself a deeper wisdom than all the sophistication and urbanity
of his own agnostic world. And certainly one aspect of K.'s
situation is to be understood, I think, in terms of his persistent
and, at times, desperate search for precisely this kind of Truth
in the world of the Village. Indeed, the very earnestness and
intensity with which he strives to establish the certitude of his
vocation as a land-surveyor, the desperate seriousness with which
he tries to relate himself organically to the on-going enterprise
of the human community by wresting a stable marriage from
his relationship with Frieda and by participating in the conventional rituals of common life, would seem to suggest that he
was preoccupied with no merely secular problem of getting a
job and marrying and "settling down," but was rather concerned to affirm our life in this world as only those can who

know that though the life of the creature is not self-sufficient, it is nevertheless infinitely worthwhile because of its relationship to its Ground. His struggle, in other words, for integration into the Village was essentially a religious struggle.

But K.'s problem does not terminate with his marginality to the community, for his consuming desire is to obtain an unequivocal declaration from the Castle concerning his station and his fate. His efforts, though, to get into touch with the Castle officials seem never to fructify. Their world is strangely remote and seems to be constituted of absurdity, beyond even the understanding of the permanent inhabitants of the Village who, when they profess to understand something of it, inevitably end by contradicting each other. They do not even hold a common mind as to which roads lead to the Castle and which do not: many roads lead to the Castle, but no one can say unerringly which one the officials take in their travels between Castle and Village, for "now one of them is in fashion, and most carriages go by that, now it's another and everything drives pell-mell there. And what governs this change of fashion has never yet been found out." Indeed, so contradictory of a common-sense view of things is the operation of this "other" world of the Castle that its officials are even said to change from time to time in appearance, so that it is impossible to predict with certainty what aspect they will wear in any given moment. Klamm, for instance, whom K. is especially bent on seeing, "after having his beer . . . looks different from what he does before it, when he's awake he's different from when he's asleep, when he's alone he's different from when he talks to people," and so on and on, endlessly. Surrounding too all these complications are the documents and the papers and the records that obscure, beyond all hope of unraveling, the actual nature of this impenetrable bureaucracy. This is the reality with

which K. has to deal, and his failure to enter into a compre-
hensible and intelligible relationship with it seems always to
be as final and as absolute as that of Amalia's father in his
never-ending attempt to determine the nature of the crime for
which he is so unremittingly punished.

D. S. Savage would define K.'s failure—and, at last, Kafka's
too—as consisting in his unwillingness to effect a simple renunciation of the Village, of "this world and its affairs." K., on his
reading, does not "hate" the world sufficiently and hence cannot "turn wholly to the eternal realm," centering his "life and
hopes *within* that realm, even if this should mean the enmity
of the world and worldly disgrace—which as a matter of fact
it usually does." He should have, according to Savage, proceeded, as it were, at once to the Castle, "taking it . . . by
storm." And so his problem, at bottom, is simply one of his
own "irresolution" and "timidity." [46] But, of course, K.'s actual
problem consists really in a felt need to synthesize these two
spheres of being—the Village and the Castle—in some such manner as that of Kierkegaard's "knight of faith." Hence, his problem
proceeds not from a kind of characterless vacillation between
passivity and activity but rather from a basic experience of cosmic
antinomy that cannot be fairly described either by a sociological
description of "the marginal man," or by a psychological description of the mystic's renunciation of history, for K. is seeking to adjust the historical, ethical task (his task in the Village) to the divine imperative. Moreover, as we saw in our
dog-hero's ascetic experiments in the "Investigations," no direct
assault upon the transcendental mystery alters the human ambiguity, for that mystery, being incommensurable with man's
"spirituality," cannot be coerced into uttering a "Yea!" to our
anguished cries.

This whole aspect of the Castle's "incommensurability" and

K.'s consequent inability to grasp its genius and enter into a
satisfactory relationship with it is, however, given a much
more forceful statement in terms of the history of Barnabas and
his family than in terms of K.'s dilemmas. Barnabas's family,
it appears, some years before K.'s arrival in the Village had
been counted among the first families; his father had held a high
post on the community's fire brigade (an organization which,
on Kafka's tantalizingly elusive and indefinite description, would
seem to have been a kind of ecclesiastical or priestly fellowship). But on the occasion of a celebration of the Castle's gift
of a new fire engine to the Village, Sortini, one of the high
officials, had come down to participate in the ceremonies, and
during his visit apparently fell in love with Amalia, Barnabas's
sister. On the following morning Amalia received from him a
letter containing an obscene proposal that she come to him at
once to be his mistress, but Amalia, finding the suggestion un-
speakably offensive, tore the note into pieces and threw them
contemptuously into the messenger's face, and by that action
cast an unalterable curse upon her family, which found itself,
from that morning on, altogether beyond the pale of decent
society. The father had been a prosperous cobbler, but his
business soon dwindled away to nothing, and Barnabas, who
had been in a promising apprenticeship, found himself ousted
from his position. There was no clear word of condemnation,
nor was there any clear word of forgiveness forthcoming from
the Castle, but the Village was unequivocal in its repudiation.
Over a period of several years the father of the family ruined
his health and finally lost his mind in his unceasing but futile
attempt to get some kind of hearing from the Castle, and the
mother was likewise reduced to mental incompetence by the
long strain of the affair. Thus did the family come finally to
live under the dark shadow of utter despair. And only just before

K.'s arrival had Barnabas succeeded in securing a tenuous position as a part-time Castle messenger, in which position he continues to hope that perhaps he may at some time be able to catch a high official in a moment of generosity and thus get some word about their "case."

Now, of course, the surrender that is demanded of Amalia is not simply to any human eroticism, for Sortini is an official of the Castle, and his demand is not that simply of another person: his demand is the Castle's demand which asks of Amalia not mere surrender to the obscene claims of another finite individual but surrender, as Herbert Tauber puts it, "to the whole of existence in general and to its Giver—God"; she is asked for "an act of comprehensive surrender to Him who . . . created the world, and therefore to existence as a whole." And that is why Sortini's proposal appears morally ambiguous: the "yea" that is being demanded of Amalia is so radical that it must inevitably cut across and shatter any merely human hierarchy of values. But "only in this extreme personal surrender is the deadly question of theodicy, which is bound to shatter any general relationship with God that exhausts itself in human conceptions of good, resolved from within." [47] Amalia clings, though, to her autonomous morality, as did Gregor Samsa and George Bendemann, and in her refusal of submission incurs a radical guilt which is radically punished. So the cost of beatitude, Kafka seems to be saying here, may involve the suspension of the ethical for the sake of fulfilling the religious demand, this suspension being made necessary by the ultimate antinomy between the categories of morality and those of religion—an antinomy which roots in the prior fact of the infinite qualitative discontinuity between our human perspectives and the perspective of God. And while these two themes are both present in *The Castle*, it is the latter—the stress on discontinuity—which determines, it seems to me, the fundamental direction of *The Trial*, which was completed in 1915, some four or five years before Kafka began work on *The Castle*.

This time our hero is less nameless. We meet Joseph K. one morning in his bedroom, as he waits for his landlady to bring his breakfast in. But instead of the landlady appearing, there come two ruffians with a curious announcement that Herr K. is under arrest—but for what they cannot say. Joseph is himself completely bewildered by the fantastic and somehow sinister intrusion of the two strangers.

Who could these men be? What were they talking about? What authority could they represent? K. lived in a country with a legal constitution, there was universal peace, all the laws were in force; who dared seize him in his own dwelling? He had always been inclined to take things easily, to believe in the worst only when the worst happened, to take no care for the morrow even when the outlook was threatening. But that struck him as being not the right policy here.

The behavior of his warders is as unintelligible as the event itself. They appropriate his breakfast and, after trying even to steal some of his shirts, are amusingly hurt when he protests. But, after a while, they depart, saying that for the time being at least, the fact of his being under arrest need not necessitate any radical alteration of the normal course of his life—with the one exception that he is to hold himself in readiness for interrogations whenever the Court sees fit to call him in.

On the following Sunday, K. goes to an outlying suburban section of the city, where the Court's chambers are housed in a tenement dwelling, for the first of these interrogations. After much difficulty he finally locates the room where the proceedings are being held, and, on entering, finds it crowded with spectators and others who have come because of their respective cases. He climbs on to the Examining Magistrate's platform and stands

crushed against the table, the crowd behind him was so great that he had to brace himself to keep from knocking the Examining Magistrate's table and perhaps the Examining Magistrate himself off the platform.

But the Examining Magistrate did not seem to worry, he sat quite comfortably in his chair and after a few final words to the man behind him took up a small notebook, the only object lying on the table. It was like an ancient school exercise-book, grown dog's-eared from much thumbing. "Well, then," said the Examining Magistrate, turning over the leaves and addressing K. with an air of authority, "you are a house-painter?" "No," said K., "I'm the junior manager of a large Bank." This answer evoked such a hearty outburst of laughter from the Right party that K. had to laugh too. People doubled up with their hands on their knees and shook as if in spasms of coughing. There were even a few guffaws from the gallery. The Examining Magistrate, now indignant, and having apparently no authority to control the people in the body of the hall, proceeded to vent his displeasure on those in the gallery, springing up and scowling at them till his eyebrows, hitherto inconspicuous, contracted to great black bushes above his eyes.

This incident casts an absurd color over the whole business for K., and so he begins to speak with great self-confidence, saying that the trial "is only a trial if I recognize it as such." But of course his very presence there constitutes a recognition of the trial and perhaps even an acknowledgment of his guilt —otherwise, he would have simply laughed at his summons. He admits in the course of his remarks that there must undoubtedly be a vast and complex organization of judges and servants and clerks and police behind these proceedings, but he declares that the significance of this organization consists only in this, that innocent persons are accused of guilt and senseless proceedings are put in motion against them, mostly without effect, it is true, as in my own case. But considering the senselessness of the whole, how is it possible for the higher ranks to prevent gross corruption in this court. So the warders try to steal the clothes off the bodies of the people they arrest, the Inspectors break into strange houses, and innocent men, instead of being fairly examined, are humiliated in the presence of public assemblies.

Thus does K.'s year-long "trial" begin.

After this first interrogation K.'s initial attitude of innocent astonishment and defiance becomes one of desperation as he vainly tries to get a clear statement from the Court concerning the precise nature of his offense against the Law and the possibility of his acquittal. So absorbed does he become in his case that he finds his work at the bank becoming less effective. But at every step along the way he encounters frustration. Finally, an uncle who lives in the country, hearing that his nephew is involved in a "case" and fearful of the disgrace that may fall upon the family as a consequence, comes to town to look into K.'s difficulties and to see if he can possibly assist him. He takes K. to a lawyer-friend of his who reportedly has great influence in the Court and a large clientele of people facing charges similar to K.'s. It has been years since the uncle and his friend have had any contact with each other. They find him to be an old man in very poor health; because of his semi-invalidism he is reluctant to accept the case, but finally does, after the repeated insistence of K.'s uncle. Months go by, however, and the advocate seems to be accomplishing nothing, and in desperation K. seeks out an artist who, he is told, as a kind of official portrait painter for the judges of the Court, is in a position to be of great influence in cases like this, and who, as K. finds to his surprise, lives in the vicinity of the Court. The painter tells K. that in cases such as this there are three possible kinds of acquittal—"definitive acquittal," which is, he reminds him, extremely rare, since for a man to be unconditionally released would mean that the Court had been initially mistaken in its indictment, and the Court is, needless to say, never wrong; and then it is possible, he says, to gain an "ostensible acquittal," or an "indefinite postponement." The last simply consists "in preventing the case from ever getting farther than its first stages," and as for the "ostensible acquittal," it seems to issue in a man's gaining his freedom, at least ostensibly, but actually, he says, the Court's file on the accused man is not destroyed and

continues to circulate, as the regular official routine demands, passing on to the higher courts, being referred to the lower courts again, and thus swinging backwards and forwards with greater or smaller oscillations, longer or shorter delays. These peregrinations are incalculable. A detached observer might sometimes fancy that the whole case had been forgotten, the documents lost, the acquittal made absolute. No one really acquainted with the Court could think such a thing. No document is ever lost, the Court never forgets anything. One day—quite unexpectedly—some Judge will take up the documents and look at them attentively, recognize that in this case the charge is still valid, and order an immediate arrest. I have been speaking on the assumption that a long time elapses between the ostensible acquittal and the new arrest, that is possible and I have known of such cases, but it is just as possible for the acquitted man to go home from the Court and find officers already waiting to arrest him again. Then, of course, all his freedom is at an end.

These, then, are Joseph K.'s three possible fates.

Some mornings later he finds himself having to perform a somewhat distasteful task. A visitor from Italy who has certain very important connections with his bank is in the city, and because of K.'s knowledge of Italian and his interest in art, his colleagues expect him to escort the visitor through the cathedral and some of the art galleries. Normally, of course,

K. would find this very pleasant, but on this particular morning he is so preoccupied with his case that it is only an annoying distraction. Nevertheless, he agrees to meet the visitor at the cathedral at ten o'clock. But for some reason the Italian does not turn up, and finally, after waiting for some time at the front entrance, K. decides to go into the cathedral for a brief rest. He finds it dark and empty, and yet, curiously enough, there is a light just above the pulpit which normally indicates, of course, that a sermon is about to be preached, but surely no cleric would be preaching to the empty pews. So K. reasons. But when a priest enters the pulpit, K. grows so disturbed by the eerie strangeness of it all that he gets up to take his leave of the place as quickly as possible. And just as he is about to make good his flight, at the cathedral-narthex, the empty cathedral resounds with the sound of his name: "Joseph K.!" It is the priest, calling him back.

The priest tells K. that he belongs to the Court and is the prison chaplain. He comes down from his pulpit and explains to K. that the only means by which he can avail himself of the justice of the Court is to accept its demands; he must, in other words, admit his guilt in real contrition. But this, of course, is precisely what Herr K. refuses to do. The priest concludes his remarks to K. by recounting the parable of the doorkeeper at the Lord's gate and the poor man who wanted to enter but who, after first being put off by the doorkeeper, waited outside the gate for the rest of his life for an encouraging sign from the keeper only to learn just before his death that had he taken it upon himself to enter at any time subsequent to his first effort he would have gained admittance, since the gate was for him alone. The priest's last words to K. are: "The Court makes no claims upon you. It receives you when you come and it relinquishes you when you go."

And then, on the evening before K.'s thirty-first birthday, two warders of the Court come to his lodging and escort him to an old quarry on the outskirts of the city where, with ceremonious fastidiousness, they plunge a knife into his back. "Nothing is said about any verdict; the two men are almost dumb; the frightful and total disregard by destiny of human speech and human wisdom finds truly gruesome expression in this scene." [48]

We have here something that one really comes on very rarely in modern literature—and that is a novel of justification, a novel in which the drama grows out of what happens when a man is called upon by God to validate the premises upon which his life has been built. For this, after all, is what K. has to deal with: a divine challenge, an overwhelming question.

The special life-failure represented by Joseph K. is, of course, one to which by now we have become accustomed on the Kafkan landscape: it is the self's failure to lay hold of itself in its actual situation because of its easy conscience which prevents the recovery of integrity. That K. has failed to come to terms with his existence is clearly shown in the constant power exerted over his life by the Court from the time of the first arrest: he is not aware, on the surface of his mind, of any radical fault within himself, but on the deeper levels of his consciousness he must surely be aware of the hidden flaw, since for no other reason, we feel, would he be impelled to return again and again to the Court. His tragedy is, again, the tragedy of the autonomous personality whose autonomy must finally be broken by divine nemesis. He suddenly awakes one morning, as did Gregor Samsa, to find his whole self-contained, egocentric, complacent existence being called into question; and, like Amalia with Sortini, he cannot bring himself to "the awful daring of a moment's surrender." [49] He refuses to acknowledge the possibility that his life may have another dimension of significance beyond that of a junior manager of a large bank who pays his debts, lives soberly and sees a girl once a week. Yet he has a deep, threatening intuition of the emptiness of a life that flows into no other life in charity and love, or else he would not feel driven back to the Court time after time. But he cannot give articulate form to this intuition, because he does not have humility: he has not the habit of self-criticism. So he comes before the Court not as a penitent, contrite sinner but as a self-righteous pharisee, furiously protesting his innocence. But he is guilty not, as the priest suggests in the cathedral, of any particular moral lapse or crime but of a "general lack of contact with the whole, a falling away from the eternal," [50] of an incomplete manhood. And so, when measured by the eternal yardstick and found wanting, the nullity of a human life alienated from its divine foundation must give way.

Albert Camus has suggested that The Trial and The Castle "complete one another," [51] and this is true, for the religious experience that is central to The Castle is formulated problematically in the earlier book, and contrariwise, The Castle is a transformation of the fatality of The Trial. The doom to which Joseph K. finally resigns himself is felt, in the presence of the absolute incommensurability of the Court, as implacable. For he knows, deep down within, that his guilt is absolute—indeed, as absolute as is the fact of his finitude. One feels that his very existence as a finite creature is a guilty existence and that Kafka's stress here is less upon the moral duality between the finite factor and the transcendent factor (though I have myself stressed it, and perhaps over-stressed it) than it is upon the ontological antagonism, the cosmological antinomy.

Now of course preoccupation with this kind of antinomy in the history of thought has generally issued in mysticism. Wherever selfhood has been regarded as essentially defective, simply because of its particularity, and where finitude has, in principle, been deprecated, the consequence has been—in Buddhism, in Plotinus, and frequently even in Christian mysticism—a flight from the world of finite individuality into some kind of undifferentiated ultimate reality. And yet, curiously enough, this movement of thought was never decisively characteristic of Kafka: indeed, it might well be argued that the extent to which Kafka avoids a mystical resolution of Joseph K.'s dilemma, for instance, is the measure of his religious profundity, for the recoil is from the barren hopelessness of Joseph K.'s contemplation of the *Deus absconditus*, who remains forever "wholly other" than ourselves, to K.'s attempt in *The Castle* to anchor himself in Flaubert's *le vrai*, to integrate himself simultaneously upon the level of the human community and upon the level of his relationship to a transcendent God.

When the two novels are viewed in this way, it becomes apparent why it is that *The Trial* gives the impression of being a much more finished artistic performance than *The Castle*, for the preoccupation with fatality, which is so central to the former, can much more naturally issue in a climactic culmination than can the preoccupation with "life on the border" which gives substance to the latter. This is why *The Trial* has an end and *The Castle* does not, for the latter could, logically, have no end. But even more significant is the fact that the novel which has no end is the last of the three novels, for it suggests, I think, a certain lack of finality not only in Kafka's development as a novelist but also in his conception of the human predicament.

The definition of Kafka's tendency as a novelist and a thinker must also make room for the recognition that he neither begins nor ends with the problem of theodicy in the Leibnizian sense of the term. He has little in common with the Catholicism of a Mauriac or a Graham Greene, for whom man's depravity is the primary datum of experience, though Original Sin is always in the background of his work as a significant indication of one aspect of man's misery. His sight is centered rather upon the radical discontinuity between the two terms of ontology—finitude and infinity—and the significant struggle generated on the human plane by their complicity in man's being. Man

is fettered to a chain which is long enough to give him the freedom of all earthly space, and yet only so long that nothing can drag him past the frontiers of the world. But simultaneously . . . he is also fettered by a similarly designed heavenly chain. So that if he heads, say, for the earth, his heavenly collar throttles him, and if he heads for Heaven, his earthly one does the same.

He is neither simply creature nor angel but something midway between, and this suspended position between the finite and the infinite in which the human spirit is situated constitutes the measure of its *cosmic estrangement* and *exile*. Thus does Kafka define, it seems to me, the human problem—in terms of man's impalement on the horns of this antinomy which, when existentially elaborated, becomes, as I have suggested, the antinomy between the "ethical" and the "religious." This is the theme that is variously explored in *The Trial*, in *The Castle*, in the stories— "Investigations of a Dog," "The Great Wall of China," "The Hunger Artist," "The Burrow," "The Judgment," "The Penal Colony," "Blumfeld," and *The Metamorphosis*—and in all of his major writings.

The one exception is his first novel *Amerika*, over which a good many critics have turned rather awkward somersaults in the effort to integrate it with the consistencies of his other writings; but this attempt, it would seem, must ultimately end in failure.* The protagonist is Karl Rossman, a boy of sixteen,

---

* Of all such efforts, Herbert Tauber's is the most persuasive that I have seen, but even his seems finally unconvincing.

who, after being seduced by a servant girl in his European home, is packed off to America by his parents. Here he is adopted by a rich uncle who welcomes him with great affection and showers upon him much attention and many gifts but who, after a short while, erratically casts him off. Karl successively works as an elevator boy in a large hotel and finds himself at the mercies of two cruel and unscrupulous men who share the dubious position as consort-servant to an opera singer. And then in the end he joins the Oklahoma Nature Theatre where *everyone* is welcomed and where he finds employment as an engineer's apprentice under the name of "Negro, Technical worker." Since Kafka had never visited this country, his picture of America is often, in detail, ludicrously in error, as, for instance, his description of the Statue of Liberty as a goddess with an upraised sword, but, in the large, as Klaus Mann reminds us in his introduction to the American edition, it contains great poetic truth (the tremendous country homes of millionaires, the confused jumble of our city streets, the atmosphere of impersonality and ruthless competition). But if the book is to be taken as being anything more than pure fantasy, it can only be regarded as a youthful and unsuccessful attempt to seek release from the strain of his persistent tensions by regarding his "problem as imbedded in a purely social context," for in it we discover "only faint and incomplete indications of the insights into the transcending aspects of experience which we identify as Kafka's central focus of interest and the elucidation of which constitutes his contribution." [52]

IGNAZIO SILONE: NOVELIST OF THE
REVOLUTIONARY SENSIBILITY

Whose is this horrifying face,
This putrid flesh, discolored, flayed,
Fed on by flies, scorched by the sun?
Whose are these hollow red-filmed eyes
And thorn-spiked head and spear-stuck side?
Behold the Man: He is Man's Son.

. . . in agony till the world's end,

And we must never sleep during that time!
He is suspended on the cross-tree now
And we are onlookers at the crime,
Callous contemporaries of the slow
Torture of God. . . .

. . . He hangs and suffers still:
See, the centurions wear riding-boots,
Black shirts and badges and peaked caps,
Greet one another with raised-arm salutes;
They have cold eyes, unsmiling lips;
Yet these His brothers know not what they do.

. . .

He who wept for Jerusalem
Now sees His prophecy extend
Across the greatest cities of the world . . .
—David Gascoyne, "Ecce Homo,"
Poems 1937–1942

IT IS ONE of the startling ironies in the history of modern literature that the novel which, as a *genre*, has been the most dis-

tinctive gift of bourgeois-capitalist society to the world's imaginative culture has been the form most tellingly employed in the criticism of that society. Such a critical use of the form, however, is of course only a comparatively recent development. The great novelists of the eighteenth century—Defoe, Fielding, and Smollett—were not much preoccupied with the *social* dimension of modern experience. Crusoe, in his insular isolation, was indeed the perfect representative of an ethos which gained philosophic expression in Berkeley's subjective idealism and which led to the various investigations into the isolated individual consciousness later in the century in the work of Richardson and Sterne and the novelist-philosopher Rousseau. Sir Walter Scott, the first large talent of the industrial era, refused to have anything to do with the new complexities of his environment and proceeded to cultivate an inordinate nostalgia for a highly idealized medieval past. And only somewhat less was Jane Austen's sense and sensibility a retreat from a formidable present. We do, to be sure, with Dickens and Thackeray come upon a profounder vision of the socially problematic, but savage as Dickens's indictment frequently was of that "self-important and moralizing middle class who had been making such rapid progress in England and coming down like a damper on the bright fires of English life," [1] he was not really interested, as Edmund Wilson has pointed out, in close analysis of institutions and political tactics. His method, as Wilson has said, was to work "always through the observed interrelations between highly individualized human beings rather than through political or social analysis." [2] His only complexity was the melodramatic one of making "one of his noxious characters become wholesome, one of his clowns turn into a serious person." [3] And consequently, even Dickens, who was the great English master of his age, does not project the same kind of radically subversive quality that incomparably lesser contemporary talents frequently achieve. In fact, as D. S. Savage has said, the very humanitarian character of Dickens's radicalism implies, beyond all his criticisms, a basic acceptance of his period.[4]

French realist writing of the time presents, however, a force of social vision not generally to be found in its English counterpart (as, indeed, the Russian novel does also, in the hands of a Gogol), although there is no straight line of progression from Balzac through Flaubert to Zola. We know that Balzac aimed at a "natural history" of nineteenth-century society, which he came near to achieving in his *Comédie Humaine*. He had, unquestionably, a profound grasp of man as an existent in a complex of social relationships and, in terms of this setting, sought to study him in as rigorously scientific a manner as the great biological naturalists investigated their subject matter. This kind of perspective was of course a derivation of Revolutionary ideology, and Balzac was fortunate in having come into maturity when he did, at a time when the force of this ideology was still strong enough to operate creatively in the literature of the period. And that Balzac's "scientism" was sometimes narrowly zealous and somewhat naive is not, it seems to me, a crucial issue here, for the significant fact is that he had a clear and sure view of the tortuous involutions of the social process. He was never overcome with disgust by the predatoriness and vulgarity of the new moneyed upstarts, as were the Goncourts, nor did he feel moved with Flaubert to "drown" [the new] humanity in my vomit." He sought only to report the social fact with clarity and objectivity—not, in the manner of Zola, by serving up a "slice of life," but rather by mastering and distilling this fact through the alembic of artistic form.

Realism, as a method of bringing the novel into touch with contemporary social reality, was, with the Goncourts and Flaubert, not so much extended as refined, for the impact of the new all-consuming capitalist society, with its "cash estimate" of human culture, registered with them primarily as an offense against their personal elegance. By the time of Flaubert's generation the boundless enthusiasms of the Revolution, which had sustained Balzac, had petered out, and there remained only the vulgarity of the Third Empire. And his very inexhaustible concern with form and style may well have been Flaubert's way of withdrawing from a society which sanctioned only acquisitiveness and which valued only property: indeed, he once suggested that the "most beautiful books are those with the least matter," that "the more the word clings to the thought and then disappears, the more beautiful it is."

Thus was the ground laid for the new "realism," which was no longer the realism of Balzac but the naturalism of Zola, who, following Taine's psychological determinism, was, above all else, interested in giving clinical descriptions of the effects of heredity, in the interrelations between "the race, milieu and moment." He was after "the little significant facts," and "the more brutal, the more revolting, the facts, the more they dealt with the waifs and strays of society, the better material they were considered for literature." [5] Zola felt that the conscientious pursuit of this method by modern writers would enable literature to provide in time what he called "practical sociology." And this was the shape that le roman expérimental took at the turn of the century. On its delayed arrival in America it "poured sullenly out of agrarian bitterness, the class hatreds of the eighties and nineties, the bleakness of small-town life, the mockery of the nouveaux riches, and the bitterness in the great new proletarian cities." [6] Its most characteristic early expressions are of course to be found in the work of Frank Norris, Stephen Crane, and Theodore Dreiser. And here, I think, naturalism, from a developmental standpoint, reaches a dead end, for the most able subsequent practitioners of the social novel working in the tradition were those young Americans in the late twenties and thirties—Dos Passos, Farrell, Caldwell, John O'Hara and Richard Wright—for whom, with the exception of Dos Passos, naturalism, as Alfred Kazin has said, was no longer a creed but an immediate reflex.

We are concerned here to trace the general forms which the prehension of social reality has taken in the development of the modern novel, in order that the subject of this chapter may be seen in proper perspective. The novel in the twentieth century has generally tended, I think, toward three main types: on the one hand, the novel which renders the rhythms of an interior life beneath the control of intelligence (of which the work of Kafka, Joyce, Proust, Virginia Woolf, and Elizabeth Bowen furnish excellent examples); and, on the other hand, two species of the novel of society. And it is with the differences between the second two types that we are primarily concerned here. The first of these two types, which has been chiefly practiced by American writers of the naturalist school, in its current handlings represents the addition of nothing really new to the tradition that I have been describing (except, of course, in so far as our youngest writers, of the generation of Mailer in this country or Sansom in Britain, occasionally give evidence of having read Joyce or Kafka): the techniques used were developed largely in the nineteenth century. The tendency is toward what we have come to call "social criticism" of a quite delimited area of social fact: with Farrell, it is the tragedy of the Chicago poolroom loafer; with Steinbeck, it is the dispossessed California Okies of the thirties; with Caldwell, it is the disinherited "poor white trash" of Georgia; with Marquand, the Boston Brahmin gone to seed, and so on. And from the standpoint of these quite specific phenomena of social dislocation implica-

tions are drawn, by the more sensitive writers, as to the extent
to which they reflect larger movements toward crisis in contemporary society. But the novelist's powers of concentration
are largely focused on a particular social microcosm, and his
aim is documentation and "reportage." This is the one type
of which the chief examples in contemporary literature seem to
be American.

The second form which the novel of society has assumed in
quite recent times is also very much the product of contemporary history. And here some lines from Wordsworth's Preface
to the *Lyrical Ballads*, written over a hundred years ago, seem so
applicable that they deserve quotation. In speaking of the
poet's task (by which he meant not alone that of the writer
who works in the medium of verse but that of every artist who
makes language serve the demands of the imagination) he said:

In spite of differences of soil and climate, of language and manners,
of laws and customs: in spite of things silently gone out of mind,
and things violently destroyed; the Poet binds together by passion
and knowledge the vast empire of human society, as it is spread over
the whole earth.

This was indeed precisely the direction in which a number of
contemporary writers were impelled by the force of events in
the thirties and early forties, for the collective effect upon them
of the Munich Agreement of September, 1938, the final over-
throw of the Spanish Republicans in the spring of 1939, the
Russo-German Pact, and the outbreak of international war in
September of 1939 was a heightening of the sense of general
calamity. The great fact on the world's horizon was the emergence of the new Leviathan of the totalitarian state; here was
the inescapable evidence of general disorder which demanded
a radical cure. And one major expression of the response made
to these phenomena of dilapidation by the modern writer was

the revolutionary novel—which, I am suggesting, represented a genuine extension of the *genre* of the novel of society.

My term "revolutionary novel" should not be taken, however, to mean that this type of novel tended toward the doctrinaire exposition of any special Leftist ideology, for preoccupied as was this group of writers with the Fascist containment of Republican resistance in Spain, with the Italian invasion of Albania, and with the dark shadows cast over Central Europe by Nazi Germany, they were equally preoccupied with the moral ambiguities in the parties of the Left. Their disillusionment was rooted in the continued purges and the progressive snuffing out of civil liberties in the Soviet Union following the Moscow trials, and their attitude with respect to the new Russia was by no means controlled by any form of messianic optimism, but rather by increasing disappointment and apprehension. They had no simple program of political activity and allegiance. Their "revolutionism" consisted rather of a certain quality of disenchantment about all "parties" and of a conviction that the disorder within Western society could be overcome only by the most radical intellectual and practical expedients. The vast empire of contemporary human society, then, "as it is spread over the whole earth," was the field within which André Malraux, Arthur Koestler, Rex Warner, Ernest Hemingway (whose novel *For Whom the Bell Tolls* entitles him to membership in the group), Christopher Isherwood, George Orwell, and Ignazio Silone moved.

And here we come upon the first point of difference between this new form and its older counterpart within the *genre* of the social novel—its internationalism, its breadth of social and psychological reference. Although these writers deal with special continua of events within various geographical contexts of social experience, it is not the local but the universal quality of their materials in which they are primarily interested. When Malraux writes of the Kuomintang uprising in China or the horrors of confinement in a Nazi prison cell, when Hemingway writes of the Spanish war, or when Silone focuses his unique X-ray apparatus on Italian society under the Mussolini regime, it is the transparency of their situations, through which we see the agony of our age, that moves us. But when Steinbeck writes of industrial labor disputes on the California coast, when Caldwell writes of the Southern poor white's disinheritance, or when Farrell tells the life story of Studs Lonigan, we get remarkable photographs of American life—but the merely photographic quality of the regional picture cannot be gainsaid. The explanation of the difference is, I think, simply that in the one case the particular social materials which the novelist uses are used instrumentally: "society" remains in the background, and the "focus is on psychological individuation shown precisely at the point where it overlaps the general social and political interest." [7] And in the other case you have what might be called an "aerial" view of society but little more.

At bottom the really distinctive mark of the writers of the revolutionary novel in our time registers with us in the sense that they are striving to create a new myth, not a new creed but a new form, for the restatement of an ancient wisdom within the conditions of modern experience—not a new system of doctrine, but a new world of the imagination for our souls to inhabit. Their books tend to be essays in symbolism which do not simply reproduce the world of which we and the author are living members but which create a world for the exhibition of the nature of man and his destiny. Thus do they offer a counterpoise to chaos. We cannot now say whether the myths by which these writers give us that shock of recognition that liberates us from the modern ruins and "redeems from decay the visitations of the divinity in man" will prove to be only myths for our age or whether some will continue to live and have power, as the great tragic myths of Virgil and Dante, of Baudelaire and Dostoyevsky have continued to live for us. But that these men are striving to freshen our vision of human life, not only in its contemporary but in its perennial aspects, seems certain. And among them one of the most powerful and impressive talents is that of the Italian writer Ignazio Silone, to whom we now turn.

An unfortunate critical convention that has been widely adopted in recent years by commentators on contemporary literature involves the designation of fiction that does not adhere to the outrageous syntax of James Joyce's "stream-of-consciousness" language as "realist"—and when the writer asks searching questions about the nature of contemporary society that indicate, incidentally, some awareness of the Marxist hypothesis, his position is immediately identified as that of "Socialist Realism." Such unfortunate methods of typification have frequently been applied to Silone, and yet nothing could be more misleading, for the "spiritual" dimension of human life is of the very warp and woof of his books. At no point does he adhere, as a partisan bigot, to a Marxist dogma of the nature of man and history. Though he writes of the social and political problems which we have had to face in our recent history, his writing is profoundly non-political in the sense, for instance, that the work of such writers as Brecht and Koestler sometimes fails to be. The modern political problem, to be sure, gives point to his dramatic situations, but Silone's world and the human beings with whom he peoples it are as old as the hills: broadly seen it is the world of Socrates and Christ and Augustine and all noble spirits—the perennial human world in which life and the dream are at odds. It is, in Hart Crane's phrase, "a world dimensional" in which disorder derives from something approximating Original Sin and in which morality and religious faith are the factors of regeneration rather than political messianism. His is, then, an "integral" humanism of a kind which perhaps we are not altogether justified in associating with the "realist" tradition in recent literature.

Silone belongs to that generation of European intellectuals now in middle age which grew to maturity in the years between the wars. Nineteen hundred was the year of his birth, and the place was the little town of Pescina, situated near Lake Fucino in the Marsica province of the Abruzzi. His lineage was aristocratic, and his nurture was Catholic. As a boy he was educated in Catholic schools, chiefly in the arts and sciences of rural life among the peasants, with whom he early cast his lot and from whom he has never withdrawn his deepest sympathies. Silone has described the hardness of life in this simple agrarian world of pre-war Italy in the starkest terms:

For twenty years the same sky, the same earth, same rain, the same snow, the same houses, the same feast days, the same food, the same poverty. . . . The life of men, beasts and earth always seeming shut in a motionless circle, closed away from the changes of time. Closed in a natural circle of its own.

First would come the sowing, then the weeding, then the pruning, then the sulphuring, then the reaping, then the harvest. And then? Then once again.

Sowing, weeding, pruning, sulphuring, reaping, harvest.

Always the same thing, unchanging. . . . The soil was thin, dry and stony. The scanty land was saddled and subdivided by mortgages. No farmer owned more than a few square yards of it. . . . The Fucino flatland has in reality been put under a colonial system. The enormous bounty it produces annually does not remain in the locality but goes to the metropolis. . . .

The sugar beet of the Fucino is the main supply for one of the most important sugar factories in Europe. But for the farmers who grow it, sugar has always remained a delicacy, and is seen among their families only at candy time in Easter. Almost all wheat from the Fucino goes to the city, where it is used to make white bread, noodles, and biscuits, and where it also feeds cats and dogs. But the farmers that grow it are forced to eat Indian corn the best part of the year. Thus the farmers get out of the Fucino what one may term a real and true starvation existence.[8]

After going through the primary school at Pescina and spending some time in the secondary school, Silone completed his education in Catholic institutions in various towns in Italy, but never attending the University because, as he says, "In the first place I was advised not to do so by the doctors, who gave me very few years to live, and in the second place political work left me very little free time." Nevertheless, he survived, it would seem, through a kind of stubborn primary vitality which strikes one as being perhaps his characteristic quality.

Then came the war of 1914–18 and Silone, at the age of seventeen, became the secretary of a syndicalist peasant movement, the Federation of Land Workers of the Abruzzi, which was working for a more equitable redistribution of agrarian lands. Soon thereafter, however, he says, "opposition to the War caused me to join a group of young Socialists, and I was appointed secretary of the Socialist Youth of Rome." A year later, in 1918, he became editor of a socialist weekly, *Avanguardia*, and subsequently one of the founders of the Communist Youth International. In 1921 he took a leading role in Moscow in the organization of the Italian Communist Party, and throughout the late twenties he remained a member of the Central Committee of the Party and was very active in underground resistance work under the Mussolini regime. But at the end of the twenties Silone began to realize that policy in the Communist International was being increasingly dictated by the Russians from the standpoint of unilateral national interest in such a way that it was becoming well-nigh impossible for other Communists to pursue courses of action relevant to their respective national situations. So, with a large group of fellow Italians, whose disillusionment was rooted in the rapidly declining moral prestige of Marxist strategy, he resigned from the Party in 1930. He refused, however, to join either the Trotskyites or the disgruntled followers of Bukharin, preferring to regard himself, as he has put it, as an "independent Communist." And in the same year, urged on by Fascist denunciation and persecution, he fled to Switzerland, where he began to write extensively for the first time and where he remained until 1944 when, following the fall of the Fascist order, he returned to his native land.

The comparison of Silone with Malraux is, in a way, inevitable —first of all, because they are both working within this *genre* of the revolutionary novel, but chiefly because they have both extended their personal myth to the description of our public agony. Not only did both men at one time find important clues to the meaning of contemporary history in Marxist assumptions, but they have both been members of our twentieth-century Underground, actively participating in the fight against totalitarianism. Malraux's personal adventure has perhaps been more spectacular—indeed, almost Byronic in its overtones—than Silone's, but the two careers have in them an unmistakable revolutionary quality which they have themselves apprehended and embodied in the characters of their most important books. And to this extent they may be said to be autobiographical writers, for theirs is the drama of the modern revolutionary's isolation from the social collectivity—an isolation which, though self-imposed, is responsible and necessary to the regenerative work which they seek to accomplish. There is a character in T. S. Eliot's *The Family Reunion* who says at one point: "In a world of fugitives the person taking the opposite direction will appear to run away." This is, of course, the view of the modern world to which Malraux and Silone adhere. They see it as "a world of fugitives," and though in this realm foxes have holes and birds of the air have nests, "he who lives for justice and truth, without caring for the consequences," and who by reason of this fact becomes of necessity a revolutionary—as Silone's Don Benedetto says—"hath nowhere to lay his head. He goes on living according to the pure dreams of adolescence, and the Christian countries hunt him like a wild beast." [9]

Now this fact, as I have already begun to suggest, Silone gives definition in terms of the various modern social collectivisms that have so denied the dignity of human personality that the only course left open for him who somehow retains his integrity of vision has been the revolutionism of the Underground. But the vocation of protestantism has for Silone a larger dimension than merely that necessitated by the crisis of contemporary society, for the dialectical movement of human history is, in his view, always tragic: there is always a status quo whose archaism in time tends toward social demonry * and against which there must periodically be directed a mobilization of spiritual forces. The disillusioned Uliva in *Bread and Wine*, when asked by Spina to rejoin the socialist resistance movement, replies in a vein of radical skepticism:

"The situation is certainly grave. . . . There is something corpse-like even about the dictatorship that stifles us. For a long time it has

* I use this phrase in the sense that it is used by Paul Tillich in *The Interpretation of History* (New York, Charles Scribner's Sons, 1936).

not been a movement, even a reactionary movement; all it is is a bureaucracy. But what is the opposition? Another bureaucracy that aspires to totalitarian domination in its turn, in the name of different ideas and on behalf of different interests. If it does conquer, as it probably will, we shall thus pass from one tyranny to another. We shall have a so-called economic revolution, thanks to which we shall have state bread, state boots and shoes, state shirts and pants, state potatoes and state green peas, just as we now have state railways, state quinine, state salt, state matches, and state tobacco. Will that be a technical advance? Certainly it will. But it will be the basis of an official, compulsory doctrine, a totalitarian orthodoxy which will use every means, from the cinema to terrorism, to extirpate heresy and tyrannize over individual thought. A Red inquisition will succeed the present inquisition, a Red censorship the present censorship. Instead of the present deportations there will be Red deportations, of which dissident revolutionaries will be the favorite victims. Our future bureaucracy will identify itself with Labor and Socialism and persecute everyone who goes on thinking with his own head, denouncing him as a paid agent of the industrialists and the landlords, just as the present bureaucracy identifies itself with patriotism and suppresses all its opponents, denouncing them as traitors bought by foreign gold." [10]

And when Spina exclaims, ". . . you know that that is not our ideal," Uliva quietly replies, "It's not your ideal, but it is your destiny." "You have not yet won," he says,

"you are still an underground movement, you have already become simply a group of professional revolutionaries. The regenerating passion by which we were animated in the student group has become an ideology, a network of fixed ideas, a cobweb. That is the proof that there is no escape for you, either . . . every new idea invariably ends by becoming fixed, inflexible, parasitical, and reactionary. And if it becomes the official doctrine of the state, no more escape is possible. . . ." [11]

This, then, is the tragic dialectic of history—which enjoins upon the man of heroic stature and vision membership in the permanent opposition, since he finds himself at odds with both the status quo and the "party line." And though Silone is far too profound an analyst of history to suppose that anarchism covers the total ambiguity of the human situation, he unquestionably sees its partial truth.

The "revolutionary," then, in his enforced contemporary, and perennial, isolation constitutes Silone's central focus. And within the purview of this perspective on his work we cannot avoid the conclusion, I think, that his first novel *Fontamara*, though it introduces us to the atmospheric quality of Silone's world, is somewhat peripheral to the major tendency of his writing, for it has no hero. Its central character is a folk—the disinherited peasantry in Fascist Italy, "the heirs to generations of poverty," whose life, once "closed in a natural circle of its own," has now become a cheap commodity in which the Fascist overlords deal with the most unconscionable ruthlessness.

Fontamara is a little peasant village in the hills above Lake Fucino, the "racial" history of whose inhabitants is one of being continuously cheated and reduced to pauperism by the world of officialdom which they regard as a kind of organized racket. And to this long experience the new Fascist hierarchy provides no exception. So there is inbred in these poor people a deep hatred and distrust of all the "authorities"—the landlords and the tax collectors and the carabinieri and the townspeople and all the others who belong to the City. The City, whose internal life is geared by all the treacherous technical elaborations of a highly organized modern society, represents for them the alien social complex which is the source of the manifold contingencies in their existence.

Silone tells us that there was once a time when these people, by way of establishing themselves in their native country, would emigrate to the New World, there to labor hard and long in shops and factories, in order to return to the Abruzzi with enough saved from their earnings abroad to enable them to purchase a small plot of ground and a few farming implements. This was the way they acquired their land, and, quite naturally, its ownership, having been so arduously achieved, exercised on them a conservative influence. To be without land was, as we see for example in the character of Berardo Viola, to be rootless, without stake in the ordered processes of common living, and hence, a radical. But to have land, a plot of ground which was one's own, or to want or to have the prospect of such stability, as again we see in the evolution which Berardo undergoes after he sleeps with the peasant girl Elvira and determines to work hard and long for the money with which to buy some land, in order that he may not marry as a landless farmer—to want or have the prospect of such stability was to be less reckless, less venturesome, less opposed to the existing order of things. But as our story opens we find that under the new regime of Fascism the possibility of a peasant's acquiring land in this way has become more remote than ever, for emigration is now forbidden, and the young men of Berardo's generation face a future that holds out not the slightest hope of acquiring even the minimal security which their fathers attained. The peasants find themselves trapped by these circumstances within their own impoverishment, and their inchoate response is one of increasing apprehension and resentment.

The narrative begins with the arrival at Fontamara one evening in June of a Fascist official, the Honorable Mr. Pelino, who comes riding into the village on a bicycle, wearing white spats and city clothes. The villagers, as is their custom after a long day in the fields, have gathered in front of Marietta Sorcanera's wine shop. They are certain that the stranger is an official bearing notice of a new tax. Indeed, they take the big sheets of paper which the stranger reveals after greeting them as a confirmation of their suspicions. After a long explanation of his visit, which the Fontamarans of course do not understand because the man speaks the language of "the city," the Honorable Mr. Pelino bids them sign the papers, but they vehemently refuse, declaring that they will have nothing to do with another tax. "Listen here," the Honorable Mr. Pelino explains,

"the days are over when the farmers used to be despised and ignored. Now there are new authorities in charge who have great respect for the farmer and they want his opinion, so sign up! Look at the honor the authorities have done you, sending you an official just to get your opinion."

He assures them that he brings no new tax, and finally, one by one, they sign his papers, and those who are present volunteer to sign for those who are absent.

After the signatures of the village's entire population have been affixed to the Honorable Mr. Pelino's papers, he notices on a table in Marietta Sorcanera's wine shop a louse with a cross on its back. For some reason he is offended and petulantly takes it as an insult directed at him and his superiors. But the incident reminds one of the villagers, Michele Zompa, of a dream he has recently had which, with a great roar, he proceeds to relate. The dream is of a conversation between the Pope and Christ, following the historic concordat between the Pope and the government. "Here's the way it was," says Zompa:

"The Man on the Cross said:

'We might celebrate this peace of ours by giving the Fucino land to the farmers who work it.'

"The Pope answered:

'Lord, Prince Torlonia wouldn't like it. And don't forget that

Prince Torlonia makes a sizeable contribution to Saint Peter's chest.'
    "The Man on the Cross said:
    'We might celebrate this peace of ours by letting the farmers have
a dispensation from payment of taxes.'
    "The Pope answered:
    'Lord, the government won't like it. And don't forget that it's
with taxes the farmers pay that the government has to pay in that
two billion of theirs to Saint Peter's chest.'
    "The Man on the Cross said:
    'We might celebrate this peace of ours by letting the farmers and
small landholders have an especially heavy crop this year.'
    "The Pope answered:
    'Lord, if the farmers' crop is heavy the price of the farm produce
will fall. And don't forget that our bishops and cardinals are all big
landholders.' "

Finally, when the Pope could think of nothing that might be
done for the farmers that might not displease Prince Torlonia
or the government or the bishops or the cardinals, he suggested
to Christ that they fly down over the Fucino and all the Marsican
villages on the night of the Reconciliation, and so they did.
They found the farmers "complaining, cursing, fighting or
nagging at each other" as usual, in vexation at their poverty, and
the Pope being touched to the depths of his heart took from a
sack he was carrying

a cloud of lice and threw them down upon Marsica saying:
    "Take ye, O best beloved children, take ye and scratch yourselves.
So it will come to pass that in the hour of your idleness there will
be something to draw you aside from evil thoughts."

That was Michele Zompa's dream. And thus does Silone ironi-
cally project through the superstition-ridden mentality of these
peasants the corruption of official religion in their world—a
theme, incidentally, which runs throughout his work.

The Honorable Mr. Pelino is stricken with rage at what he takes to be the impudent effrontery of these people, and he screams into their uncomprehending faces:

"You're trying to make fun of me. You're trying to make fun of the authorities. . . . The government will put you where you belong. . . . The authorities will get busy on you all right. . . . Do you know who's in command today? Have you any idea who the boss is?"

He departs, trembling with anger, with a last thrust: "I give you my word that you will hear more from me."

On the following morning the Fontamarans find a gang of laborers from the town turning a stream aside, which had for years irrigated their fields, to the vineyards and fields of a rich landholder, Don Carlo Magna. The people are at first simply mystified by this occurrence, supposing that it is only a prank which the townspeople are playing upon them. But then they begin to realize the possible consequences of this prank, and since the men are busy with the crops, the women decide to investigate the matter. On entering the town, they are, as usual, ridiculed and humiliated. After a futile attempt to gain a conference with Don Circostanza, they learn that he is no longer mayor but that a powerful and unscrupulous Roman, "the Promoter," has been appointed alderman of the town. And so they decide to go directly to Don Carlos Magna's house where, on arriving, they are informed by Donna Zizzola, his wife, that her husband's fields, toward which Fontamara's stream is being changed, have been acquired by "the Promoter"—who, of course, after changing them into irrigated land, will sell them again at a much higher price than that at which he purchased them. The women begin to realize now that a day of reckoning has even come for the old landowners too.

Finally, somewhat crestfallen now, they go to "the Promoter" himself, who shows them the agreement which they and their husbands had unwittingly signed the night before, consenting to the stream being turned toward the town land. At this point Don Circostanza, whom the Fontamarans have traditionally regarded as their "representative" (and whom they have amply paid for such "representational" functions as he has performed) and who has set himself up as the "People's Friend," steps in, presumably to arbitrate the matter. Actually, of course, he is only a groveling tool of "the Promoter," but, with considerable bombast, he assures the Fontamaran women that their interests are safe in his hands and that he will see to an equitable arbitration of the matter—which he does by way of persuading "the Promoter" to consent to a division of the water in such a way as to allow each claimant to receive "three-fourths" of the stream. To this settlement of the dispute the poor women consent and return to their homes.

As the days go by, however, the laborers continue to dig out the ditch by which the precious water is to be carried through "the Promoter's" fields. At first the Fontamarans apply themselves to the explication of the subtle logic of Don Circostanza, whereby the water was to be divided into two parts of three-fourths each. Some say that the water is to be divided into two equal parts, and others say that Fontamara will retain more than a half—that is, three-fourths. But slowly the awful truth settles upon them that they are being robbed of the source of irrigation for their fields and that they face, as a consequence, a winter of hunger and starvation. Berardo Viola advocates an act of violence against "the Promoter," insisting that they not try to "talk things over with city folks." "The law," he says, "is made by city folks. It is administered by judges who are all city folks. It is interpreted by lawyers who are all city folks. How can a peasant ever be right, then?" But Berardo's advice is disregarded as the irresponsible counsel of extremism given by a man who has no land.

Some nights later a fence which "the Promoter" had built along a sheep trail that had for generations belonged to all and that he had recently confiscated is burned down. A second fence is erected, at the expense of the township, and this one is burned down also. Then comes the reprisal. One evening, before the men have returned from the fields, a large motorized unit of Fascist militia comes roaring into Fontamara. The soldiers fire on the inhabitants, but finding no men in the village, they alight from their vehicles to break up the homes and rape the defenseless women.

This last outrage leaves the Fontamarans completely stunned.

What was quite clear was that the militia had come to Fontamara and raped a number of women. But they had done so in the name of the law, and in the presence of a police commissary, and that was not so clear. . . .

Each one of our misfortunes, examined separately, was not new, for similar misfortunes had often happened in the past. But the way they befell us was new and strange.

The whole thing was absolutely beyond our understanding.

Following the reprisal, Berardo Viola goes to Rome with a friend in the hope of finding work and earning sufficient money to return home to marry Elvira, the village dyer. But there he is baffled by the endless complexities of this strange urban world, rebuffed and victimized by numerous confidence men who promise him assistance for a price, only to desert him in the end. And finally he finds himself in jail, along with his friend from Fontamara and a young revolutionary, all of whom are suspected of being the "Unknown Hand"—a mysterious figure who has been spreading anti-Fascist propaganda. Berardo, while in prison, relates to the young revolutionary, who is really the Unknown Hand, the story of Fontamara's troubles and then sacrifices himself by declaring to the police that he is himself the criminal. Whereupon the real felon is set free and goes to Fontamara, there to publish, with the help of the peasants, a subversive newspaper. Our story ends with the invasion of Fontamara by Fascist militia who murder *en masse* the inhabitants of the village.

Now it is quite probably true that to summarize any fully developed novelistic idea, as I have done here, is in some measure to betray it, but if, on the other hand, as Lionel Trilling has suggested, "plot is to the novelist what experiment is to the scientist," [12] we ought not then to disregard the *story* that the writer wants to tell. And especially is this true of Silone's first novel, for here we get the stuff out of which he will build his later books. Here we get a first statement of many of the major themes which are to punctuate all of his novels—the theme of opposition between the simple rhythms of the agrarian village and the artificial, morally ambiguous complexities of the "City" (which are used as symbolic of the highly synthetic quality of life in the totalitarian society); the themes of the capitulation of official religion, of the corruption of the middle-class intellectuals and government functionaries (Don Circostanza), and the tragedy of the peasant's victimization. Finally, the question is posed as to what must be the revolutionary's relation to this whole agonized world—and I say *posed*, for, though the Unknown Hand has a strategy of action, it is itself morally ambiguous, not in the sense of the impurity of his motives but in the sense of its unintended tragic issue, for it unquestionably contributes to the perpetration of the peasants' final anguish. Significantly, this last episode culminates in the disintegrating question asked by those few Fontamarans who manage to escape into the hills: What, then, must we do?

We are here now.
We reached here over the border, through the Unknown Hand.
But it is clear that we cannot stay here.
What must we do?
After all this suffering and all this fighting, all these tears and all
this anguish, all this blood, all this hate, and all this hopelessness,
What must we do?

This is a question, I say, which Silone in this book asks but does
not answer, for, as we have seen, it is essentially a story of the
folk and its tragedy, and only incidentally, of the revolutionary
who becomes the central figure in the two later novels, *Bread
and Wine* and *The Seed beneath the Snow*.

In characterizing the polarities within which the modern
writer has conceived and come to terms with his spiritual situation, the late F. O. Matthiessen spoke of Lawrence, on the
one hand, as a leading example of those who have created
private religions of their own as surrogates for the Christian
tradition, and, of "others, like Malraux and the younger radical
poets and novelists, [who] have tended to subsume the religious
impulse under the breadth of their devotion to purposive social
action." [13] And to this latter group Silone certainly belonged during the period of his development out of which came *Bread and
Wine*. His progress, to be sure, has steadily been toward a more
unambiguous, explicit use of Christian categories, and it would
be more probably true to say even of *Bread and Wine* that not
so much is the religious impulse subsumed under preoccupations
with political strategy as are the two elements held in constant
tension. *Fontamara*, as a novel of the folk and its victimization by
the synthetic cohesions of Italian Fascism, is, I think, a master-
piece of its kind. Its simplicity, the tightness of its structure, the
baldness of its pathos, the brilliant seizures of peasant humor—
all these things contribute to the richness of its texture. And in

spite of its tragic climax in the failure of the Unknown Hand
one strongly feels that the book was bodied forth out of an im-
perious revolutionary passion, out of the feeling that there is
something which "we must do," and that this something is to
be discovered and actualized within a context of Marxist thought
and strategy. To this last the book seems to offer no alternative.
But when we come to *Bread and Wine* we meet a new tension
that runs across the entire novel—between Arthur Koestler's
"yogi and the commissar," between the saint and the revolutionary, between Christ and Marx. And this tension finds its
full embodiment in the character of Pietro Spina, who dominates
the stage not only here but in the subsequent novel *The Seed
beneath the Snow* and the play *And He Hid Himself.*

The time span of *Bread and Wine* begins just prior to the rape
of Ethiopia. The peasants remain in a state of oppression and
misery, the helpless victims of the new bosses. At the center of
the story is one Pietro Spina, who, unlike many of his childhood
friends who chose to temporize with the Fascist regime, has
chosen the lonely road of intransigeance and revolution—
through which, though he has preserved his integrity and self-
respect, he has lost his health. The narrative opens with his
return to Italy, worn out by long months of exile and anxious
to help his people, his body racked with consumptive pains and
his mind perturbed by the dark shadows cast over his native
land. Though still in his early thirties, he looks like an old man,
partly because of his ill-health and great fatigue, and partly
because of the wrinkled visage he has achieved through the use
of iodine to aid his disguise, a disguise completed by priestly
vestments that take on in time, as Isaac Rosenfeld suggests,
thematic as well as strategic significance.[14] Spina wants to renew his connections with the Underground by way of re-
establishing a living relationship with the people, and in terms

of the pilgrimage that he enters upon Silone accomplishes a rich integration of social antinomies—the peasantry and the landed gentry, the Fascist bureaucrats and the urban proletariat, the obsequious upholders of a decadent official religion and the faithful village priest, the workers in the Underground and the Party members in the cities.

When Spina arrives in Italy he is at the point of physical collapse. Nunzio Sacca, a boyhood friend now a doctor of medicine, who has made his peace with the Fascists but who remains sufficiently intelligent and sensitive to realize his own moral failure, arranges for Spina, disguised as a priest, to go to a little village in the foothills of the Apennines called Pietrasecca, where he may rest and regain his health. Spina adopts the name Don Paolo Spada, and there, because of his disguise, he is trusted and accepted by the simple people of the little village. As Don Paolo slowly regains his strength amidst the peace of this quiet countryside he uses his unaccustomed leisure to meditate on the course of his life and the meaning of his career. Indeed he finds himself carrying on a kind of "internal dialogue," which grows out of his experiences with two girls whom he encounters in Pietrasecca and who become greatly devoted to him.

The first of the girls is Bianchina, whose home is in Fossa dei Marsi and whom Don Paolo first meets when he is called from Pietrasecca to her bedside one night, when it is thought that she is about to die after having tried to rid herself of her unborn illegitimate child. The idea of lending himself to such an imposture is repugnant to him, but he knows that to refuse the priestly office might be to betray his disguise, and so he reluctantly enters the bedroom. The girl expects to be rebuked and berated by the strange priest, but, instead, he refuses to hear her confession, saying:

"My dear girl, I know everything. I beg you to tell me nothing. I beg you not to humiliate yourself and not to renew your sufferings. You have no need to confess. You are confessed already. . . . You have already done penance, and it has been too hard. . . . Have no fear; you are forgiven. What will not be forgiven is this evil society that forced you to choose between death and dishonor."

Bianchina subsequently recovers, and, after being evicted by her aunt who is, she says, "against liberty," she comes to Pietrasecca to thank Don Paolo for his kindness and to seek the assistance of a friend, Cristina Colamartini. Following her arrival she meets Don Paolo, and, on a lovely summer morning in the little garden beside his inn, the priest and the girl begin to talk:

Bianchina started laughing. Her pretty face looked even prettier against the dark rectangle of the door. Perhaps her neck was a little too thin, and her mouth was large and red; when she laughed it was really too large; although she certainly knew this, she laughed all the same. She had tiny ears. She picked up two pairs of cherries from the table and hung them over her ears, like a child. Then she started laughing again. Then she grew serious.

"You mustn't think ill of me," she said.

Round her neck, under her chemise, she wore the scapular of the Madonna del Carmine. She unbuttoned her blouse, opened her chemise and showed it. The scapular was green and her breasts were milky white.

Don Paolo felt his heart beating faster at the sight, after long abstinence, of this tender and fresh fruit of his own country. It was a pity, it really was a pity, that he had to be prudent.

Bianchina is, then, "the desire to enjoy freely the physical, worldly side of life" [15] and reveals to Spina one dimension of his being which he has failed to affirm and which he has indeed lost sight of in his practice of the political life.

It is the overtones of his relationship with Bianchina's friend Cristina, however, which are profounder and which awake in him the "internal dialogue," of which I have spoken, between the faithful Catholic adolescent boy of his youth, whom he has long suppressed, and the revolutionary. Cristina belongs to the old and respected Colamartini family of Pietrasecca and has long wanted to enter a convent, but has been unable to do so because her aged parents would then have no one on whom they could depend, all the other children having gone away from home. One morning Cristina comes to Don Paolo's inn to see its proprietress, and while she is there the priest engages her in conversation about the relevance of the cloistered life of spirituality to the flux and turmoil of life in the world. And he finds himself disarmed by the simple, unwavering faith of the girl.

Cristina's voice recalled Don Paolo's own dialogue between the adolescent and the revolutionary in him. Thus he had himself been greedy for the absolute and in love with righteousness when he had cut himself from the Church and gone over to Socialism. But much time had passed since then. What had remained in him of that generous impulse towards the masses of the people? He had broken with a decadent Church, rejected opportunism, and declined to compromise with society. But had he not succumbed to another kind of opportunism, the opportunism dictated by the interests of a political party? He had broken with the old world and all its comforts, cut himself off from his family, abandoned his favorite studies, set himself to live for justice and truth alone, and entered a party in which he was told that justice and truth were petty-bourgeois prejudices. Did he not feel himself betrayed? Had he, perhaps, taken the wrong road?

The pressure of such questions is so strong that he begins that night a notebook which he calls "Dialogues with Cristina," and in his first entry he asks himself:

Is it possible to take part in political life, to devote oneself to the service of a party, and remain sincere?

Has not truth, for me, become party truth? Has not justice, for me, become party justice?

Have not party interests ended by deadening all my discrimination between moral values? Do I, too, not despise them as petty-bourgeois prejudices?

Have I escaped from the opportunism of a decadent Church only to fall into bondage to the opportunism of a party?

What has become of my enthusiasm of that time? By putting politics before anything else, before all other spiritual needs, have I not impoverished, sterilized my life? Has it not meant that I have neglected deeper interests?

It is at this point that a circle of definition is drawn around the theme that is to prevail throughout the rest of the book: Spina's desire for a dimension of spiritual fulfillment that transcends anything to be envisaged through a purely political analysis of the human situation and that is symbolized by Cristina. Indeed, his "Dialogues with Cristina" develop into "a kind of examination of conscience, a kind of audit of his past life." As the summer draws to a close, his strength begins to return, but, significantly, we find him engaging in no real political activity. He does, to be sure, begin to make trips back and forth between Rome and Pietrasecca in an effort to re-establish contact with the Underground, and though each return to Rome suggests a resumption of the political life, each return to Pietrasecca suggests its renunciation. His main work appears to be confined to what Harry Slochower, in discussing the book, has called "a pilgrimage of good deeds." [16] He rarely enters into political discussions with the peasants but rather seeks to enter into a vital personal relation with them, to *practice the human presence* through an act of friendship. He does not want, it seems, any longer to offer a therapy of political conversion but, rather, a therapy of love.

Although the peasants talked quite freely in his presence, these casual encounters left him dissatisfied. He felt more like a tourist talking to people casually encountered by the wayside than a revolutionary working among the masses he represented . . . to establish relations between man and man, to inspire confidence and have confidence, to exchange ideas and not words, two men must be alone together, talk softly and with many pauses, the better to be able to reflect. One by one Don Paolo reviewed in his mind those peasants whom he already knew, wishing to select one to make friends with.

And yet Spina's indecision concerning the ultimate grounds of his assurance and the true direction of his vocation is never altogether overcome. We have already noted, for instance, his stubborn unwillingness to accede to Uliva's view of the fate of political revolution. When he visits his former comrade in Rome, Uliva bitterly remarks upon the inevitable corruption of the revolutionary idealist by his own legalism. Spina seizes the lapels of his coat and cries into his face:

"But why should that be our destiny? Why should there be no way out? Are we hens shut up in a hen-coop? Why should we remain the victims of an inexorable fate, powerless to fight against it? Why condemn a regime which does not yet exist and which we wish to create in man's image?"

But deep down Spina really sees and feels a terrible perplexity.

Meanwhile, Silone all the time casts Don Paolo's spiritual struggle against a broad panoramic background of social decline and individual failure. We see, for example, the mesmerization of the herd under "the new eloquence" on the occasion of The Leader's declaration of war against Ethiopia before a great throng at Avezzano. His voice is broadcast through a loudspeaker, but the hoarse mutterings of the apparatus pass unnoticed as the great crowd, though really not knowing at all the significance of the occasion, proceeds with a rhythmical cry to an impassioned invocation of their nameless leader, The Great Chief. Their enthusiasm is, of course, artifically created by the propitiatory magic of the government officials which makes them gladly surrender to the spurious unanimity contrived by the authorities, and they shout

That name which nobody dared pronounce privately, either in praise or in blame, because to name it brought misfortune . . . with all the force of their lungs in this general gathering, in the presence of his feared image, in the presence of the patriotic fetishes, as a piece of propitiatory magic, in a kind of religious frenzy. ". . . CHAY DOO! CHAY DOO! CHAY DOO! CHAY DOO! CHAY DOO! . . ."

As Spina witnesses this act of collective hypnotism the enormity of his task impresses itself upon him, and, as in a gesture of despair, his arms sink to his side. The orthodoxies of both Church and Party seeming now equally impervious to the dignity of the individual, he feels himself to have reached a dead end.

Along with such pictures of the capitulation of men in the broad mass, Silone gives us remarkably telling portraits of the individual's failure to retain integrity under the pressures exerted by totalitarian society. There is, for example, the cleric Don Piccirilli, whom we meet early in the novel at a gathering of Don Benedetto's former students who have come to the old priest's home to observe with him his seventieth birthday. When Don Piccirilli arrives somewhat late, with the rather breathless air of the fat, well-fed young divine, he says that he was detained by the necessity of finishing for the diocesan journal an article which is to be entitled "The Scourge of Our Time." When Don Benedetto asks whether it is about war or unemployment, the young priest is visibly annoyed. "Those are political questions," he says. "Only spiritual questions are dealt with in the diocesan journal. From the purely spiritual point of view, the scourge of our time, in my opinion, is immodesty in dress." He goes on to boast of the success he has achieved, the enormous spiritual progress that has been realized in his parish in recent years: "The number of confessions has increased by forty per cent, and the number of communions by thirty per cent." His old schoolmaster replies: "Poor Piccirilli. You talk of pure spirit and spiritual progress, and you express yourself in calculations and percentages, just like a baker." This, then, is the state of official religion.

We have already met Nunzio Sacca, whose opportunism is so typical of the compromised middle-class intellectual, but there is also the immensely pathetic figure of Don Zabaglione, the corrupt old orator, almost Falstaffian in his comic dimensions, once a socialist of sorts and therefore now suspect by the authorities, who is so eager to sell his "eloquence" to the new regime and who is so hurt by its refusal to accept him. Or there is the Colamartini family, so typical of the old landowning class, who can only cope with the disintegration of their traditional world by a kind of desperate insistence upon the prerogatives of name and birth and lineage. Or again there is the curiously dissolute figure of Signor Achilles, the professional *galant*, who, as he makes his living in the streets and bedrooms of Rome by rescuing young ladies from the assault of his assistant Lamorra, embodies all the moral disaffirmance of his society.

It is such human beings as these that constitute the world within which Don Paolo gropes for redemption. And the event which wrests him finally from his circuity into lucidity of thought and feeling is the murder of Don Benedetto, the fine old priest who had taught Spina as a boy and whose intransigeance finally provokes the Fascist authorities to poison the wine in the chalice from which he drinks in the celebration of

the Mass. After his death Spina begins fully to realize for the
first time the great influence his former teacher had exerted
upon the shaping of his mind. He realizes too, now that his
attempt over the past fifteen years to escape the Christian
truth which Don Benedetto had early inculcated in him has
failed, that all during this time, when he had substituted Marx-
ism for Christianity, he was only "half alive," having substituted
"logic and intellectual ideas taken from the world of economics
and politics for those deeper forces which I felt myself compelled to distrust." And so now he draws upon the wisdom
which had sustained the old priest in his last days when, in
speaking to the young radical, Murica, who has come seeking
some further insight into the great purposes that should guide
the revolutionary in our time, he says that they have to do not
with "new formulas, new gestures, or shirts of a different color"
but rather "a new way of living. To use an old expression,"
he says, "it is a matter of conversion. It is a matter of becoming a new man. . . . At heart every revolution puts this elementary question afresh: What, it asks, is man? What is this
human life?" And Murica, grasping his meaning, concurs: "The
revolution is a need of being no longer alone, one man against
another; it is an attempt to stand together and to be afraid no
longer; a need of brotherliness."

Toward the end of the book Murica is overtaken by the authorities and executed, and we find Spina in the Murica home
at the funeral meal. The boy's father welcomes his guests by
saying, "Eat and drink. This is his bread and this is his wine."
And here Silone strikes his deepest note, which is subsequently
to be elaborated in *The Seed beneath the Snow* and the play
And He Hid Himself: we suddenly discover that the entire book
has been poised in the direction of revealing the revolutionary
figure in our time as the real extension of the Incarnation, as

the foundation stone of the modern communion of saints. It is his body, broken and disfigured by a society which hunts him down "like a wild beast," that is our modern sacrament.

What Silone is presenting here is, I believe, an essentially liturgical conception of the problem of society: he is suggesting that the Incarnation of the Son of God, which is the manifestation of God's goodness in the flesh, must be seen as involving "the redemption of the body, and therefore also of the social relations of the life lived in the body, and of the whole social, economic and political structure." [17] And those who devote themselves to this work of redemption, that was initiated by Christ, are in truth extensions of His Presence: in their action is contained a sacramental quality which we must apprehend and lay hold of, if we are to be saved from the wreckage and disorder of contemporary history. "In times of conspiratorial and secret struggle," says Don Benedetto, "the Lord is obliged to hide Himself and assume pseudonyms," and so His name becomes that of those who "live outside the law," who, finding their society intolerable, seek to show men "a different way of living." Thus there is born a new type of saint in whom the old distinction between the "sacred" and the "secular" is broken down, who, for the sake of re-creating our social life, has rejected the temptation of political messianism. Take ye, then, and eat of his *bread*, and drink of his *wine*, and pronounce the Amen.

The novel ends on an echo of the Crucifixion as Spina is pursued out into the snow-covered mountains above Pietrasecca by the authorities, where he must meet the certain annihilation of all those followers of the Nazarene whose goodness cannot maintain itself in history against the hostile forces of Caesar. And Cristina, who loves him, follows him out into the great nocturnal silence of the mountain, herself to die under the attack of a pack of wolves; as she sees them galloping toward her, she kneels, closes her eyes, and makes the sign of the Cross.

In the later book, *The Seed beneath the Snow,* Spina is "reborn" through, as Harry Slochower suggests, a kind of immaculate conception—the rebirth coming about through the patient ministrations of his grandmother and through the renewal of spirit to which he is brought by living in a stable with mice and a donkey and a deaf-mute. We find now that his former priestly posture has become a real habit of his soul; it is no longer as a political revolutionary that he goes among the peasants of the Abruzzi but rather as a kind of St. Francis, motivated no longer by considerations of political tactics but simply by the Christian impulse of love and charity. Yet he regards his efforts to *practice the human presence* as being not a retreat from the political task but as rather a new approach to it: his conviction is that unless there is love among men there can be no real health in the body politic. Thus the political task can be discharged, then, on his present view, only when it is seen to have an ultimate moral and religious dimension.

Indeed, the great fact with which we now see Spina contending is that of man's persistent denial of Christ. Don Severino, the organist of the little church at Colle, at one point asks Mastro Eutimio, the village carpenter:

"Do you really believe, Mastro Eutimio, that the people of Colle would choose Jesus rather than Barabbas, if Barabbas were to appear on horseback, in a gala uniform, his chest covered with decorations, at the head of a legion of armed men, acclaimed by a crowd of flunkeys in the livery of scribes and public speakers and priests, and if Jesus were in the guise of a poor Christian, or of a poor, dirty, hunchbacked little Jew, a refugee, a man outside the law, without a country and without any 'papers'? . . . I'm just asking you a simple question, Mastro Eutimio, and to relieve your embarrassment I'll confess that I've often asked myself the same thing. I'm curious to hear your answer."

Mastro Eutimio scratched his chin, looked at the ground and remained for some time painfully silent.

"Truly, by the living Christ!" he exclaimed at last. "That's no question, Don Severino, it's the answer to a question, you know that yourself, Don Severino; the most tragic, humiliating and hopeless of answers. If you wanted to make me say that we all usurp the name of Christian, Don Severino, you've found the right tactics. . . . Excuse me, Don Severino, but which way are you going? May I walk down a piece of the road with you?"

Thus does Silone set forth the human tragedy in its perennial aspect; its contemporary manifestation is, of course, the new blasphemy of the monolithic totalitarian state.

It is, therefore, logical, since Christ continues to be denied even unto our own time, that there should be throughout Silone's novels "those who do not believe in the death and resurrection of Jesus but do believe in his agony." I spoke at the outset, in relating Silone's work to the revolutionary novel generally and especially to the work of André Malraux, of his having created a personal myth and made it central to his work. And one of the things I had in mind was that though he has drawn liberally upon traditional Christian mythology, he has adapted it to his own temperament to suit his own purposes; particularly do we sense this in the ever recurrent refrain that I have just noted which comes from his characters' lips, the insistence that Jesus is not dead but still hanging on the Cross, his body racked with pain. We hear, for instance, the government orator, Cavaliere Marcantonio, trying to persuade Mastro Eutimio, the carpenter at Colle, to alter a great wooden cross which he has made for a village Lenten celebration in such a way that it can serve as a suitable symbol of the new order. Marcantonio wants to superimpose a bundle of rods on the trunk of the cross and add an axe to its upper extremity. But Mastro Eutimio wants to know where, then, will Jesus lay his head. Marcantonio replies:

"You have forgotten, Mastro Eutimio, that Jesus is no longer hanging on the cross; such is the teaching of the Church itself."

"There are people, Cavaliere, who believe He is still hanging there in agony," Mastro Eutimio explained in a low voice. "There are people who are convinced that He never died and never rose again, that He is still living His agony here on earth. This, they say, explains a good many things."

And, indeed, this does explain a good many things for Silone. It illuminates basically the tragic disorder at the heart of human life, the anarchy of sin, which made Christ's suffering inevitable, for, as Donna Maria Vincenza, Spina's grandmother, maintains one day in conversation with Don Severino, as they try to analyze the meaning of Pietro's career:

"There is an original sin that was present in the handful of clay upon which Our Lord breathed to create Adam, an hereditary sin, an inner weakness, inherent in man, a sort of physical infection, an incurable fault that Christians must combat; if at times they delude themselves that they have uprooted it, it returns as surely as the weeds among the wheat return in the spring."

Don Severino's reply suggests Silone's complementary truth, when he says:

"There, Maria Vincenza; it seems to me that we have come back to where we started. In order to escape even the contamination of evil, sensitive souls have no choice but to take refuge in poverty and re-nunciation; they must flee the world, flee even life itself or at least reduce it to that mere breath that is passed on from generation to generation. Even the ways of the new secret organizations, Maria Vincenza, seem to me a sort of flight from evil."

But within the terms of Silone's total vision Don Severino's word is to be seen not simply as a doctrine of defeatist withdrawal but rather as a statement of one aspect of a duality of movement which is completed by a "return." For though the Christian revolutionary may be forced either by the necessities of the unpropitious occasion or of his own inner nature or by both to withdraw from the arena of political decision and activity, such a withdrawal, profoundly considered, is an opportunity, and, as Arnold Toynbee suggests, "perhaps a necessary condition for the anchorite's transfiguration." [18] To be sure, such transfiguration-in-solitude has little relevance for the field of social action except, as Toynbee goes on to say, "as a prelude to the return of the transfigured personality into the social milieu out of which he had originally come. . . . The return is the essence of the whole movement as well as its final cause." [19]

Spina's "return" assumes the form of what I have called the *practice of the human presence,* whereby the political act is transformed into an act of friendship and love. He first discovers the profoundly therapeutic power of friendship in his relationship with a young peasant, a deaf-mute, whose name is Infante. Infante comes devotedly to sit with him each day in the donkey's stable in Pietrasecca where, broken in body, he is hiding from the Fascist police. His grandmother subsequently arranges for his transport from Pietrasecca to Colle, giving him secret refuge in her own home. Spina tries afterwards to explain to her the experience he has undergone.

"How can I possibly give you an idea, Grandmother, of the simple, silent, deep friendship between us? I could barely see the dark bulk of his heavy body and hear his deep slow breathing, but there was a certain affinity between his body and the bodies of the other objects in that cave—the donkey, myself, the mice, the trough, the straw, the packsaddle and the broken lantern—a communion, a brotherhood whose discovery flooded my heart with a new feeling which perhaps I should call peace or even happiness. . . . And "companion" was the first new word that Infante learned from me. He knew how to say bread, 'pane,' which he pronounced 'paan,' and I explained to him with gestures that those who break bread together are called 'companions' from 'cumpane.' . . . Grandmother, I should tell you at length about my stay in the stable, I should refer to it every time that I try to explain my present frame of mind because I came out of it, if not a new man, at least stripped and bare. I feel now as if I had never really been myself before, as if I had been playing a part like an actor on the stage, wearing a mask and declaiming prepared speeches. This life and this civilization of ours seem to me a theatrical, conventional, lying sham. . . . I have come to think that the quiet, the peace, the happiness, the well-being, the homeliness, the companionship which I found in that stable derived from a contact with simple, true, difficult, painful forms of life, immune from the plague of rhetoric."

When Infante comes to Colle, Spina leaves his grandmother's home, fearing that her efforts in his behalf may involve her in dangerous complications with the authorities. Spina and his dumb friend are given refuge by the peasant Simone the Polecat, a village radical. In Simone's little hut, just outside Colle, these three live together in a spirit of love and friendship, more deeply satisfying than anything Spina has ever known before. One day Simone asks Spina why it is that in all their talks together he has never spoken of his old friends in the Party. Pietro answers:

"I didn't have any real friends in the Party. . . . All in all, I must have been acquainted with several thousand persons in the Party more or less and known a few dozen among them a little better. But in fifteen years I never knew a soul as well as I know you and Infante.

I used to think it was my own fault but I came to see that the same thing was true of others. To tell the truth, they didn't hold much with friendship in the Party; there was something suspicious about it, as if it might engender the formation of cliques and gangs. For this reason I should even rightly admit that friendship, in the true and human meaning of the word, was regarded and despised as a remnant of bourgeois individualism. . . ."

Simone, saddened by his friend's revelation, after a long silence, murmurs: "I didn't know how widespread was the decay."

Sometime later Spina has to flee from Colle to Acquaviva, a little town in the mountains. He is accompanied by Faustina, an intelligent and attractive girl, who "embodies the qualities represented by the two girls in Bread and Wine. She represents the union of physical and spiritual happiness and fulfillment." [20] With Faustina he discusses his discoveries of the past months.

"It was more painful to me than I can tell you, Faustina, after I had come back from exile abroad in order to work and fight against the dictatorship, to spend almost a whole year in inactivity here in the country, rusting away, all because I was going through a spiritual crisis. But this much I learned at my own expense: that before we can give something of ourselves to others, we must first possess ourselves. A man who is spiritually a slave cannot work for true freedom. To look after one's own soul no longer seems to me a waste of time or, as I once used to say pontifically, a sign of bourgeois decadence. When all is said and done, there is no better and more necessary occupation than man's effort to know himself and the meaning of his life on earth. Everything else must follow, as the cart follows the horse."

Simone and Infante shortly follow Pietro to Acquaviva; and there Spina and Simone decide to look up a number of their old friends whom they have not seen for many years. And suddenly this desire of theirs to renew old friendships begins to spread contagiously over the entire region; the episode culminates in a kind of mystery play with the whole countryside overrun with "old friends, looking for one another." "An old, faithful and disinterested friendship," says Simone to Pietro, "is in itself a total negation of death." Man's disinterested offer of love to his fellow man is, in other words, finally, the greatest act of revolution and the surest antidote to the world's evil. It is upon such a vision of the human problem that, at bottom, the entire book rests.

But what has been said thus far must not be taken to mean that Silone is a simple moralist who regards the mere exhortation that we ought to love one another more than we do as a sufficient resolution of our world's dilemmas. For he has no simple faith in the human heart: he knows its radical weakness, its secret fault. His presiding mood is one of pessimism, or at least of disenchantment. Nor is this pessimism truncated by any simple recapitulation of that particular humanistic optimism that has been so characteristic of radical socialism in our time and that might well be summed up in the proposition: Though men of might and power may reveal the taint of Original Sin, you may trust the poor man, for, since he has no interests to defend, he can be relied upon to see the truth. We recall, for instance, Spina's disclaiming any illusions about the " 'good savage,' the simple and ridiculous 'natural man' painted by Rousseau," in the course of his attempt to explain to his grandmother his relationship with Infante. And he is mindful of the fact that the peasant in whose stable he hid during his stay in Pietrasecca, though poor and simple in mind, was a thoroughgoing opportunist and only failed to betray him because he felt he could make capital of his person. But beyond this isolated instance of explicit rejection of romantic feeling about the peasants as a class of humanity Silone consistently refuses to falsify his representation of the human fact by intro-

ducing any sentimental illusions about the nature of man—
even the poorest and most humble of men. The human beings
who make up his world do not love one another easily, for
theirs is, primarily, a community of Original Sin, from which
they can be lured into love and friendship only by the "revolutionary" activity of him who is what Toynbee has called a
"creative saviour." And here, I think, Silone's grasp of the process
of social salvation parallels to a remarkable degree that of Bergson, who was himself centrally preoccupied with those

privileged souls who have felt themselves related to all souls, and
who, instead of remaining within the limits of their group and keeping to the restricted solidarity which has been established by nature,
have addressed themselves to humanity in general in an *élan* of love.
The apparition of each of these souls has been like the creation of a
new species composed of one unique individual.[21]

It is the vocation of Silone's "creative saviour," as with Bergson's
"mystic," "to make a movement out of something which, by
definition, is a halt." His task is that of luring contemporary
man back into the direction of the *élan* of life itself, which is
love and friendship. This, Silone is saying, is the true business
of the "revolutionary" in our time: he must somehow overcome
the alienation and estrangement that separate man from man.
But he remains himself an isolated figure, forever an "outlaw"
(and again, the parallel with Bergson holds), for the saint—and
this is finally the category in terms of which Silone comprehends the revolutionary—can be no other; the normal entanglements of human living are powerless to contain him. When
Donna Maria mourns that her grandson cannot remain with
her as her sons once stayed around their parents, she is reminded
that those whom Christ "chooses and draws after him are, in
a way, lost to their families." And not only is Spina free of the
normal entanglements of blood and family, but of all others

as well. As we have seen, he not only stands against the apostasies of his society but against the various protestant orthodoxies as well; but finally he stands apart from society as an order of life really, by reason of his being constituted in the manner that he is—as a hero, as a saint, as a revolutionary, as an extension of the Incarnation, and is characterized, in Don Severino's words, by "an intimate sadness which comes to chosen souls simply from their consciousness of man's fate." It is a sadness, though, which we can understand, for, as Don Severino goes on to say, "if we stop to think deeply and quietly about man's fate, Maria Vincenza, you will agree that there's not much cause for rejoicing." Donna Maria concurs, saying that she supposes her grandson's sorrow comes finally not "from any particular way of living but from life itself."

In the Preface to his most recent work, the play *And He Hid Himself*, which is based on an episode drawn from *Bread and Wine*, Silone insists that the rediscovery of the Christian tradition remains the most significant gain for the revolutionary conscience of our generation. "In all these two thousand years," he says,

the Christian revolution has not succeeded in destroying the classical human relationships of ancient comedy and tragedy, but it has enabled us to judge them from a radically new standpoint. In the Middle Ages this judgment was personified by the saints and martyrs, but for some time past it would seem as if the men who "hunger and thirst after righteousness" had "gone out of the temple." None the less it is they who carry within themselves the truth of Christ.

Hence it is the libertarian socialist revolutionary who bears in his being the presence of Christ. It is he who is the foundation of our modern communion of saints, and so, Annina, a young woman who is one of Spina's comrades, says to him that, though as a schoolgirl she dreamed of entering a convent and becoming a nun, she feels now that she has after all "entered the novitiate of a way of life that is pure and consecrated to duty, a way of life which in its own way is also sacred, because in its own way it's difficult, and farther removed than any other from the compromises of ordinary life." But this community of those who have "gone out of the temple" but who yet "carry within themselves the truth of Christ" is itself outlawed, as was Christ Himself, and is hunted down by an apostate society "like a wild beast." "In the sacred history of man on earth," then, as Silone goes on to say in this Preface, "it is still, alas, Good Friday." And so we encounter once more the insistence upon the continuing agony of Our Lord. Brother Gioacchino, the Capuchin friar, declares early in the play:

"The crucified Just Man is not dead, as they tell; neither has He risen again and ascended into heaven, as they tell; He is still and forever in agony on the cross. Nailed hands and feet to the tree of torment, His side pierced deep by a lance, His head crowned with sharpest thorns, spat upon, mocked and abused by the rabble of armed hirelings, forsaken, denied, forgotten by His dearest friends, He, the Just Man, is still on the cross today, hanging between life and death, in atrocious, unending, fearful, maddening agony. The world knows nothing of him, and the Church, maybe out of pity for us, tries to make us believe that He is dead and risen again and departed from this earth, but He is still down here, alive, on the cross, in agony. That is the truth."

And He Hid Himself may, then, I think, be legitimately viewed as a "Passion play," as a "Good Friday play," set against the background of the world made familiar by the novels. The main thread of the action has to do with Luigi Murica's betrayal of his comrades in the Underground to the Fascist authorities. Murica, however, cannot suppress the condemnations of his conscience, and so, in his distress, he goes to Don Benedetto for counsel. The old priest sends him back to Spina, confident that the boy will be dealt with mercifully by his former pupil. When Murica meets Spina, he tells him that it was not so much fear of punishment that made him want to confess his sin to his old comrades whom he had betrayed and to be forgiven, not so much fear of punishment as the frightful possibility that he might really get away with his crime. One question, he says, overrode all others:

". . . if technical competence in the craft of evil were to eliminate all risk of sanction, would this mean also that all distinction between good and evil would thereby be effaced? . . . My whole being was seized by a new, painful, implacable tension. . . . I simply couldn't and wouldn't resign myself to impunity. I hadn't believed in God for many years, but I suddenly began longing, with all the strength of my soul, for Him to exist. I began to invoke Him, crying into the void. I needed Him urgently in order not to succumb to insanity and chaos. The most frightful punishment imaginable seemed to me infinitely preferable to placid acceptance of a world in which the problem of evil could be solved by a little cunning and dexterity of execution. . . ."

With this, Spina's faith in Murica is restored; he forgives him, and accepts him back into the movement.

The close parallel which Silone wants to establish between this drama and the Christian myth becomes manifest in the subsequent events of the play. Murica, after resuming his activities in the Underground, is overtaken by the authorities and executed by the state police for distributing subversive pamphlets. Thus, through the ultimate sacrifice of death, he finally achieves his own expiation—but, even more, makes possible the redemption of others, to the extent at least of arousing the peasants to engage in revolutionary work and overcoming their reluctance to associate with Underground movements. And again, as in the closing sections of *Bread and Wine*, we find his father welcoming his guests at the funeral meal by saying:

"This is his bread, you know, the bread he can no longer eat. This is his wine, the wine he can drink no longer. The bread that for us now has a taste of ashes. The wine that for us now has a taste of gall. But for each one of you let it be the bread of strength and the wine of healthfulness, and I beseech God, our most merciful Father, to grant my prayer."

Thus does Silone place the drama of the Passion at the very center of human life, making it the basic event in terms of which all others are to be construed, which is itself in some measure recapitulated in every moment that the human spirit, in penitent confession of its sinfulness and acknowledgment of its subjection to God, extends itself in sacrificial love toward other life, working for its redemption and thereby transmuting the temporal order into an earnest of the Kingdom of God.

Here, then, is what Ignazio Silone is saying to the intellectual bewilderment and moral confusion that attend the crisis of radical thought in our period. It is, indeed, his distinction to have proclaimed the possibility of a redemption of politics in a time when radical thought has been almost overcome with despair of politics by reason of the inordinate elephantiasis of the modern state, which, in its exacerbation of the tensions between the various national communities, has threatened to destroy all power of discrimination as to the areas in which politics is valid. And he has done this within the terms of the Christian distinction between the natural and the supernatural. Silone has seen, as few of his generation have been able to, that, though man is by nature a political animal, as Aristotle contended, his full stature transcends the political organism and therefore cannot be defined in terms of political categories alone, that consequently no purely political statement of man's destiny can do justice to the subtleties of the human situation, for when the political order seeks to embrace the whole of the natural community it obstructs our natural proclivities, thereby finally exhausting and destroying itself. Such a false politic has, of course, been the bane of contemporary history and has presented us with the present occasion that demands, in Silone's view, a reorientation of the political task in the light of Christian principles. Politics thus reorientated will proceed from the basic presupposition of the ontological duality of man, a duality consisting in the natural and supernatural dimensions of his being. It will then be seen that, though the necessities of man's nature dictate his existence in the order of common life presided over by the political executive, the whole of his being is not comprehended by such relationships, that he has certain essential loyalties, beyond those of a citizen, of a supernatural order, the observance of which the political community is ordained to make possible, and that when it fails to do so it places its own integrity in jeopardy. Such a revivification of political consciousness Silone would accomplish, as we have seen, through the transmutation of the revolutionary act (which is, presumably, in the service of that *Real-Politik* which ignores man's supernatural character) into an act of brotherhood, of love and friendship—whereby "the sacred history of man on earth" might move beyond the agony of Good Friday.*

* There are two volumes of Silone's which I have not considered in this essay: the collection of stories and sketches under the title *Mr. Aristotle* and the systematic prose-critique of Fascism in dialogue form under the title *The School for Dictators*. Though both books are at one with the consistencies of the novels, neither throws sufficient light on Silone the novelist to justify integration into the kind of analysis that has been set forth above. The review of the history of his affiliations with Communism that Silone contributed to *The God that Failed*, edited by Richard Crossman (New York, 1950), is also a highly interesting document which many readers of this essay may want to examine.

D. H. LAWRENCE: CHARTIST OF THE VIA MYSTICA

Is it not without reason
That this hollow
Has been put away in a wilderness.
It means
That the place of love
Lies not in beaten ways
Nor about our human dwellings.
Love haunts the deserts.
The road that leads to its retreat
Is a hard and toilsome road.
—Gottfried of Strasbourg's *Tristan*

There is love whenever desire is so great as to
go beyond the confines of natural love.
—Guido Cavalcanti

Real life is *elsewhere.*—Rimbaud

It is probably true now that to venture to contribute anything further to the literature on Lawrence without apology or explanation must constitute in the minds of many a considerable *faute d'inattention*, especially after the excellent criticisms of J. Middleton Murry, Horace Gregory, F. R. Leavis, and William York Tindall. But perhaps the only excuse I need really offer is that which Santayana gave many years ago for writing on Lucretius, Dante, and Goethe—"the human excuse which every new poet has for writing about the spring." He has "attracted me" and "moved me to reflection"; he has "revealed to me certain aspects of nature and of philosophy which I am prompted by mere sincerity to express, if anybody seems interested or willing to listen." And yet perhaps the more serious apology for the pages which follow was suggested some years ago by Horace Gregory when, in the Preface to his little book on Lawrence, he said that "it will be some time before we exhaust a number of possible attitudes toward D. H. Lawrence, for since his death and through his published letters we have become sensitively aware of a great personality, the exact likeness of which we shall never experience again."

This essay proceeds, then, from the conviction that in the eighteen years that have elapsed since Mr. Gregory penned these lines all such possible attitudes have not yet been exhausted by those who, either out of excessive devotion or excessive impatience with the man and his work, have attempted to define his meaning for our time. Indeed, when one looks back over the large body of critical and biographical material that has been produced since, say, 1930, one is soon struck by the extent to which the great bulk of it has ceased to be useful or even interesting. There was, of course, a time in the early thirties, shortly after Lawrence's death, when almost everyone who had known the man or who had attended a few dinner parties at which he had been present brought out some kind of informally written volume of personal recollections, in an effort, one imagines, at once to ride to immortality in the light of his glory (which was perhaps, after all, a not wholly ignoble aspiration) and to exploit what was then a fairly good market for such hack-writing. Lawrence's glory, though, is not now quite what it then was, nor is the market as good today as it was then, but, judging from the personal memoirs that continue to appear, this sort of writing has not yet come to an end. Of the plethora of biographical material Richard Aldington's recent book, *D. H. Lawrence: Portrait of a Genius*

But . . . , is perhaps the most valuable, chiefly because it consists very largely of a summing up of things previously said in such books as Catherine Carswell's, Mrs. Lawrence's, and that of "E.T.," the Miriam of *Sons and Lovers*—books which still deserve to be read; somewhat less valuable are the studies of Dorothy Brett and Mabel Dodge Luhan. Two French critics, Ernest Seillière and Paul de Reul, have produced serious studies of Lawrence, but one feels that Seillière overstresses Lawrence's affinities with the German Rousseauists (Bachofen, Bleibtreu, and Ludwig Klages), and both somehow fail to give us a sufficiently whole view and do not altogether disengage themselves from their materials. And so we are left with the one indispensable study, Murry's *Son of Woman*, which, though it is not always reliable on factual matters of personal history and is at times governed by a too determined preoccupation with self-defense, remains the deepest and most revealing exploration of Lawrence's character that we have. Murry was chiefly interested in reconstructing the psychological foundations on the basis of the books, and though it is clear that Lawrence's doctrines root in a tragic personal dilemma it is also true that he looked upon his work as not merely an objectification of self-knowledge but also as a new gospel for modern man. And, therefore, it would seem that he asks us to consider his ideas as ideas and not alone as vehicles of self-revelation. To this extent, then, the methods of analysis which Murry employed must be supplemented by other methods. We have also the excellent little studies of F. R. Leavis and Horace Gregory, the first of which is hardly obtainable in this country now, even in university libraries; and at the end of the thirties there appeared William York Tindall's brilliantly mordant analysis, *D. H. Lawrence and Susan His Cow*, which, though it places rather more emphasis on Lawrence's critical writings and polemical writings (which I take to be essentially subordinate to and by-products of the poetry and the novels) and his affinities with theosophy, yoga, and astrology than I should care to do, yet contains many stimulating insights. There is also the essay of R. P. Blackmur and that of D. S. Savage, in each of which fundamental and important considerations are cogently set forth concerning Lawrence's achievement in poetry.*

There is, of course, a great body of criticism now bearing upon Lawrence's work, but these things which I have mentioned are the texts to which we must turn when we seek help from other critics in understanding his problems. It is, then, astonishing, in view of the magnitude of his achievement, both quantitatively and qualitatively considered, that so few things of solid worth can be discovered in all the literature that has grown up about him in the last twenty years. And it would therefore seem that the attitude of reluctance to read still another analysis of his ideas which I anticipate on the part of many who may come to this book derives not from their being surfeited by excellent Laurentian studies but, more probably, from a currently pervasive hostility to Lawrence himself. Or perhaps I should not say hostility but rather indifference, for I do not think I am wrong in feeling that the younger generation which has grown into ma-

* Since these lines were written there have appeared other studies of Lawrence, the most important of which are Harry T. Moore's *The Life and Works of D. H. Lawrence* (New York, 1951) and Father William Tiverton's *D. H. Lawrence and Human Existence* (London, 1951); Father Tiverton's study, the work of an Anglican priest writing on this occasion pseudonymously, belongs, I believe, among the most searching analyses of Lawrence that have yet been produced. F. R. Leavis's latest studies of Lawrence, which have been appearing in recent issues of *Scrutiny*, appear also to be breaking new ground, particularly in their defense of him against the charge, which is made here, that he was frequently a careless craftsman. And it may well be that Leavis's vigorous defense, partly by reason of the solidity of his own reputation now, will accomplish the renewal of interest in Lawrence for which many have long hoped. Unfortunately, the present study was completed prior to the appearance of these works and could not benefit from the new insights which they have made available.

turity during the past decade do not read him and that their elders now feel obliged to apologize for once having read him. It may, of course, be true that the cyclical histories of literary reputations, as Elizabeth Bowen suggests, "follow some beneficial, restorative natural law," that after judgments cease and controversies die down we naturally proceed to a new and profounder seizure of a great writer's legacy, and that Lawrence's present "winter sleep" is only prelusive to his re-emergence as a vital and living monument of the great tradition.[1] But however this may be, the sad condition of his current reputation is unarguable. Diana Trilling has recently tried to elucidate the serious disproportion between what would seem to be Lawrence's achievement and our present opinion of him, and the best of her reasons is, I think, given when she says:

We have insisted that our renovators of the spirit—our poets, novelists, and critics—renovate, instead, the body politic, that they be public health officers, criers of economic and political cures, anything except, like Lawrence, spokesmen for the self and the self's mysterious possibilities.[2]

Lawrence has, in other words, been the victim of a deceit which we have practiced upon ourselves and by which doubtless we shall be done more harm than his ultimate stature.

But where Lawrence has been the object of carefully enunciated and sustained analysis, the critical attitude that has been frequently taken toward his craftsmanship seems now to have considerable justification. He appears to us today to belong, as R. P. Blackmur has said, "to that great race of English writers whose work totters precisely where it towers, collapses exactly in its strength: work written out of a tortured Protestant sensibility and upon the foundation of an incomplete, uncomposed mind: a mind without defences against the material with which it builds and therefore at every point of stress horribly succumbing to it." [3] And again, Blackmur, with immaculate precision, defines his magnitude as "the magnitude of ruins—and the ruins for the most part of an intended life rather than an achieved art." [4] This is just it. Indeed we find ourselves in the uncomfortable position, if we would consider Lawrence as an artist, of being unable to discover in all but a few of the poems and the novels the significant formal complexities which we usually associate with the internally coherent and self-subsisting aesthetic organism. Lawrence rarely gives us that characteristic cerebral sensation which we expect from the pure artist—of being at the second remove from experience and of having for a moment a vantage-point over the obscurities of life itself.* He could not do this, for he was too casual a craftsman to interpose that formal apparatus between the diffuseness of personal experience and the objectivity of language which transmutes the concrete stuff of experience into a seizable imaginative prehension. And the consequence is thus that we do not often get in Lawrence that same intensity of form, that same universalized particularity, that we get in the best work of his contemporaries—in Eliot and Yeats, in E. M. Forster and Virginia Woolf (the excellences of the latter two being, though, minor excellences, whereas Lawrence, on the other hand, for all of his monumental faults is a major figure in modern literature). His undeniable power and greatness as a writer seem rather to reside chiefly in his highly sensitive faculties of observation and his really masterful command of the English language.

This kind of evaluation could easily be extended and fully documented, but this work has already been ably carried out by D. S. Savage, R. P. Blackmur, and others; and it is not, at

---

* It should, of course, be borne in mind, though, that many great writers—and perhaps even some of the greatest—are not *pure* artists, a discrimination which a certain rigorism among contemporary critics often prevents them from making.

any rate, my primary purpose here to continue this enterprise of aesthetic analysis. I propose, rather, to attempt an elucidation of the interrelations between his ideas, of the structure of his thought, as it relates to the context of discussion established by this book. And this is by no means an easy task, both because of Lawrence's inordinate capacity for self-contradiction and also because his work has always been subsumed—and rightly so—under a category of thought and culture than which there is none more difficult to define. That is to say, we speak of Lawrence as a *romantic*, and what we mean by this, or should mean, is precisely the question with which this essay must begin.

Our present impatience with the term is well expressed by William York Tindall, when he says: "Romantic and romanticism are tiresome labels, perhaps better left alone, but of some use when narrowly limited and applied to the art of the last one hundred and fifty years as aids to the understanding of its character." [5] Or again, Emery Neff rejects the term "as having no meaning common to the four literatures [of modern European poetry] and as often foreign to the creative intentions of the poets." [6] That the attitude of these critics springs from a profound realization of the inability of any simple formula to do justice to the endless complexities that have attended the growth of modern literature seems clear. But it seems to me to be equally clear that the classical-romantic antithesis is an integral part of the furniture of our minds which corresponds with real and recognizable—though elusive, to be sure, and difficult to define—aspects of art and literature which have some measure of historical significance. Indeed, it seems somehow to keep on reappearing, in spite of and to the distraction of scholars, in order to separate what men in every generation deeply feel needs to be separated.

And yet it appears that not a great deal of progress has been made by way of elucidating the nature of this distinction. Ever since T. E. Hulme wrote his now celebrated essay, "Romanticism and Classicism," over thirty-five years ago, it has been the subject of a main segment of the most important critical controversy of our time. Pronunciamentos on the matter have been handed down by T. S. Eliot, Herbert Read, Middleton Murry, Wyndham Lewis, and, more recently, the controversy has been energetically reopened by Jacques Barzun and Hoxie Neale Fairchild. Though all of these writers have made fresh and vital contributions to the theory of literature, most of them, on the point of this particular controversy, have largely tended to proclaim their personal bias toward one or the other of the two antithetical principles, and most, excepting Barzun and Fairchild, have tended to define the "classic" and the "romantic," almost exclusively, in "qualificatory" rather than in "historical" terms. And at the other extreme is Mario Praz, who would have the terms understood as meaningful only when they function as purely empirical categories, designating special characteristics of fixed historical periods, and who finds Croce's dictum that "romantic" and "classic" are moments of the human spirit, coexisting as systole and diastole in the human heart, to be meaningless.[7] Though I am in no way disposed to enter the controversy here, I should be willing to venture the suggestion that the appropriate position to be defended lies somewhere between the two extremes and is more nearly approximated by the perspective on the history of European literature offered some years ago by Sir Herbert Grierson.[8]

Grierson's analysis, to be sure, is contextualistic; that is to say, he defines what he means by "classic" and "romantic" in primarily historical terms, although he does not exclude the "qualificatory" sense of these designations. A classical literature, he says, is the product of a nation and a generation which has consciously achieved a definite advance, moral, political, intellectual; and is filled with the belief that its view of life is more natural, human, universal, and wise than that from which it has escaped. It has effected a synthesis which enables it to look round on life with a sense of its wholeness, its unity in variety; and the work of the artist is to give expression to that consciousness, hence the solidarity of his work and hence too its definiteness, and in the hands of great artists its beauty. . . . The work of the classical artist is to give individual expression, the beauty of form, to a body of common sentiments and thoughts which he shares with his audience, thoughts and views which have for his generation the validity of universal truths.[9]

D. S. Savage's description of the Augustan age of eighteenth-century English literature represents, for instance, what Grierson would take to be a "classical" ethos:

At this period society had reached a high degree of outward homogeneity. Common values permeated the entire social structure; the growth of the city made possible a predominantly urban mode of existence for the upper and middle classes, with an attendant social life centering around the Court but not rigidly bound to it. In this society the writer was completely at home; his values were society's, and society's values were his own. This is to be seen in the close connection that held between the literary and the social career. Success in literature, on one's purely literary merits, was practically synonymous with social success. The writer might legitimately, therefore, set out on a literary career with social ambitions. He would not deliberately have to adapt himself to the taste of the time, because he was almost certain to share it. Dr. Johnson's much quoted remark that no one but a fool wrote except for money reflects this state of cultural homogeneity. One has only to transpose the application of this remark to our own time to see the vast gulf that exists between the conditions of eighteenth- and of twentieth-century England. Other conditions, too, were favourable to the socialization of literature. The life of the time was not only homogeneous but compact.

It was therefore possible for a certain identification to obtain between private and public values. The man of letters today is, virtually, a specialist: at least he is driven in upon his experience as a private individual. The vast complexity of the modern social structure and the specialized nature of political problems and issues make politics, too, a specialist's concern. This was not at all the case in Dryden's, Pope's or Johnson's day, when the man of letters was almost invariably a political pamphleteer, a man of the world and a self-conscious citizen. . . . There was neither need nor excuse for specialization. Life was a whole, and demanded to be comprehended as such. The literary personality, which has since then become divided into its several components, was a unity.[10]

But, as Brunetière showed in his *La Nationalisation de la littérature*, there has been a frequently recurring tendency in the history of the human spirit toward a periodic "déformation de l'idéal classique." The classical synthesis becomes demonic; reason becomes dogmatic and begins to ignore the fragmentariness of its premises, and as the process of desiccation goes on, disintegration becomes

violent disruption, because a fresh sap is beginning to rise in the veins of the human spirit, a wave of fresh thought and emotion is pouring over the nation or the world of which this or that nation is a conscious part. The minds of men become aware of what has been left out in the synthesis, the balance of which a classical art is the reflection. The *spiritual*, or it may be the *secular*, side of man's nature has been repressed or ignored. A new vision dawns on the imagination. In some of its manifestations the new movement, and the literature which expresses it, will be sentimental and fanciful, a literature of *Sturm und Drang*; to some minds it will come, at some period at any rate, as almost entirely an artistic movement, a rejection of old forms, a delight in new experiments in vocabulary and metres; but for its greatest minds it is a spiritual and philosophical movement also. . . . But this spiritual quickening reacts on the form of literature, hence the qualities which distinguish the literature of such a movement from classical literature.[11]

Applying this antithesis to the history of thought and culture, Grierson seeks to show that each principle has received three great expressions. The first of the great classical epochs, he says, was the age of Pericles, the imaginative flower of which was the Attic drama; the second gained expression in the great culture of Rome, extending through the later republic and reign of Augustus, from Cicero to Virgil and Horace; and the third such age, says Grierson, was that of Louis XIV in France and that which in England was initiated by Dryden. And in like manner he delineates three great Romantic movements: the first appears in the tragedies of Euripides and the dialogues of Plato and culminates in the revolution both in religious thought and Greek prose embodied by St. Paul; the second, he says, coincides with the emergence of that spirit in the twelfth and thirteenth centuries which took shape in the love lyrics of the Provençals and the profane romances of *Lancelot and Guinevere, Tristan and Iseult,* and *Aucassin et Nicolette;* and the third is that more popularly associated with the word Romanticism, the movement which started from "the flame which Rousseau kindled and which spread to Germany and England," and which was to project a radical criticism of that bondage to the secular which we associate with the *Aufklärung.*

Now it is interesting and essential to our argument to ¬ote that still another and more recent writer on the "romantic agony," Denis de Rougemont, in his fascinating book, *Love in the Western World,* has remarked upon this antagonism between the spirituality of Romance and that of medieval Christianity, which Grierson uses to illustrate a second major outburst of Romanticism in the history of European culture. Though de Rougemont takes this cleft in medieval culture as the *point de l'origine* of the

Romantic movement, it will be seen later on that there is no
real incompatibility between his conception and Grierson's somewhat broader view on the subject. So germane is his argument
to the perspective which I propose to cast on the subject of this
chapter that it will be helpful to have its main outlines before us.

De Rougemont, at first somewhat disconcertingly, locates the
metaphysical foundation of Romanticism in a spiritual movement which, from its earliest years, Christianity had opposed but
which gained somehow a new power and attractiveness in the
Middle Ages, a movement generally subsumed under the generic
name of Gnosticism or Manicheism. We know, of course, that
this movement assumed widely diverse forms, for its basic tendency, both philosophical and religious, was syncretistic. It was
never simply a local cult, for, as early as the third century it had
spread over the geographical and historical area now marked off
by India on the one hand and by Britain on the other. From
Persian culture and religion it acquired its radical moral dualism,
from Eastern mysticism the antithesis between Darkness and
Light, and from Alexandria and the Near East its universalism.
Though this religion assumed various forms and provided the
basic impulse for many Christian heresies, de Rougemont finds
its presiding strain to have been a metaphysic of death that represented the world as essentially evil and held forth as the only
possible salvation a kind of *askésis*, a kind of death into the
Darkness where union with the Magna Mater could be achieved.
It was based on a theory of emanation, the implication of which
was that the soul is imprisoned in matter and that its redemption
is dependent upon a denial of the world and a mystical reunion
with the divine element from which it originally descended.
The original sin was birth itself, from which the human soul
could be redeemed, it was held, only by returning into "the One
of luminous indistinction."

Though much recent scholarship has, in its study of the history of primitive Christianity, noted the many evidences of rivalry between Gnosticism and Christianity, it has frequently been overlooked in the past, for, as Father D'Arcy has reminded us, the contradiction between the two systems is not so immediately apparent, say, as is that between a purely naturalistic gospel such as Epicureanism and Christianity. We do not so readily "grasp the truth that a too spiritual ideal which despises the body and this earth is also anti-Christian." [12]

This curious religion of despair was the product of a union between that aspect of the Greek genius designated by Nietzsche as "Dionysiac" and the dark ecstasy of Eastern religions, and it was one of the significant bequests of Graeco-Roman culture to early Christian civilization, in which it lived on subterraneously, appearing in Spain in the heresy which is called Priscillianism and then, at the beginning of the Middle Ages, in the form of the Catharist heresy. To this whole movement the Church's doctrine of the Incarnation, its sacramental conception of the world, its gospel of love for neighbor as for God Himself, appeared as scandal and blasphemy. Its foundation-principles are well summarized by de Rougemont:

God is love. But the world is evil. Therefore God cannot be the author of the world, of its darkness, or of the sin by which we are hemmed in. A first creation of the world was being carried out by God when while still unfinished it was interrupted by the rebel Angel —Satan or the Demiurge—who then completed it. Man is a fallen angel, imprisoned in matter, and on that account subject to the laws of the body—in particular the most oppressive of these, the law of procreation. But the Son of God came to show the way back to the Light. The Christ was not incarnated; he but put on the appearance of a man. In this way the Cathars were brought to reject the dogma of the Incarnation, and consequently the sacrament of the Lord's Supper in which the Incarnation is expressed.[13]

De Rougemont also notes three further points of Catharist doctrine: that the third Person of the Trinity is the Mother of God,
that those who seek to be perfect must avoid intercourse with
their wives if they are married, and that of the two classes in the
Church of love—the perfect and the mere believers—the latter
alone may marry and participate in mundane affairs.

It appears that the Church felt the Catharist movement to be
as dangerous a menace to herself as Arianism had been earlier
and sought through the Inquisition to root out its disruptive
influences. But this was made difficult by reason of the fact that
the "Cathars were compelled to promise, at the moment of
initiation, never to disclose the nature of their faith, and that
they looked upon this promise as binding even in the face of
death." [14]

Now for some time we have been growing aware that the
rhetoric of the Provençal poetry written in the twelfth and thirteenth centuries by the troubadours of Languedoc, and that of
the Arthurian legends, and perhaps above all that of the Tristan–
Iseult story contains an esoteric doctrine that, contrary to what
we once supposed, was in sharp contradiction to the premises of
the Christian culture in which it first flourished.[15] And it is
de Rougemont's bold contention that this body of literature
represents basically a "lyrical and psalmodic" projection of a
spiritual movement which, because of its heretical character, was
forced to live "underground," to conceal itself, and to express
itself under disguised symbols. It is his suggestion that "courtly
rhetoric was *at least inspired*" by that Neo-Manichean movement
known as Catharism.[16]

De Rougemont takes the story of Tristan and Iseult as being
the most representative example of these literary expressions of
the Catharist metaphysic and proceeds, with extraordinary penetration, to unfold its inner logic. The large outlines of the story

are familiar: Tristan, who is orphaned in infancy, is taken under the care of his uncle, King Mark of Cornwall, and on reaching manhood becomes one of the King's sworn knights. One day a bird brings the King a golden hair, and Mark, determining to marry the woman from whose head the hair has come, selects Tristan to go out in quest of her. Tristan finds her and brings her back to Cornwall, but on the way, while at sea, the heat grows oppressive, and Iseult's maid, Brengain, gives them a drink; by mistake she gives them the love potion which the young princess's mother had brewed for the King and his bride. Tristan and Iseult drink it. And "the effect," says de Rougemont, "is to commit them to a fate which they can never enjoy during the remainder of their lives, *for they have drunk their destruction and death.*"

Here we have the essential clue to the subsequent ambivalence of Tristan's conduct. At times Tristan seems disposed to maintain an almost heroic fidelity to his pledge to King Mark; at still other times he seems disposed, out of love for the King's chosen lady, to betray his lord at the most opportune moment. At times it is suggested that Tristan's passionate love is a consequence of the fateful love potion which he is powerless to resist, though on other occasions it is made to appear as Tristan's own true love. Nor are we certain as to whether his love is purely an affair of the heart or as to whether it also embraces the physical. De Rougemont reminds us that one of the very early versions of the story represents Tristan as never having any physical contact with Iseult. And then when King Mark comes upon the lovers sleeping side by side in the Forest of Morrois, he finds Tristan's drawn sword lying between them which, presumably, symbolizes their innocence. De Rougemont goes on to point out that, contrary to appearance, Tristan and Iseult do not really love each other: their admission is quite explicit: "Il ne m'aime pas, ne je lui."

What they love is love and being in love. They behave as if aware that whatever obstructs love must ensure and consolidate it in the heart of each and intensify it infinitely in the moment they reach the complete obstruction, which is death. Tristan loves the awareness that he is loving far more than he loves Iseult the Fair. And Iseult does nothing to hold Tristan. All she needs is her passionate dream. Their need of one another is in order to be aflame, and they do not need one another as they are. What they need is not one another's presence, but one another's absence. *Thus the partings of the lovers are dictated by their passion itself*, and by the love they bestow on their passion rather than on its satisfaction or on its living object.[17]

Finally Tristan delivers Iseult up to King Mark, but as soon as they are absent from each other the passion rises again to a new intensity. And so the romance draws its dynamic, its motive power, from the repeated partings and reunions of the lovers; and their predilection for the pain attendant upon such partings seems really to represent a desire for death—but for a death which is for love, and for a death which comes at the end of a series of ordeals by which they are purified and transfigured out of their human finitude into union with the One behind the One. Thus it is that in dying for love they redeem their destiny, the struggle between passion and obstruction being inverted into a new relation in which "the obstruction is no longer serving irresistible passion, but has itself become the goal and end wished for for its own sake. Passion has thus only played the part of a purifying ordeal, it might almost be said of a penance, in the service of this transfiguring death." [18] And here, says de Rougemont, "we are within sight of the ultimate secret," for we now see that both Tristan and Iseult have been smitten by Eros, that dark Gnostic passion, which motivates its victims not to any love for a concrete object but for love itself. It is a love which is beyond concern for anything earthly; it is in truth a passion for *askésis*, for the *via mystica* of the "Perfect," for deliverance out of the body of this earthly death.

The initial ambiguity in the romance, de Rougemont suggests, resides in the mingling of the motif of *sexual* attraction with *eternal* desire, but, as he goes on to remind us, we must not allow the deceptiveness of the symbol to obscure the fact that the main thrust of the story is beyond sexual love, beyond the contingent world of relative and finite goods, to a transcendent world in which the finite is swallowed up in Infinity. Thus we see the lovers in our story being forced to pursue the *intensification* of passion rather than its satisfactory appeasement, for the keener their passion and the more it can free them from created, imperfect worldly persons or things the more readily do they feel that they are on the way toward achieving the death *in endura* which spells for them the salvation of the soul. Love, for all followers of the Catharist heresy, in other words, involved a kind of flight from the world of creation *in passion*.

De Rougemont argues, then, that this whole poetry of courtly love, of which the story of Tristan and Iseult is a consummate expression and which has for so long baffled interpreters of the medieval mind, was based not at all upon the Christian religion, as was once thought to be the case (though it frequently used Christian symbolism to disguise itself), but was rather based upon a theory of the soul and its destiny which had many non-Christian roots: the Platonism of Plotinus,* the mystical re-

---

* Indeed, de Rougemont discovers roots of the medieval heresy in Plato himself, when, in speaking of *Eros*, he describes it as a kind of frenzy or ecstasy which culminates in the soul's union with the divine. And so, it seems that de Rougemont, if pressed, would agree with Grierson, who tends somewhat more unequivocally to regard the medieval heresy as a recapitulation of this aspect of Greek thought. But, of course, the two would be in radical disagreement at the point where Grierson subsumes Pauline Christianity under the category of Romanticism, for, on de Rougemont's view, the constitutive metaphysical principle of Romanticism is a theory of

ligions of the East, the ancient mythology of the Celts, the radical dualism of Persian religion, and the ancient Gnosticism of Alexandria—all of which somehow came together in the medieval heresy of Catharism. And the contradiction between this heresy and Catholic Christianity he defines in terms of the radical antinomy between *Eros* and *Agape.*

There can be little doubt but that this heresy pervaded the whole of the medieval world. We know, for instance, and de Rougemont reminds us again, how greatly influenced St. Francis of Assisi was by the ideal of courtly love and that certainly part of the ambiguity of Dante's symbolism derives from the questionableness of the figure of Beatrice. It would also seem that the notion of love which informs Provençal poetry generally in no way represents a depiction of conditions prevailing at the time in the environing Christian culture but is rather to be derived from an alien source that in time domesticated itself within the European tradition.

The latter part of de Rougemont's book is largely given over to an account of the process whereby this sensibility insinuated itself into the warp and woof of a tradition of European literature and morals. It is not, however, a linear progression, as he traces it. He finds the great Spanish mystics of the sixteenth century, Saint Teresa and Saint John of the Cross, employing the whole rhetoric of courtly love, using in common with the troubadours such topics as: *The "salute" of love; Passion that sets one apart from the world and other beings; Love as a purifying emotion that drives away all vile thoughts; "To die of not being able to die"; The "sweet cautery."* Thus did a rhetoric originally devised for use against the Church reappear in the language of Christian saints, now wrested from its original source. But de Rougemont

---

the soul and of love (*Eros*) which is in direct opposition to the Christian conception of love as *Agape.*

goes on to trace the gradual degradation or profanation of the myth

as it passed from Thomas's *Tristan* via Petrarch and *L'Astrée* down to French classical tragedy. Little by little it was made humane and broken up into components less and less mysterious. Finally Racine felled it, though not before he had suffered a most grievous wound in the course of his struggles with the dark angel. Then Don Juan sprang on the stage, and from Molière to Mozart the myth underwent a major eclipse. But with the reappearance of Rousseau's novel [*La Nouvelle Héloïse*], which was produced on the margin, so to speak, of the eighteenth century, we are launched upon a new journey, a journey over the same road, but in the opposite direction. Via *Werther* . . . we come to Jean Paul, Hölderlin, and Novalis. Amid the commotion of the French Revolution, the Terror, and the ensuing European wars, it became possible to make certain admissions and a certain anguish was enabled to proclaim its true nature. For the first time the worship of Night and Death rose up into the field of lyric *awareness*. Hardly had Napoleon been overcome than Europe was invaded by a more insidious tyranny, which lasted till the day Wagner caused the myth all at once to stand forth to its full height and charged with its full virulence. Music alone could utter the unutterable, and music forced the final secret of Tristan.[19]

In German Romanticism, then, the scattered fragments of the myth came together again, being finally fashioned into a great monumental synthesis for the nineteenth century by Wagner. De Rougemont quotes broadly from the literature of the period to indicate how sweeping was the recapitulation of the Catharist theme of unhappy mutual love. There is the letter to Hölderlin, for example, from his Diotima:

Last evening I reflected for a long time about passion. No doubt *the passion of supreme* love is never fulfilled here below! Be sure to understand my feeling: to seek *this* satisfaction would be madness. To die together! . . . Such is the only fulfillment. . . .

Or there are the maxims of Novalis:

All passions end like a tragedy. Whatever is finite ends in death. All poetry has a tragic element.

A union formed even unto death is a marriage bestowing on each a companion for night. It is in death that love is sweetest. Death appears to one still alive as a nuptial night, the heart of sweet mysteries.

We are spirits that have come out of God; we are divine seed. One day we shall become even as our Father Himself.

And there is the melancholy of Tieck and Jean Paul and Kleist which turns in the case of each upon this constant theme of *death for the sake of love and absorption into the divine*. Then finally comes Wagner whose *Tristan und Isolde* restores the significance of the myth in all its virulence, giving it the completion of consummate expression. After Wagner it becomes increasingly popularized by the mass-produced novels of the twentieth century, the popular stage successes, and, "above all," says de Rougemont, by the modern cinema. Thus

The *claim to passion* put forward by the romantics becomes a vague yearning after affluent surroundings and exotic adventures, such as a low grade of melodramatic novel can satisfy symbolically. . . . That the yearning is entirely meaningless becomes evident as soon as we realize how impossible it is for the readers of these novels to imagine a mystic reality, an *askésis*, or any effort on the part of the mind to throw off its sensual fetters; and yet courtly passion had no other purpose, its language no other key. . . .[20]

It is in these terms that de Rougemont traces the history of that melancholic, frustrated love of love which, originating in a Gnostic Eros, first gained coherent literary expression in the poetry of courtly love and which subsequently influenced a main segment of European culture. And this history he regards as being the history of that tradition of literature and morality which we confusedly invoke by the term Romanticism. That his book advances a richly complicated and deeply persuasive argument no one intimately acquainted with it will deny. It may, of course, be true that scholars on any one of the numerous subjects about which he ventures to generalize are disposed to quarrel with details of his analysis, and perhaps with good reason. I suspect, however, that de Rougemont is himself far too wise and good-humored a scholar to want his work to be taken in a literalistic and textbookish manner. He is doubtless aware that there is much else to be said by way of defining the Romantic tradition, and it is unlikely that he would want to insist that he has pronounced the last word on the origins of Provençal literature; I am, at any rate, not myself disposed to enter a controversy in behalf of his entire thesis. But, whatever the deficiencies of his analysis, I should only want to insist that he has set forth a tradition of sensibility in European literature and has most cogently illustrated its unity and consistency. And the point for us is that it is to this tradition of thought that D. H. Lawrence belongs. De Rougemont remarks toward the close of his book that "the love of Tristan and Iseult was the anguish of being *two*; and its culmination was a headlong fall into the limitless bosom of Night, there where individual shapes, faces, and destinies all vanish: 'Iseult is no more, Tristan no more, and no name can any longer part us!' " [21] And this is precisely the theme which runs throughout all of Lawrence's characteristic work of the middle and later years. It is the anguish of what I have called man's *ontological solitude*, the discrete particularity of man as individual separated from other finite individuals by the qualitative, ontological gulf that separates finite creatures from one another—it is this *ontological tragedy* which constitutes Lawrence's central focus.

Tennyson once sang that the main miracle of our universe

is that "Thou art thou," that "I am I." But for Lawrence and the whole tradition in which he stands it is not only the main miracle but also the main tragedy of the universe that we are as human beings thus confined to an ontological particularity of existence, for the fragmentary character of human life is apprehended as being an essentially evil thing, a corruption of an originally undifferentiated divine unity. Lawrence speaks, for instance, in *Sons and Lovers* of Paul Morel's and Clara Dawes's desire

to know their own nothingness, to know the tremendous living flood which carried them always, [that] gave them rest within themselves. If so great a magnificent power could overwhelm them, identify them altogether with itself, so that they knew they were only grains in the tremendous heave that lifted every grass-blade its little height, and every tree, and living thing, then why fret about themselves? They could let themselves be carried by life, and they felt a sort of peace each in the other.[22]

Thus the effort at transcension of individuality culminates in the effort to achieve absorption into the universality of some mystical life-force whose nocturnal unity cancels out the separation and the loneliness of the Day. Here we see the true character of Lawrence's "mysticism" which, together with the "courtly mysticism" that de Rougemont is concerned to explicate in connection with the Tristan myth, differs from that mysticism derivative from Christian orthodoxy not in form but in the content of the spiritual state, for, as de Rougemont points out, it aims at a state of mind in which

"the others" cease to be present; and there are no longer either neighbors or duties, or binding ties, or earth or sky: one is alone with all that one loves. "We have lost the world, and the world us." Such is ecstasy, a flight inward from all created things. . . .[23]

Orthodox mysticism, on the other hand,

brings about a "spiritual marriage" of God and the individual soul already in this life, whereas the heretical looks to union and complete fusion, and this only after the demise of the body.[24]

The special quality of Lawrence's thought which I am seeking to establish has, I think, been so frequently overlooked because, in overresponding to his sexual ideas (to borrow an excellent phrase of Diana Trilling's), we have mistakenly supposed that Lawrence was simply idealizing carnal desire, that he was simply recommending more and better coition as the sufficient panacea for the human problem. But we must remember that Lawrence talks so long and so hard about sex only because it is on the level of sexual experience that he discovers this ontological polarity that separates us from those in whom we might find completion. And then the dialectic that controls Lawrence's thought is, too, partly responsible for this misunderstanding, for his Eros, having assumed the guise of Woman, symbolizes both the other world and the nostalgia which makes us despise earthly joys: the Passion which figures so prominently in the spiritual drama of his books, in other words, contains within itself a profound hatred of the sexual rhythms of the human body. His Desire, as de Rougemont would say, "despises Venus even when he is in the throes of carnal desire and imagines himself to be in love." That is to say, the characteristic Laurentian ambiguity resides in the language which affirms at once the sexual impulse and the impulse toward the glorious indistinction of that mystic Night wherein the particularizations of human existence, without which the sexual impulse is unthinkable, are transcended. And so, though at first he would seem to be our great modern lyricist of sexual joy, I hope to show that, in terms of twentieth-century life, he was really carrying out the logic of the Tristan myth.

Lest the affinity that is being stressed between Lawrence and the Romantic tradition (as described by de Rougemont) be taken too literally, it must be said that the suggestion is not being made that in any conscious and deliberate way Lawrence sought to appropriate any of the texts which de Rougemont regards as definitive expressions of the Tristan myth in modern culture. On the contrary, from what we know of his reading, chiefly through the researches of Professor Tindall, his philosophical peregrinations were largely guided, it appears, by Darwin, Huxley, Haeckel, Spencer, Stuart Mill, Hegel, and William James. Though he was given some feeling for archetypal mythical patterns by Jane Harrison, Frazer, Tylor, Maspero, and Gilbert Murray, it would not seem that his reading in this area was of a kind to establish any direct connection between him and the tradition of thought with which de Rougemont is dealing. And though he knew Rousseau and Wordsworth and others of the great Romantics, he frequently spoke of them with considerable disparagement. So there is no simple, direct line of influence between our subject and this tradition; the affinity is, rather, qualitative and structural, but yet of sufficient strength as to justify the explication of the character and tendency of his thought in terms of such external references as those to which I have turned.

It is, I think, in the light of such a perspective on Lawrence that T. S. Eliot's appraisal of him some years ago gains in validity, in spite of the animus from which one feels it sprang. In lucubrating on his now familiar theories of tradition and orthodoxy in the little "primer of modern heresy," *After Strange Gods*, Eliot, by way of contrasting the respective ethical orientations of Lawrence and Joyce, spoke of the essential *orthodoxy* of Joyce—and he was perhaps the first to discern that Joyce's mind, for all of its eclecticism and dazzling vivacity, was most deeply determined by Catholic Christianity—and of the radically heretical character of

Lawrence's sensibility. The ambiguity of Eliot's analysis, though, was rooted in the fact that he did not on this occasion define, as he subsequently has, what he meant by *tradition* and *orthodoxy* in explicitly religious terms but appeared rather to be defining them purely in terms of European cultural history. And if they be so considered, it would then seem to be impossible to speak of Lawrence as heretical, for, as de Rougemont has shown, the tradition to which I have been relating Lawrence is as deeply endemic to modern culture as is Christianity to the classical phases of European civilization. But if the two traditions, though both European, be considered spiritually antithetical, as they are, and if Christianity, for historical reasons, be considered as morally and spiritually normative for our culture, the distance between Lawrence and the moral and spiritual premises of our whole Christian ethos may then be clearly seen. Indeed, his work provides what is perhaps the extreme example of the *alienation* upon which this book is focused.

(David Herbert Lawrence was born on the eleventh day of September, 1885, in the little town of Eastwood, near Nottingham, England, the fourth child of a Methodist coal miner and his middle-class wife. "The father," says John Middleton Murry, "was almost the pure animal, in the good and bad senses of the phrase: warm, quick, careless, irresponsible, living in the moment and a liar." [25] The mother, on the other hand, seems to have been a person of superior sensibilities—which were, however, constantly being offended by her mate's easy intemperance —whose yearnings for the genteel life became in time exaggerated by her husband's grossness and vulgarity.

That Lawrence from early childhood "disapproved" of his father and was strongly drawn to his mother is the obvious implication of the book which, above all others, gives the clearest and most unambiguous account of the source of his emotional experience, *Sons and Lovers*. Indeed, the presence of the Oedipal element in the circumstances of his childhood seems unarguable and has been remarked upon by almost every analyst of his personal history. The early poems bear strong witness to this attachment, notable among which is the lyrical paean to "The Virgin Mother," which commemorates his mother's death:

> My little love, my darling,
> You were a doorway to me;
> You let me out of the confines
> Into this strange countrie
> Where people are crowded like thistles,
> Yet are shapely and comely to see.
>
> My little love, my dearest
> Twice have you issued me,
> Once from your womb, sweet mother,
> Once from your soul, to be
> Free of all hearts, my darling,
> Of each heart's entrance free.
>
> And so, my love, my mother,
> I shall always be true to you.
> Twice I am born, my dearest:
> To life, and to death, in you;
> And this is the life hereafter
> Wherein I am true.
>
> I kiss you good-bye, my darling,
> Our ways are different now;
> You are a seed in the night-time,
> I am a man, to plough
> The difficult glebe of the future
> For seed to endow.
>
> I kiss you good-bye, my dearest,
> It is finished between us here.
> Oh, if I were as calm as you are,

Sweet and still on your bier!
Oh God, if I had not to leave you
Alone, my dear!

Is the last word now uttered?
Is the farewell said?
Spare me the strength to leave you
Now you are dead.
I must go, but my soul lies helpless
Beside your bed.

But that Lawrence's delight in his relationship with his mother
came, in time, to be qualified by feelings of resentment at its
compulsions is revealed by the logic of the latter part of *Sons
and Lovers*, for the central motif there is Paul Morel's desperate
attempt to liberate himself from an attachment whose restric-
tions had grown oppressive. Mrs. Morel, having failed to find
fulfillment in her marriage, had turned to her son for that which
her husband should have given her; and thus the mother's
diverted affection prematurely thrust upon the boy the emotional
responsibilities of a man: the effect was to arouse in him feelings
for his mother which should have come years later for the girl
of his choice. "She bore him," he says in *Sons and Lovers*, "loved
him, kept him, and his love turned back into her, so that he
could not be free to go forward with his own life, really love
another woman."

But Paul is not at ease in this relationship; he senses its
wrongness, and so he turns first to Miriam Leivers and then to
Clara Dawes, seeking in each the release for which he dumbly
yearns. And here we find Lawrence unable to continue to
record his experience with honesty and candor. He cannot endure
the ultimate truth of his personal history, and so he begins to
misrepresent the facts. He seeks, for instance, to represent
Miriam as the one who is really at fault in her relationship with

Paul; it is she who shrinks from the sexual mystery: it is she who is frigid. "I held forth with rapture to her, positively with rapture. I simply went up in smoke. . . . The serpent in the grass was sex. She somehow didn't have any, at least not where it's supposed to be." But Paul does not really desire Miriam; he desires *"it"* and because he does not love her for herself but only as a possible instrument of release he fails to evoke in her the response that he wants. Miriam loves him in the mind but not in the body, but, loving him in the mind and knowing the intensity of his physical need, she forces herself to love him in the body out of pity.

She looked at him and was sorry for him; his eyes were dark with torture. She was sorry for him. . . . He was restless, for ever surging forward and trying to find a way out. He might do as he liked, and have what he liked of her.

Paul appeals, in other words, to Miriam's charity, and her generosity impels her to sacrifice herself. Paul knows that he does not feel that for her which would justify his demand, but, nevertheless, he takes what she has to give. And so the consummation of their passion is only an agony of unrelieved self-consciousness.

Then he turns to Clara Dawes, who is estranged from her husband Baxter Dawes. But again, the woman's response is motivated by pity rather than by desire.

He needed her badly. She had him in her arms, and he was miserable. With her warmth she folded him over, loved him. . . . She could not bear the suffering in his voice. She was afraid in her soul. He might have anything of her—anything; but she did not want to *know*. She felt she could not bear it. . . . She knew how stark and alone he was, and she felt it was great that he came to her; and she took him simply because his need was bigger either than her or him. . . . She did this for him in his need.

Thus it is, as Middleton Murry says, that

This feverish effort to become a man turns fatally upon itself; it makes him more a child than before. He struggles frenziedly to escape being a child-man to his mother, and he becomes only child-man again to other women, and the first great bond is not broken. If the woman is virgin like Miriam, he breaks her, by communicating to her the agony of his own division; if the woman is married like Clara, she breaks him, by abasing him in his own eyes.[26]

We get, then, in *Sons and Lovers* the characteristic form of Lawrence's personal dilemma as it was determined by the inner structure of his relationship with his mother. He feels that relationship to involve an assault upon his manhood: he feels it to be something from which he must somehow escape, and so he uses other women as means to that liberation. /But he can approach them only as extensions of the maternal presence; so, they take him to themselves as a mother takes a child to her breast, out of a love which, whatever else it is, has in it an essential pity and compassion for a helpless, incomplete human being. / But this humiliates the man, and, in his embarrassment, he comes, therefore (as we see, for instance, in the story of Annable and Lady Chrystable in *The White Peacock* or in the story of Mellors and Bertha Coutts in *Lady Chatterley*), to fear and hate the woman who has thus unintentionally done violence to his manhood. He clings, however, to sex—no longer, though, as a possible means of escape from his mother but rather as a possible means of flight from the general failure of love. It is, says Murry, for Lawrence a "chance of oblivion."

Here, then, we have the personal root of his sexual ideas, of the *idée fixe* which presided over the whole of his life and thought—the preoccupation with the ultimate isolation of the human spirit, as it is apprehended in the sexual relation. Indeed, the fundamentally monolithic character of Lawrence's thought suggests that his nature was governed by what amounted to a tic, an obsessive compulsion to recapitulate a single, fixed idea. R. P. Blackmur has used an even better word: hysteria.[27] Indeed, Lawrence's habit of imagination was hysterical, and the reality which it framed was of an hysterical order. The reader need hardly be reminded, however, that his hysteria was "an affair of genius not of insanity."

Ignoring the chronological order in which Lawrence's books were written, we have begun with *Sons and Lovers*, and rightly so, for here we get the emotional source of his doctrines. The two earlier books, *The White Peacock* and *The Trespasser*, contain suggestions and prefigurations of what was to become in his middle and later years his characteristic manner, but they represent, basically, the first awkward efforts of a young man of genius to prove himself a writer to be reckoned with, and beyond that, the halting but determined efforts of a young Englishman in the first decade of this century to liberate himself from the sweetness-and-light of the Georgians. And so, though they are not of sufficient importance to require attention here, they yet represent a stage of growth that appears now to have been an integral part of Lawrence's development.

With the completion of *Sons and Lovers* in 1912 we find that this young man has mastered the solid narrative technique of the Victorian novel and is well on the way into a new phase in which the preoccupation with questions of form that is echoed in his letter of November, 1912, to Edward Garnett [28] will be left behind for new interests, a phase that is heralded in lines from his "New Heaven and Earth":

> I was so weary of the world,
> I was so sick of it,
> everything was tainted with myself,

skies, trees, flowers, birds, water
people, houses, streets, vehicles, machines,
nations, armies, war, peace-talking,
work, recreation, governing, anarchy,
it was all tainted with myself, I knew it all
    to start with because it was all myself. . . .

I shall never forget the maniacal horror of it
    all in the end
when everything was me, I knew it already, I
    anticipated it all in my soul
because I was the author and the result
I was the God and the creation at once;
creator, I looked at my creation;
created, I looked at myself, the creator:
it was a maniacal horror in the end.

I was a lover, I kissed the woman I loved,
And God of horror, I was kissing also myself.
I was a father and a begetter of children,
And oh, oh horror, I was begetting and conceiving
    in my own body.

At last came death, sufficiency of death,
and that at last relieved me, I died.
I buried my beloved! it was good, I buried myself
    and was gone. . . .

God, but it is good to have died and been trodden out,
trodden to nought in sour, dead earth,
quite to nought,
absolutely to nothing
nothing
nothing
nothing . . .

Thus the self is projected into the *living death* toward which
the two subsequent novels, *The Rainbow* and *Women in Love*,
are poised.

When we come to *The Rainbow* and *Women in Love* we no longer encounter characters who are recognizably living personal entities, contributing each to the other's destiny in the sense to which we are accustomed by the narrative conventions of the English novel from Fielding to Forster and Maugham. The chief characters—the Brangwens, Anna Lensky, and Skrebensky of *The Rainbow*, Birkin, Gerald Crich, Ursula, and Gudrun of *Women in Love*—are now mainly larger-than-life embodiments of a poetic mood; they are all vehicles used to project the vision of a Darkness, beyond the fragmentariness of human existence, in which the disunities of human life are negated and overcome: they are all servants of the Mystery that lies beyond the "Phallic," automatons of Lawrence's imagination.

(*The Rainbow* begins with a highly congested account of the history of the Brangwen family of Nottinghamshire which brings us down to Tom Brangwen, who, with his Polish wife Anna Lensky, is in the foreground of the opening section of the story. And though their story is mainly prelusive to that of Will Brangwen and Tom's stepdaughter Anna, it introduces certain of the prevailing motifs that run throughout the book. Tom Brangwen has for many years been living a lonely bachelor existence on the family farm when there comes into the little community of Cossethay a foreigner, a young Polish widow, who enters the service of the vicar as his housekeeper. Tom soon falls in love with her and eventually brings her to the Marsh as his wife. "She wanted it, this new life from him, with him, yet she must defend herself against it, for it was a destruction. . . . And the dawn blazed in them, their new life came to pass, it was beyond all conceiving good. . . ." But immediately their love is consummated in marriage, there begins that pattern of ordeal, struggle, and passion that we identify as the characteristic Laurentian dialectic, which eternally interrupts the emotional immediacies of human love. The source of this agitation in his characters seems to reside in their sudden intuitions of their fundamental separateness from each other. Tom Brangwen and his wife Anna, after beginning their life together at the Marsh, make the discovery that

They were such strangers, they must for ever be such strangers, that his passion was a clanging torment to him. Such intimacy of embrace and such utter foreignness of contact! It was unbearable. He could not bear to be near her, and know the utter foreignness between them, know how entirely they were strangers to each other.

And strangers not in the sense that their "foreignness" would pass away in time as they lived with each other from day to day and their separate lives merged into the common life of their family, but strangers in the sense of having fundamentally separate human identities. Tom moves "in violent, gloomy, wordless passion": "he could not get definitely into touch with her . . . he could never quite reach her, he could never quite be satisfied, never be at peace, because she might go away." She "was something strange and foreign and outside his life," and "gradually he grew into a raging fury against her," becoming "a solid power of antagonism to her." Of this his wife "became gradually aware. And it irritated her to be made aware of him as a separate power. . . . Then suddenly, out of nowhere, there was connection between them again. . . . Then he burst into flame for her, and lost himself."

What did it matter who they were, whether they knew each other or not?

The hour passed away again, there was severance between them, and rage and misery and bereavement for her. . . . But no matter. They had had their hour, and should it chime again, they were ready for it, ready to renew the game at the point where it was left off, on the edge of the outer darkness, when the secrets within the woman are game for the man, hunted doggedly, when the secrets

of the woman are the man's adventure, and they both give themselves to the adventure.

And again,

He felt he wanted to break her into acknowledgment of him, into
awareness of him. It was insufferable that she had so obliterated him.
He would smash her into regarding him. He had a raging agony of
desire to do so.

Out of this nightmarish struggle comes Tom's little stepdaughter, the child of his wife's first marriage, whom he loves
more dearly than his own son. Hers is a wild, untamed feminine
will that hurries her quickly through childhood into an early
maturity, and it is her life with her young husband Will Brangwen, Tom's nephew, that forms the central and most beautiful
section of the book. Their life with each other is already prefigured, too, in the few pages that Lawrence devotes to their
brief courtship. We find them one evening walking through the
farm buildings at the Marsh.

They did not want to turn back, yet whither were they to go,
towards the moon? For they were separate, single.
"We will put up some sheaves," said Anna. So they could remain
there in the broad, open place. . . .
They worked together, coming and going, in a rhythm, which
carried their feet and their bodies in a tune. . . .
And always she was gone before he came. As he came, she drew
away, as he drew away, she came. Were they never to meet? Gradually a low, deep-sounding will in him vibrated to her, tried to set her
in accord, tried to bring her gradually to him, to a meeting, till they
should be together, till they should meet as the sheaves that swished
together. . . .
Why was there always a space between them, why were they
apart? Why, as she came up from under the moon, would she halt
and stand off from him? Why was he held away from her?

But during the honeymoon their young love transports them in careless rapture to an ecstasy beyond all "the hard rind of worldly knowledge and experience," and they are "unutterably glad." Then comes the recurrence of estrangement and conflict, when

His hovering near her, wanting her to be with him, the futility of him, the way his hands hung, irritated her beyond bearing. She turned on him blindly and destructively, he became a mad creature, black and electric with fury. The dark storms rose in him, his eyes glowed black and evil, he was fiendish in his thwarted soul.

There followed two black and ghastly days, when she was set in anguish against him, and he felt as if he were in a black, violent underworld, and his wrists quivered murderously. And she resisted him. . . .

But again the reconciliation, and then the conflict, and so on and on. Gradually, as the weeks go by she begins to realize

more and more that he did not alter, that he was something dark, alien to herself. . . . As the weeks and months went by she realized that he was a dark opposite to her, that they were opposites, not complements.

And Will

was afraid. He was afraid to know he was alone. . . . He could not bear to know that he was cut off. Why could he not be always one with her? . . . Why must he be set in this separateness, why could she not be with him, close, close, as one with him? She must be one with him. . . . He wanted her to come to him, to complete him, to stand before him so that his eyes did not, should not meet the naked darkness . . . he wanted her to come and liberate him into the whole.

Even after the conception of their child, the struggle goes on unabated—she, turning "fiercely on him," and he, resenting her aloofness, yet needing her desperately and going on from day to day in a blackness of rage and shame and frustration. . . . She was as the rock on which he stood, with deep, heaving water all round, and he was unable to swim. He *must* take his stand on her, he must depend on her.

What had he in life, save her? Nothing. The rest was a great heaving flood. . . .

Finally the two escape one day into Lincoln Cathedral,

Away from time, always outside of time! . . .

Here in the church, "before" and "after" were folded together, all was contained in oneness. . . .

Here the stone leapt up from the plain of earth, leapt up in a manifold, clustered desire each time, up, away from the horizontal earth, through twilight and dusk and the whole range of desire, through the swerving, the declination, ah, to the ecstasy, the touch, to the meeting and the consummation, the meeting, the clasp, the close embrace, the neutrality, the perfect, swooning consummation, the timeless ecstasy. There his soul remained, at the apex of the arch, clinched in the timeless ecstasy, consummated.

The entrance of Will and Anna Brangwen into Lincoln Cathedral thus introduces a motif into the logic of the book which is at one with certain of the consistencies that are native to Lawrence's entire work. The Cathedral-arch is obviously a sexual symbol, but it also has more extensive symbolic ramifications which suggest a transcendent world of Mystery, in the attainment of which the idiom of the sex act is merely instrumental and evocative. We breathe throughout this chapter the rarefied atmosphere of pure spirituality in which the anxiety, the antagonism, and the loneliness that root in our human bifurcation and that manifest themselves in the sexual relation have disappeared, because, an identification with a non-personal Ground having been achieved, the bifurcation no longer exists, and hence the motive power of the sexual relation itself has been canceled out.

Here we begin to see clearly for the first time Lawrence's profound despair over the possibility of our achieving a "balanced polarity" in the sexual relation—a despair which probably derives, as Middleton Murry suggests, from his persistent distrust of Woman, of her irrationality and unpredictability. And this wariness has, of course, its roots in his personal history. We remember, for instance, that throughout the book, first with Tom Brangwen and Anna Lensky and then with Will and Anna Brangwen, it is the Woman who appears as self-sufficient and complete and whose self-sufficiency is apprehended by Tom and by Will as an assault upon their masculinity (and this is clearly a projection of Lawrence's personal dilemma). They resent Her independence and are ashamed of the extremity of their need of Her, and She, feeling their demands upon Her to be oppressive, strikes back, undermining their faith in themselves and their own separate creative purposes, forcing them "to the spirit of her laws." And finally, Anna, in the presence of the awe-inspiring majesty of Lincoln Cathedral, deliberately wrests herself out of her own enthrallment in order to shatter Will's and does so by forcing upon his attention the little gargoyles carved in stone, whose sly, impish faces were so out of harmony with the great, throbbing pulse of the church; in the case of one she insists that the mason had put into the "plump, sly, malicious little face" the features of his detested wife. "You hate to think he put his wife in your cathedral, don't you?" she says to Will, and of course he does, for this transcendent world of pure spirituality which the Cathedral represents is his only refuge from the exasperations of the sexual life, and into it the sexual fact cannot be admitted, the two being deeply antithetical.

But finally Lawrence and his men get satisfaction in their battle with the feminine principle when, in the last chapter of the book, Ursula, the child of Will and Anna, whose sexual life, as Horace Gregory has said, is "stamped with the signature of the Cathedral arch," [29] is annihilated under a stampede of horses and is resurrected not as "victrix," not as "triumphans," but as subordinate to that *Darkness* for which the male has hitherto been the chief spokesman.

This inner circle of light in which she lived and moved . . . suddenly seemed like the area under an arc-lamp, wherein the moths and the children played in the security of blinding light, not even knowing there was any darkness, because they stayed in the light. . . .
Nevertheless the darkness wheeled round about, with grey shadow-shapes of wild beasts, and also with dark shadow-shapes of the angels, whom the light fenced out, as it fenced out the more familiar beasts of darkness. And some, having for a moment seen the darkness, saw it bristling with the tufts of the hyaena and the wolf; and some, having given up their vanity of the light, having died in their own conceit, saw the gleam in the eyes of the wolf and the hyaena, that it was the flash of the sword of angels, flashing at the door to come in, that the angels in the darkness were lordly and terrible and not to be denied, like the flash of fangs.

Now it seems that just as *Sons and Lovers* is the pivotal book for an understanding of the personal source of Lawrence's doctrines so also is *The Rainbow* the pivotal book for an understanding of the schematic structure in terms of which he is to articulate his vision. Here we find him developing for the projection of his basic convictions a symbolic convention which at times suggests a larger frame of reference, a larger design, that has many significant affinities with the structure of thought embodied in the Tristan myth. As with the lovers in the romance, Lawrence's men and women desire that ravishment into a transcendental state beyond, and incommensurable with, the world which, *considered from the standpoint of life,* is Death: Law-

rence's name for it is *Darkness*. And so their "love," again, as
with Tristan and Iseult, reaches toward a kind of fulfillment, as
prefigured in the Cathedral chapter, that involves essentially a
denial of any particular terrestrial love and, instead of drawing
them together, impels them to feel that they have everything
to gain from a separation. We recall that

Tristan, having landed in Ireland, meets Iseult and then parts from
her without being "in love." He turns up in Ireland again, and this
time Iseult wants to kill him. They take ship together and drink
the love-potion, and then sin. Next, Iseult is delivered up to Mark,
and Tristan is banished from the castle. He and Iseult meet under
a pine-tree, their talk being overheard by Mark. Tristan comes back
to the castle, and Frocin and the barons discover evidence of his
crime. They are parted. They meet again, and for three years go to
live in the forest. Then, once more, they part. They meet at the
hut of Orri the Woodman. Tristan goes away. He comes back,
disguised as a poor pilgrim. He goes away again. The separation this
time is prolonged, and he marries Iseult of the White Hand. Iseult
the Fair is about to rejoin him when he dies. She dies too. More
briefly still: They have one long spell together ("L'aspre vie"—
"The harsh life"), to which corresponds a lengthy separation—and
Tristan's marriage. First, the love-potion; lastly, the death of both.
In between, furtive meetings.[30]

Thus the motive power of the romance, as we have already noticed, seems to consist in the repeated separations of the lovers,
and these partings appear to answer to an internal necessity of
their passion: they "behave as if aware that whatever obstructs
love must ensure and consolidate it in the heart of each and intensify it infinitely in the moment they reach the complete obstruction, which is death." [31] Indeed, every significant situation
seems to mark a stage in a mystical career that has as its goal
the ultimately impracticable transcension of human limitations.
Their passion, which necessitates their pursuance of a deliberate

askésis, functions, in other words, as a purifying ordeal in the service of a salvation whereby they may be redeemed from their *separate identities* into a mystic oneness in which the agonizing particularity of selfhood will be annihilated by the fecundity of mystical transcendence. Tristan and Iseult, then, do not love each other but love itself, and this "love" reaches its culmination in "a headlong fall into the limitless bosom of Night, there where individual shapes, faces, and destinies all vanish," where "Iseult is no more, Tristan no more, and no name can any longer part" them—for theirs was "the anguish of being two."

And so too does one feel that Lawrence's men and women desire, basically, a mutual immolation, a total eclipse, an utter lapse from Day into Night. This orientation of his characters is presaged as much in many of the poems from *Look! We Have Come Through* as it is explicitly drawn in *The Rainbow.* In "In the Dark," the man, in his dialogue with the woman, utters the constant cry of the Laurentian family:

> In the darkness we all are gone, we are gone with the
>   trees
> And the restless river;—we are lost and gone with
>   all these.

He desires

> Not sleep, which is grey with dreams,
> nor death, which quivers with birth,
> but heavy, sealing darkness, silence, all immovable . . .

It is true that Lawrence sometimes wrote not simply out of a desire for unity but out of a desire for *unity-in-division,* and at times he seems prepared to acknowledge, simply and resignedly, the necessity of finite human beings being *bounded* by other finite human presences, between which there is an ultimate ontological discontinuity that must simply be accepted. He admits, for instance, in "The Manifesto" that

> ultimately, she is all beyond me,
> She is all not-me, ultimately.
> It is that that one comes to.
> A curious agony, and a relief, when I touched that which
>   is not me in any sense,

and yet

> it wounds me to death with my own not-being; definite,
>   inviolable limitation,
> and something beyond, quite beyond, if you understand
>   what that means.

That Lawrence desired a true unity, however—which, for him, is symbolized by "the rainbow," the great heavenly arch that spans and unites conflicting and antagonistic elements—is clear, but that he failed to achieve it is equally clear, for, by way of dealing with this "anguish of being *two*," he resorts always, finally, to an effort at mystical transcendence, invoking the Darkness of the Mystery beyond the Phallic, in which men and women are so transfigured by the "spiritual ecstasy of unanimity" (a phrase Lawrence used in *Twilight in Italy*) that sexuality, as it is normally experienced in the world of everyday, disappears.

John Middleton Murry, in a book brought out in England during World War II which he calls *Adam and Eve: an Essay towards a New and Better Society*, has tried to reassess and redefine the continuing relevance of Lawrence's thought for our period, and, in the course of his discussion, he remarks:

It is quite impossible to discuss Lawrence's prophetic message without reference to Jesus. Because, consciously or unconsciously at all times, and very consciously indeed at some times, Lawrence was answering the question he put to himself: "What think ye of Christ?" . . . Lawrence was, to an extent beyond any of his con-

temporary writers, absolutely saturated in Christianity. To leave
Jesus out of any attempt to understand Lawrence is like playing
Hamlet without the Prince of Denmark.[32]

Though we take Murry seriously when he discusses Keats and
Shakespeare and indeed Lawrence too, those who have tried to
follow the convolutions of his attempt to formulate a theological
doctrine of "metabiology" can hardly escape recognizing the extent of his failure to come to terms with the complexities of
Christian thought. And though he is quite right in suggesting
that Lawrence somehow makes us want to talk about Jesus and
Christianity, when he declares that Lawrence was "of Jesus's
party without knowing it, preaching and suffering for a gospel
of salvation," [33] we feel that he has considerably missed the
mark.

Let us approach the matter in this way. The profound and
radical difference between Lawrence's religion and the Christian
faith may be very simply put. The deep basic tone that resounds
throughout the Gospel symphony is most beautifully expressed
in the Fourth Gospel when the writer declares: "In the beginning was the Word, and the Word was with God, and the Word
was God. . . . And the Word was made flesh, and dwelt among
us (and we beheld his glory, glory as of the only begotten from
the Father), full of grace and truth." The distinctively Christian fact is, in other words, the fact of the Incarnation which, in
endowing the whole of creation with a sacramental quality, enables us to affirm our existence in the world and, to use de Rougemont's apt phrase, delivers us "from the woe of being alive."
Thus the final term of the Christian faith is neither *Death* nor
Darkness, but life and "life more abundantly." When the Gospel
speaks of *dying to the old man*, it apprehends this death as the
precondition for a re-creation of the self *in history*, not as a precondition for a flight out of the world. The "light shineth in
darkness," and pierces the darkness, restoring its inhabitants to

wholeness of mind and newness of life. Christian love—the New Testament name for which is *agape*—therefore presupposes a death to the self and the world, in so far as they have been corrupted by sin, but this death is the precondition for a reassertion of life, sanctified and made whole, *in the world.* Hence, *agape* has as its aim the affirmation not only of oneself, as *imago Dei*, but of the neighbor as well. As de Rougemont puts it,

The symbol of love is no longer the infinite *passion* of a soul in quest of light, but the *marriage* of Christ and the Church. And in this way human love itself has been transformed. Whereas, according to the doctrines of mystical paganism, human love was sublimated so thoroughly as to be made into a god even while it was being dedicated to death, Christianity has restored human love to its proper status, and in this status has hallowed it by means of marriage. Such a love, being understood according to the image of Christ's love for His Church is able to be truly mutual. For its object, from having been the actual notion of love and the exquisite and fatal branding of love, has become the other as *he or she really is.* And, in spite of the hindrances of sin, human love is a happy love, since already here below it can by obedience attain to the fullness of its own status.[34]

This is, then, the love of "Jesus' party." But what of Lawrence's love"? It receives its clearest and most unambiguous expression in *The Rainbow*, in the last pages of the book, which are largely devoted to the latter phase of Ursula's affair with Skrebensky. Here we see the true character of Lawrence's *Eros*, as he manipulates once again the old antithesis between the *Darkness* that surrounds the social life of mankind and the conventional world of everyday. He shows the two young people as deeply resentful of this conventional social world. Ursula, as she looks at the little town of Beldover, is exasperated by

The stupid lights. . . . The stupid, artificial, exaggerated town, fuming its lights. It does not exist really. It rests upon the unlimited

darkness, like a gleam of coloured oil on dark water, but what is it?—
nothing, just nothing."

She goes about "in the sensual sub-consciousness all the time,
mocking at the ready-made, artificial daylight of the rest." And
Skrebensky "knew no one in this town, he had no civic self to
maintain. He was free." Their "antagonism to the social imposi-
tion" is "complete and final." They linger on the edge of the
Darkness. "As for her temporal, social self," Ursula "let it look
after itself," for her "whole soul was implicated with Skrebensky
—not the young man of the world, but the undifferentiated man
he was." And Skrebensky shares in common with Ursula a reluctance to marry:

To make public their connection would be to put it in range with
all the things which nullified him, and from which he was for the
moment entirely dissociated. If he married he would have to assume
his social self. And the thought of assuming his social self made him
at once diffident and abstract.

This love that flees from "the Norm of Day" to the deserts of
the Night is, of course, a lovers' *askésis*, whereby they will
eventually escape out of life, since for them, as for Rimbaud,
"Real life is *elsewhere*." They want to have nothing to do with
the troth of marriage, for their vows, in the words of Novalis,
"were not exchanged for this world," but, as de Rougemont and
all Christian writers on the subject insist, "the troth of marriage
is . . . given unreservedly for *this* world." But Lawrence's men
and women seek constantly to deny *this* world and to prevent its
encroachment upon their private passion, for, being blinded by
"the anguish of being *two*," they know nothing of their neighbor. "Old tune so full of sadness"—this is clearly not the love
of "Jesus's party" but is rather that of an ancient heresy.

In a letter written to the London publisher Martin Secker on
January 16, 1920, Lawrence suggested that "*The Rainbow* and

Women in Love are really an organistic artistic whole." [35] And one does feel a certain continuity, though primarily of a doctrinal sort, between the two books. Lawrence apparently intended *Women in Love* to be a sequel to the earlier book, as is indicated, for instance, in his continuation of the history of the Brangwen family which he had there begun. And the use to which it is put brings it into the same service of the "Gods of the living Darkness" as that of its predecessor: the dialectic that governs the personal relations of its characters—or that renders them impersonal—remains that to which we grew accustomed in *The Rainbow*. And both books posit the same black, claustrophobic airlessness that we have come to associate with Lawrence's nirvana-like underworld. Hence a detailed analysis of *Women in Love* would, in many of its aspects, be merely repetitious of what we have said about *The Rainbow*.

When the book is viewed, however, in its relation to the Laurentian corpus as a whole, its larger significance may well be defined in terms of the transitional position it bears with respect to what had come before and what was to come after. It is, I think, mainly anticipatory of the direction in which Lawrence was to extend his preoccupation with human isolation—that is, toward an analysis of the factors in modern culture which have tended to aggravate the *perennial* isolation of man that we have found him to be defining. And this movement toward cultural criticism was in time to bring him to a devastating polemic against the foundations of liberal modernity (reason, science, materialism, and technology), a polemic which is most fully and systematically formulated in *Psychoanalysis and the Unconscious* and *Fantasia of the Unconscious*, but which is also suggestively adumbrated in his sequel to *The Rainbow*.

Lawrence considered the whole of modern culture to lie under the condemnation of *too much mind*. "I would rather listen now to a negro witch-doctor," he once said, "than to

Science."[36] Thus was he fond of dismissing all those proud citadels of the modern intellect which, in his judgment, were only disruptive of the original unities of the blood. Indeed, one might say that the basic event to which Lawrence's private mythology refers is a Fall, which, for him, occurs in the moment of *gnosis*, in the moment when knowledge and self-consciousness are achieved, when the mind becomes the director of the human psyche and through its rational, discursive processes sets ego against ego, thus disconnecting mankind from that original, premental, unitive Darkness of "mindless animation" in which there were no *individuals* but only a *folk*. He regarded the state of culture itself as involving a tragic declension from the grace of nature and was, therefore, in this most radical sense, a primitivist. But the great weight of his polemic fell upon the particular apostasies embodied in the post-Renaissance period of European history, of which the machine, and all that it represented in terms of the rationalization of human life, was for him the most suggestive symbol. To the machine Lawrence boldly opposed the pure mindlessness of animality for which, on his view, we were intended and which was variously symbolized for him in the figure of a horse (as in the last chapter of *The Rainbow* or again in *St. Mawr*) and in Susan, the cow which he kept in his back yard at Taos.[37]

It was, then, out of such an extreme repudiation of the whole style of modern life that Lawrence composed his allegorical sequel to *The Rainbow*, *Women in Love*. In the portraits of Hermione Roddice and Gerald Crich he exteriorized all the lower middle-class hatred of the rich and their irreligious materialism which the circumstances of his birth and nurture had given him and which he never lost. And in his portraits of Ursula Brangwen, Rupert Birkin, and Loerke he tried to draw to scale several versions of a Laurentian saint—that is, a human being who, though continuing to live in the modern world, has, in surrender to the Phallic Mystery, gained liberation from the disruptions introduced into life by the intellect and its tool, the machine, and has thereby been enabled to achieve "relationship."

But not only does *Women in Love* prefigure, in its attacks on "mentalism," the fuller polemical statements of *Psychoanalysis* and the *Fantasia* and, especially in the portrait of Gerald Crich, the portrait of Clifford in *Lady Chatterley*; it also foreshadows a new line that Lawrence is to take, in *Aaron's Rod*, *The Lost Girl*, *Kangaroo*, and *The Plumed Serpent*, when Birkin says to Crich:

"You've got to take down the love-and-marriage ideal from its pedestal. We want something broader. I believe in the *additional* perfect relationship between man and man—additional to marriage."

Now far too much nonsense has been written about this ideal relationship between men, for which Gerald and Birkin struggled and which Lilly and Aaron Sisson tried to achieve in *Aaron's Rod*. Lawrence's detractors have leaped upon it as providing sufficient justification for combing the man's personal history for evidences of sexual perversion, and though it seems to me that his deepest psychological involvements, as I characterized them in the course of my analysis of *Sons and Lovers*, might possibly have constituted the basis for the development of a homosexual personality, so far as I know he was not a homosexual. But, on the other hand, his defenders have very often tried, somewhat too facilely, to obscure the patent apology for homosexuality which is to be found in his writing. Diana Trilling, for instance, comes perilously near to casuistry when she admits, as she is forced to do, that the male relationship which Lawrence was advocating had a physical dimension, then denies that he was "seeking a license for homosexuality for his male characters," and finally declares that if we are "to recognize his sexual ideas without the shadow of perversity, we must accept the bisexuality of our own infant pasts." [38]

The plain truth of the matter is that Lawrence included homosexuality in his concept of *the natural* and held it forth as a means of possible relief from the antagonism between the sexes which, in his view, has been so greatly increased by the special tensions created by modern life. Lawrence's Man (in this case Birkin) says to Lawrence's Woman (Ursula): "What I want is a strange conjunction with you . . . an equilibrium, a pure balance of two single beings:—as the stars balance each other." But this "pure balance," this "strange conjunction," never quite comes off, or when it is occasionally managed in fleeting moments of ecstasy, it does not endure, for, as Lawrence is constantly saying throughout his later period, all of us have been so affected by modernity's deification of "mind" and "will" (which are fatal to "relationship") that this "equilibrium" between men and women inevitably disintegrates into "disconnection." And so, Lawrence's men say to each other: "We ought to swear to love each other, you and I . . . implicitly and perfectly, finally, without any possibility of going back." To "enter into the bond of pure trust and love with the other man, and then subsequently with the woman"—this is the only way, for, as Gerald reasons,

If he pledged himself with the man he would later be able to pledge himself with the woman: not merely in legal marriage, but in absolute, mystic marriage.

And to refuse to enter into such a relation, as Gerald finally refuses to do with Birkin, is to be destroyed, as Gerald is himself finally destroyed. The book comes to a close with Rupert and Ursula talking about their dead friend.

"Did you need Gerald?" she asked one evening.

"Yes," he said.

"Aren't I enough for you?" she asked.

"No," he said. "You are enough for me, as far as a woman is concerned. You are all women to me. But I wanted a man friend, as eternal as you and I are eternal."

"Why aren't I enough?" she said. "You are enough for me. I don't want anybody else but you. Why isn't it the same with you?"

"Having you, I can live all my life without anybody else, any other sheer intimacy. But to make it complete, really happy, I wanted eternal union with a man too: another kind of love," he said.

"I don't believe it," she said. "It's an obstinacy, a theory, a perversity."

"Well—" he said.

"You can't have two kinds of love. Why should you?"

"It seems as if I can't," he said. "Yet I wanted it."

"You can't have it, because it's false, impossible," she said.

"I don't believe that," he answered.

Professor Hocking, in the course of explicating that tradition in Western philosophy which goes by the name of "Idealism," has suggested that, in terms of its basic tenets, it would really make better sense to refer to it as "Ideaism," since "the 'I' was added for the sake of euphony and not for sense." [39] And this might also be said of the "idealism" which we find Lawrence to be denouncing with such heat and constancy, when we come to the polemical pamphlets, *Psychoanalysis and the Unconscious* and *Fantasia of the Unconscious*, in which his main focus, as Middleton Murry has said, rests upon "the assertion of the supremacy of the idea in the passional sphere." [40] In our modern deification of the intellect, Lawrence argued, we have lost all sense of the *mysterium tremendum* that is the basic datum of human life, all capacity for the experience of mystery. We can instead understand now only machines and the automatic gadgets of a culture largely given over to technology and its inhuman creations. And not only the larger aspects of our common life, but, what is even more tragic, the most private and intimate of all human relations, the relation between man and woman, has become saturated with mental consciousness. The blood and the flesh have been repudiated for the sake of the inhuman intellect, and our last state, as with the Biblical figure whose house was left empty, becometh worse than the first.

Taking this kind of perspective on modern life, Lawrence's estimate of Freud, whom he considered to be a consummate expression of the whole modern ethos, should not be at all surprising. He considered the basic implication of Freudian theory (and at this point he was right) to hinge upon the presumed necessity of the invasion of the unconscious by mind. And this "motivizing of the passional sphere from the ideal," Lawrence contended, "is the final peril of human consciousness. It is the death of all spontaneous creative life and the substituting of the mechanical principle." He saw, in other words, and saw clearly, that the basic presuppositions of Freudian psychology were unalterably opposed to his own beliefs, for the unconscious or preconscious was, for him, the primordially normative principle of life. It is that condition of life in which we are not aware of our separateness and our isolation from each other—because there is no awareness, no thought, no mind. So the "emergence" of mind in the evolutionary process of nature and society is not to be simply accepted with "natural piety" (in Samuel Alexander's familiar phrase): its givenness must be in some way adjusted to, but the adjustment must not involve capitulation but rather an effort aimed at control of its power and delimitation of its activity. And above all, it must not be allowed to encroach upon the sacred preserves of those lower levels of our being where all is dark and vital, unconscious and immediate, where all "is pristine, not in any way ideal . . . the spontaneous origin from which it behoves us to live."

But Freud and his followers and the whole decadent modern ideology which they represent, so Lawrence argues, are not content to let this be so. They are not content simply to experience the mystery of the unconscious: they must know it *mentally*; they must generalize it out into insipidity. And so it is in our age that love between man and woman is more an affair of the head than it is of the "bowels of compassion." We have forgotten what was understood in the old pre-Christian mysteries: that our human tragedy *can* be transcended, but through the blood, not through the mind. And so we must abandon ourselves once more to "mindless progressive knowledge through the senses . . . mystical knowledge," blood-consciousness, if we would be delivered from the body of this death —and down this path Freud cannot help us.

So much for *Psychoanalysis and the Unconscious*, which ends on this note of rejection of psychoanalytic salvationism. When we come to the *Fantasia*, we find in the earlier sections mainly a repetition of the basic ideas of *Psychoanalysis*, but the latter half of the book is largely given over to an analysis of what Lawrence considers to be the chief manifestation in human relations of modern "idealism"—the Oedipal situation. His charge is that because we have been so unwilling to seek the kind of fulfillment which he has been advocating, in "absolute, mystic marriage," because we have refused to surrender the "mind" to "the lower centres" of vitality, men and women have been unable to gain relief from the torment of their separateness, and the result has been the dissolution of the primitive unity of the family. "In the woman particularly, the love-craving" runs "to frenzy and disaster. . . ." She "beats about for her insatiable satisfaction, seeking whom she may devour. And usually, she turns to her child." Here, of course, he is patently generalizing again his own private history, as we found him doing earlier in *Sons and Lovers*. He feels that it is in her own son that the frustrated woman

seems to find the last perfect response for which she is craving. He is a medium to her, she provokes from him her own answer. So she throws herself into a last great love for her son, a final and fatal devotion which would have been the richness and strength of her husband and is poison to her boy.

Thus the mother, frustrated in her marriage, "now feels for the first time as a true wife might feel. And her feeling is towards her son." But this frustrated and diverted love is devastating for the child in whom sexual awareness is prematurely awakened, and awakened in such a way that when he grows to maturity he will be inhibited from achieving the right and proper satisfactions in the sexual life and thus doomed to "ideal" satisfactions—for "you will not easily get a man to believe that his carnal love for the woman he has made his wife is as high a love as that he felt for his mother."

Now the demand at which Lawrence quite logically arrives is for a new kind of society which will make a decent marriage possible; and, conversely, he holds, it is only upon the basis of such a marriage that the new society of the future can be built. The sexual mystery must, in his view, be reinstated as a religious mystery before we can come to a new understanding of our ecumenical human task. Until, that is, a man and his wife have learned to love their love, from the standpoint of its "ultra-phallic" reference, their children will be spiritually and emotionally crippled, and they will themselves be unfit for the demands of "absolute, mystic" marriage. When one life-pattern is in ruins, its offspring will suffer from the same disease: this is the inexorable logic of human generation. Lawrence would, indeed, have heartily concurred with Middleton Murry's estimate a few years ago that the

> number of men who, having been bound by inordinate affection to their mothers, and scared by inordinate fear of their fathers, unconsciously seek a mother where they should be looking for a lover, a wife, and a companion; the number of women who, having been bound by inordinate affection to their fathers, and estranged by subtle jealousy from their mothers, unconsciously seek a father where they should be looking for a lover and a husband and a leader, is Legion today.[41]

But this vicious circle must be broken, if we are to move into "a new heaven and a new earth," if Christ is to be increasingly reincarnated "in a long and steadily increasing succession of true marriages." [42] For only in such marriage of man with woman will the burden of the separate ego, the separate self which is *against* life, disappear. The regeneration of the sexual relation is, then, the fundamental postulate of the new society toward which history must move. This is the ultimate implication of the *Fantasia*.

But Lawrence would have this regenerative process begin with a "blood-relationship" between men, through which their spirits might be so renewed as to enable them to pledge themselves with a woman later on "not merely in legal marriage," but in the "absolute, mystic marriage" of which we have already found Gerald and Birkin speaking in *Women in Love*. This conception gains its sharpest definition in *Aaron's Rod*, for it is in Aaron Sisson that Lawrence presented "the friend and brother who should form with him the nucleus of a new society." [43] He is himself Rawdon Lilly, and, as Middleton Murry says, "Aaron is the friend of his dream." [44]

The details of the narrative—which is, by the way, more carefully wrought than anything since *Sons and Lovers*, with the possible exception of a few of the short stories—do not require recapitulation in their minutiae: it is sufficient to say that the central issue of the book brings us back to the blood-brother business between Gerald and Birkin in *Women in Love*. Aaron has left his children and his whining, nagging wife and gone to London, where he meets Lilly, who, when he falls ill with pneumonia, takes him into his London flat and nurses him through to recovery. He subsequently follows Lilly to Italy where, in this ancient land, he discovers the final truth of his manhood—his loneliness, the ultimate isolation of his being.

Break it, and he broke his being. Break this central aloneness, and he broke everything. . . . By the innermost isolation and singleness of his own soul he would abide though the skies fell on top of one another, and seven heavens collapsed.

Lilly also, though not permanently estranged from her, is separated from his wife Tanny, who is, for some unexplained reason, in Norway. So the two men turn toward each other in their need and longing. Lawrence wants to say to us that what they make of their relation must serve as the basis for "the new Jerusalem." And what do they make of it? Lawrence calls it "sticking together," and Lilly calls it "extending" marriage. I think we should want to call it more plainly a homosexual "extension" of the heterosexual relation.

The ultimate implication of their relation is most clearly revealed in the chapter devoted to the period of Aaron's illness in Lilly's London flat, and here once again I draw upon Murry, who describes the situation with admirable concision:

The women are far away, the underlying tension of hostility that is always felt when Lawrence is describing a woman and a man together dissolves peacefully away. Lilly is blissfully happy looking after Aaron, with a more than wifely tenderness.[45]

And then he quotes the following passage to illustrate his remarks:

He put on the kettle, and quietly set cups and plates on a tray. The room was clean and cosy and pleasant. He did the cleaning himself, and was as efficient and unobtrusive a housewife as any woman. While the kettle boiled, he sat darning the socks which he had taken off Aaron's feet when the flautist arrived, and which he had washed. He preferred that no outsider should see him doing these things. Yet he preferred also to do them himself, so that he should be independent of outside aid.

His face was dark and hollow, he seemed frail, sitting there in the London afternoon darning the black woolen socks. His full brow was knotted slightly, there was a tension. At the same time, there was an indomitable stillness about him, as it were in the atmosphere about him. His hands, though small, were not very thin. He bit off the wool as he finished his darn.

Gradually Aaron's condition grows worse, and the crisis of his illness approaches. The physician in attendance is disturbed about some obstruction that appears to be creating excretory difficulties, and he is also worried by Aaron's refusal to fight for his life. Finally Lilly decides that massage will be helpful.

"I'm going to rub you with oil," he said. "I'm going to rub you as mothers do their babies whose bowels won't work."

Aaron frowned slightly as he glanced at the dark, self-possessed face of the little man.

"What's the good of that?" he said irritably. "I'd rather be left alone."

"Then you won't be."

Quickly he uncovered the blond lower body of his patient, and began to rub the abdomen with oil, using a slow, rhythmic circulating motion, a sort of massage. For a long time he rubbed finely and steadily, then went over the whole of the lower body, mindless, as if in a sort of incantation. He rubbed every speck of the man's lower body—the abdomen, the buttocks, the thighs and knees, down to the feet, rubbed it all warm and glowing with camphorated oil, every bit of it, chafing the toes swiftly, till he was almost exhausted.

And immediately we are aware that the crisis has been successfully weathered, that Aaron has been restored to health through the commingling of his body with Lilly's body, just as Gerald was restored to health on that night when he and Birkin threw off their clothes and wrestled with each other in Gerald's living room at Shortlands. "We are mentally, spiritually intimate," said Birkin to Gerald, "therefore we should be more or less physically intimate too—it is more whole." And so, here too, the "blood-relationship" between Aaron and Lilly is completed through the crucial stress of physical contact—by which he who is sick is healed. Try to comprehend this in terms of "the bisexuality of our own infant pasts," if you will, but its real meaning is surely plain enough to make unnecessary such fine subtlety.

Lawrence's abhorrence of British and European culture generally is, of course, spattered throughout his vast correspondence and is there for all those to see who care to go through the Huxley edition of the letters (which belongs among the great bodies of correspondence in English literature). But that England, both through Mrs. Grundy and Aspatia, returned his contempt with animus and venom, no one who knows his constant harassments by publishers and censors and critics, both highbrow and low-brow, can deny. Never did he know the sweet content that comes to a writer from the kind of wide public adulation and esteem to which the Wellses and the Galsworthys and the Bennetts gained access. And so he came in time to hope that, though it seemed impossible for him to make common cause with England, perhaps in America he could find a refuge and a home.* England, he thought, has

got to pick up a lost trail. . . . The Englishman, *per se*, is not enough. He has to modify himself to a distant end. He has to balance with something that is not himself. . . . England is only one end of the broken rope.[46]

And he felt that perhaps the other end of this broken rope, this lost trail, this thing with which England must balance herself, was perhaps to be found somewhere on this vast new continent that is, he felt, as yet unspoiled by the "older life-modes" of European mind and culture. The expression of this hope was, I think, his *Studies in Classic American Literature.*

Now it seems clear that Lawrence's essays on Franklin, St. John de Crèvecoeur, Fenimore Cooper, Poe, Hawthorne, Dana, Melville, and Whitman, just as is the case with his writings on Freud, do not represent a body of sustained and disinterested criticism, in the usual sense of that term. Indeed, they represent a triumph not of intelligence but of a uniquely personal imagination, and thus constitute an important document that continues to be very much worth reading, not perhaps because of what it tells us of Hawthorne's *Blithedale Romance* or Melville's *Moby Dick*, though it contains flashes of true and remarkably penetrating insight into these and other classic American texts, but rather for what it tells us of Lawrence and the world within which his own spirit was contained. The scope of this essay makes impossible a detailed examination of this fascinating book, but let us turn at least to one of the most characteristic chapters, the one devoted to Whitman, whose presiding mood, it is true, perhaps of all American writers, most closely

* This was, of course, after he had despaired of Italy and Australia.

resembles that of Lawrence, though the equivalence is manifestly overstated and exaggerated in the *Studies*.

The chapter which precedes the Whitman section is devoted to an analysis of Melville's *Moby Dick*, and what an analysis! *Moby Dick* becomes, on Lawrence's reading, an allegorical statement of our "crucifixion into sex." The great white whale, says Lawrence, is "our deepest blood-nature."

And he is hunted, hunted, hunted by the maniacal fanaticism of our white mental consciousness. We want to hunt him down. To subject him to our will. And in this maniacal conscious hunt of ourselves we get dark races and pale to help us, red, and yellow, and black, east and west, Quaker and fire-worshipper, we get them all to help us in this ghastly maniacal hunt which is our doom and our suicide.[47]

Now as every schoolboy knows, the great whale finally sinks the Pequod, which Lawrence takes to be Melville's vision of a final victory in modern society of the "blood-consciousness" over the "ideal" consciousness—and then *"Boom!* as Vachel Lindsay would say. To use the words of Jesus, IT IS FINISHED. *Consummatum est."* [48]

So he begins his essay on Whitman by flaying "Walt" with pejoratives for having killed his "isolate Moby Dick." "You have mentalized your deep sensual body," he says, "and that's the death of it." He quotes the little poem from Whitman's *Children of Adam*, "I am He that aches with Love," that goes:

> I am he that aches with amorous love;
> Does the earth gravitate? does not all matter,
>   aching, attract all matter?
> So the body of me to all I meet or know.

And, as if resentful at finding his own deepest feelings so fully bodied forth in the poetry of another, he professes bewilderment as to what these lines really mean:

I am he that aches with Amorous Love.

What do you make of that? *I am he that aches.* First generaliza-tion. First uncomfortable universalization. *With amorous love!* O God! Better a bellyache. A bellyache is at least specific. But the *ache of Amorous Love!*
Think of having that under your skin. All that!

I am he that aches with Amorous Love.

Walter, leave off. You are not *he.* You are just a limited Walter. And your ache doesn't include all Amorous Love, by any means. If you ache you only ache with a small bit of amorous love, and there's so much more stays outside the cover of your ache, that you might be a bit milder about it.

I am he that aches with Amorous Love.

Chuff! chuff! chuff!
Chu-chu-chu-chu-chuff! [49]

And he continues to castigate Whitman for having asserted that he embraced *all,* weaving all things into himself. "Do you really!" explodes Lawrence. "There can't be much left of *you* when you've done. When you've cooked the awful pudding of One Identity." "Walt," he says,

becomes in his own person the whole world, the whole universe, the whole eternity of time, as far as his rather sketchy knowledge of history will carry him, that is. Because to *be* a thing he had to know it. In order to assume the identity of a thing he had to know that thing. He was not able to assume one identity with Charlie Chaplin, for example, because Walt didn't know Charlie. What a pity! He'd have done poems, paeans and what not, Chants, Songs of Cine-maternity.

Oh, Charlie, my Charlie, another film is done— [50]

Lawrence is, then, attacking Whitman, really, for having been too intent upon *knowing* to embrace the "One Identity" as com-pletely as he himself wishes he might have done. But his true attitude is rendered ambiguous by the apparent attack upon the principle of *identification* itself—which was, I think, motivated only by his embarrassment at confronting in Whitman a spirit so near a replica of his own. Lawrence too "aches with Amorous Love," as I suggested earlier, in a manner that is evocative of that whole tradition which we found de Rougemont to be defining, and he too seeks relief from his singleness in the "En Masse," the "One Identity," of which Whitman sang so stirringly. He too, in every fibre of his being, was interested in the "Allness," and so we think it not quite sporting of him to rib poor old Walt so mercilessly for being a kindred spirit. As Lawrence once said in a letter to Middleton Murry, "One hand in space is not enough. It needs the other hand from the opposite end of space, to clasp and form the bridge." We found him making this discovery in the sexual experience, wherein we found him also making the discovery that this "other hand" could be grasped only in that Night, beyond the Day, where the *two* vanish away in "absolute, mystic marriage," and the anguish of finite individuality is transcended in the ecstasy of a mystic union which cancels out the mutuality of the sexual relation.

But with *Calamus* Lawrence begins to approve of Whitman, for here he finds him singing

of the mystery of manly love, the love of comrades. Over and over he says the same thing: the new world will be built on the love of comrades, the new great dynamic of life will be manly love. Out of this manly love will come the inspiration for the future.[51]

And when he finds him whispering in a strangely beautiful way:

> Yet you are beautiful to me, you faint-tinged
> roots, you make me think of death.
> Death is beautiful from you (what indeed is
> finally beautiful except death and love?)
> I think it is not for life I am chanting here

> my chant of lovers, I think it must be
>   for death,
> For how calm, how solemn it grows to ascend
>   to the atmosphere of lovers,
> Death or life, I am then indifferent, my soul
>   declines to prefer
> (I am not sure but the high soul of lovers
>   welcomes death most)
> Indeed, O death, I think now these leaves
>   mean precisely the same as you mean—

—when Lawrence comes upon this Whitman, a lusty *Amen* springs almost involuntarily from his heart, and he is forced to acknowledge with an unwonted humility:

Whitman, the great poet, has meant so much to me. Whitman, the one man breaking a way ahead. Whitman, the one pioneer. And only Whitman. No English pioneers, no French. No European pioneer-poets. In Europe the would-be pioneers are mere innovators. . . . Ahead of Whitman, nothing. Ahead of all poets, pioneering into the wilderness of unopened life, Whitman. Beyond him, none. His wide, strange camp at the end of the great highroad. And lots of new little poets camping on Whitman's camping ground now. But none going really beyond. Because Whitman's camp is at the end of the road, and on the edge of a great precipice, blue distances, and the blue hollow of the future. But there is no way down. It is a dead end.[52]

What was the movement of Whitman's soul? "Merging!" shouts Lawrence. "And Death! Which is the final merge. . . ."

The great merge into the womb. Woman.

And after that, the merge of comrades: man-for-man love.

And almost immediately with this, death, the final merge of death.

There you have the progression of merging. For the great mergers, woman at least becomes inadequate. For those who love to extremes. Woman is inadequate for the last merging. So the next step

is the merging of man-for-man love. And this is on the brink of
death. It slides over into death.
    David and Jonathan. And the death of Jonathan.
    It always slides into death.
    The love of comrades.
    Merging.

This may not perhaps have been the dialectic of Whitman's
experience, but it was surely Lawrence's, for he was himself a
great merger, and for mergers there must always be death. This,
it seems to me, was the utter extremity of the man's life and his
doctrine.

    It is in *The Plumed Serpent* that Lawrence gives us his Utopia.
The story is largely devoted to a description of a successful attempt by Don Ramon, a Columbia graduate, and Don Cipriano,
an Oxford man, to revive in Mexico, the ancient religion of the
pre-Aztec god Quetzalcoatl.

It was as if, from Ramon and Cipriano, from Jamiltepec and the
lake region, a new world was unfolding, unrolling, as softly and
subtly as twilight falling and removing the clutter of day.

Professor Tindall has reminded us of the identity of the book's
theme with that of Mme. Blavatsky's *Secret Doctrine:*

the recovery of lost Atlantis by means of myths and symbols. More
practical than Mme. Blavatsky, however, and not content merely
to talk about a primitive Utopia, Don Ramon erects a past Utopia
in the present, generally according to Mme. Blavatsky's plan, but
with modern improvements. The ends and means are hers, the
improvements Frazer's.[53]

Atlantis recaptured—that's it: "the old, antediluvian silence" of
that "old pre-Flood world."
    Quetzalcoatl was apparently for Lawrence the symbol of the
primitive truth which he sought to make his own. He was the

god of the union of rain with earth. His name means bird-serpent and twin, thus indicating not only a certain duality but transcension of the duality in union. And it appears that Lawrence for a while supposed that in the ritual of worship surrounding the person of this god the tragic problem of human isolation could be solved. But the book which is based upon this phase in the evolution of his thought has a more strikingly abstract, and consequently irritating, quality than do most of the novels, for there is involved in it a curious kind of failure, which has to do not simply with the distastefully authoritarian character of this ideal society whose overlord, Ramon, is the prototype of the modern political dictator. Lawrence, of course, justifies the authoritarianism that Ramon and Cipriano represent on the ground that they are servants of the "ultra-phallic" mystery; and though ir this were to be taken seriously it would be the perversest kind of nonsense, it yet has a certain validity in terms of the premises of his poetic logic. The primary failure embodied in the book involves a failure to realize this very logic. His premise is, of course, that he has found in Mexico something with which to minister to the sickness in the larger community of the modern world. And so the only chance he has for giving the novel the slightest appeal to our credulousness is so to thrust us into the spiritual climate of this ethos that we do for a moment glimpse the splendor and majesty of its ancient mysteries and surrender our hearts to their charm. But this he seems consistently to fail to do, for he is so intent upon his homily, so preoccupied with his theosophic doctrine, that he never gives us a sense of place, which is necessary for the maintenance of the unity of his mood. The result is that Mexico never shines through, as it does so beautifully in the earlier books, *St. Mawr*, *Mornings in Mexico*, and *The Woman Who Rode Away*. And so when we glance back at the course of his travels, we are not surprised to learn that shortly after this book was written he returned to Europe, for already, as we had begun to suspect in reading the story and realizing the cause of its inadequacy, he had begun again to despair of still another land as the land of his salvation.

There remain now, of the work of Lawrence's later years, three books of which something must yet be said; and the first of these is *Lady Chatterley's Lover*. Of all the texts in twentieth-century literature generally regarded as of first importance, for one reason or another this has perhaps been one of the most heatedly discussed, and critical reaction to it has been diversified in the extreme. Henry Miller, for example, regards it as a superlative example of Lawrence's genius, but Middleton Murry regards it as only "wearisome and oppressive." F. R. Leavis speaks of its "splendid artistic maturity," but Horace Gregory feels that Lawrence's "sense of aesthetic structure had barely recovered from the complete lapse in *The Plumed Serpent*." And then again, Aldous Huxley finds it "a strange and beautiful book," and Diana Trilling discovers in it "a quality both of reality and humanity that is not often present in Lawrence's fiction." My own feeling is that one's reaction to the novel will be largely governed by the degree to which one has become anaesthetized to the special quality of redundancy (W. H. Auden calls it "wooziness") that pervades so much of his writing, and whose characteristic manner is laid out so barely in *Lady Chatterley*.

The novel revolves around Constance Chatterley, whose husband, Sir Clifford, is paralyzed from the waist down as a result of injuries received in the War of 1918. Lawrence would have us, one feels, understand his affliction in a symbolic sense: Sir Clifford is not only technically impotent but sensually impotent as well (a distinction which he drew, in the autumn of 1922, in writing about Ben Hecht's *Fantazius Mallare*, in a letter to Willard Johnson).[54] So Constance, in her desire for a child, turns to her husband's gamekeeper, Mellors, who lives on the Chatterley estate, and it is their love affair that is made the dramatic center of the book. Here we get all the old arguments, but the old hysteria which, when Lawrence is at his best, somehow supports the scaffolding of his stories, seems here to be lacking, and the whole thing strikes us as being curiously abstract. The sufficient and most appropriate word of appraisal to be pronounced upon it is simply that here is probably the supreme instance of Lawrence thumbing his nose at the censor.

But in the little book *The Man Who Died*, the last upsurge of his creative power, we come to the most beautiful and perfect jewel that ever came from his hands—and, what is more, an intensely personal document that belongs with Rimbaud's *Une Saison en Enfer*, Gide's *L'Immoraliste* and *Corydon*, Ezra Pound's *Draft of XXX Cantos*, and José García Villa's *Have Come; Am Here* in being one of the purest examples of modern blasphemy. It was as if Lawrence toward the end of his life had a deep intuition of the radically heretical nature of his religion and, rejoicing in it, wanted at last to cry out boldly, unequivocally: "I am not of Jesus's party, or, belonging to his party, I have no traffic with his Church, for my Jesus was, yes, crucified dead and buried, but rose again not to sit on the right hand of the Father in Heaven but to cohabit with a virgin priestess of Isis and by her ministrations to be made whole again."

Then came in the *Apocalypse* his final word of revelation, his final vision of a new world, of a possibly available future, which would be a recapitulation really of a very old world, wherein man's divinity would be restored, wherein we would be reunited with the cosmos and all ideas of "creation" and "separateness" and "God versus world" would have disappeared, wherein the cosmos would simply *be* and we would *be* with it, oblivious to all the extreme conceptions of mind and personality and self-hood that have burdened the modern world. "What we want," said Lawrence, "is to destroy our false, inorganic connexions, especially those related to money, and re-establish the living connexions, with the cosmos, the sun and earth, with mankind and nation and family. Start with the sun, and the rest will slowly, slowly happen." Thus his last word was a word of hope, of faith in a possible atonement and reconciliation beyond our present alienation, but as to the attainability or even desirability of such a reconciliation as Lawrence envisaged, each of his readers must finally judge for himself in terms of his own *Weltanschauung*.

Whatever ultimate conclusions one reaches about Lawrence, though, it is difficult to avoid, finally, the paradoxical position of at once according him a kind of sainthood and yet withholding from him the kind of reverence and veneration that we give to the saints. We have had, I think, two types of saint (if the term may be loosely used without primary reference to Catholic dogma) in the modern world: on the one hand, of course, the men and women of great faith, whose lives and works are a constant source of instruction in belief and edification of piety, among whom we number such gracious spirits as Albert Schweitzer, Baron von Hügel, Bishop Andrews, Evelyn Underhill, Charles Péguy, and the painter Rouault. But, on the other hand, there have been those whose despair has been so profound that, in hovering on the verge of prayer, it has been evocative of faith —Baudelaire, Nietzsche, Picasso, Cocteau, and Sartre—and among these limbic saints sits D. H. Lawrence as our great modern chartist of the *via mystica*. And if, as Bergson contended, our salvation is to be accomplished by our saints, we shall need him too.

> . . . this soul hath been
> Alone on a wide, wide sea:
> So lonely 'twas, that God himself
> Scarce seemed there to be.
>
> Oh sweeter than the marriage-feast,
> 'Tis sweeter far to me,
> To walk together to the kirk
> With a goodly company!—
>
> To walk together to the kirk,
> And all together pray,
> While each to his great Father bends,
> Old men, and babes, and loving friends,
> And youths and maidens gay!
> —Samuel Taylor Coleridge, *The Rime of
> the Ancient Mariner.*

> . . . our redemption is no longer a question of
> pursuit but of surrender to Him who is always
> and everywhere present. Therefore at every mo-
> ment we pray that, following Him, we may de-
> part from our anxiety into His peace.
> —W. H. Auden, *For the Time Being*

WE HAVE NOW reached a point at which it is possible for us to pause for a moment in consideration of the nature of the unity within which this book falls—which may perhaps appear somewhat ambiguous by reason of the way in which the modesty of one side of my purpose is counterbalanced by the largeness of still another claim.

The subject of our reflections has, of course, been the forms which a certain modern spiritual phenomenon has assumed—that phenomenon being the estrangement and the isolation which are so prominent a feature of contemporary sensibility. And we have sought a fuller understanding of this phenomenon—and thus of ourselves—through the examination of certain modern writers whose work seems constantly to be ringing the changes on this theme. The "modesty" of our effort results simply from our not having attempted primarily the more specialized task of analyzing the specific phenomenon of the alienation of the artist-personality from the modern environment. This more narrow, but very difficult, problem, it is true, has been the subject of a good deal of recent critical writing, though one feels that it is yet to receive its fullest definition in terms of the whole apparatus of sociological, psychological, and philosophical insights that is available to criticism at the present time. But this has not been the field within which we have moved—although all that we think of when we speak of the "alienation" of the modern artist has, I think, been presupposed all along the way. Our primary concern has rather been with that dimension of the writer's book which transcends self-discovery and self-definition and which reveals, beyond the terrain of the artist's private world, a collective self and a collective destiny. It has been assumed that the true artist does not misunderstand the meaning of the period in which he lives and that his art is therefore always, beyond its purely aesthetic intentions, an art of haruspicy. And so, in taking up the work of Kafka, Silone, and Lawrence, we have been interested not so much in what their books reveal of a given personality, however interesting we may feel that personality to be, but rather in what they tell us about ourselves, about contemporary man in the broad mass—from the standpoint of our special category.

It is, of course, never possible to distill from imaginative literature the kind of propositional truth about experience which we get from mathematics or the physical sciences without doing violence to the kind of truth which we have a right to expect that it will give us—which is, as John Hospers has insisted, not "truth-about" but "truth-to" experience.[1] Or, to employ the terminology of D. G. James, it is not the business of the artist, whatever his medium, to report *facts* about the world—which would, of course, have to be judged by the same canons of evidence as those by which all scientific analysis is judged—but rather to convey an "imaginative prehension" of the world. "The question of the abstract truth or otherwise of a play or poem," he says, "simply does not occur in imaginative experience; for poetry is not a number of propositions, but the conveyance of imaginative prehension."[2]

And though I have admitted to a kind of interest in these writers that focuses primarily on what they tell us "about" contemporary experience, I have done so in full awareness that what we have gotten from Kafka and Silone and Lawrence has not been a series of propositional statements, of a scientific, discursive order, but rather a vision, a seizure, a poetic organization, or, as D. G. James would say, an imaginative prehension of an aspect of the modern mind. Hence, we are, I think, relieved of the necessity of checking, say, Lawrence's psychological insights against those of Dr. Abram Kardiner, or Silone's social vision against that of Sorokin, for the two kinds of insight are of a radically different order.

To return, however, to the first paragraph, I suspect that whatever largeness of claim may be felt to be attached to this essay derives from my assumption of the typicality of the figures with whom we have been dealing. But though there may be formulations of our theme in modern literature of which neither Kafka nor Silone nor Lawrence is in some way evocative, it is, on the other hand, unarguable that each of these writers is representative of at least one aspect of a generally pervasive sensibility in our day and that when one speaks of Kafka or Silone or Lawrence, a whole habit of mind is instantly recalled.

I do not suggest, though, that either figure is, of the group of writers with whom we identify him, the most successful artist, the most accomplished practitioner of his craft—but only, for my purposes, the most convenient example. It is probably true, for instance, that of those writers to whose work I have referred by the term "revolutionary novel" Malraux is the most considerable artist, but Malraux's present activity in France as the leading spokesman for General de Gaulle, though not perhaps utterly discontinuous with his past, yet establishes a new term to which his career must be related and which, because it involves so highly problematic a political situation, probably requires a reservation of further judgments of his work for some time to come, until we see his new phase in fuller relation to the whole. And considerations of a similar order have, I think, guided the other selections of focal figures here.

That I should feel impelled, however, to approach a problem that is fundamentally psychological and philosophical from the standpoint of literature—and actually be justified in doing so—has a level of implication that extends far beyond such irrelevancies as my own special bent of mind, and demands that we take a synoptic view of the position of art in the total economy of man's spiritual life, particularly in the modern world.

In one of his last books Professor Ernst Cassirer, in the course of restating the problems of philosophical anthropology that exist for our time, defined man as an "*animal symbolicum*," as that being who, considered from the standpoint of what he *does*, is distinguished by his comprehension of his environment in

terms of *symbolic systems*.[3] And if we do not seek a definition
of man in terms of "essence" or "substantiality," this is about
as good a definition as we can find, for it places before us the
most distinctively human faculty—namely, the faculty of *imagination*, which, in its transmutation of the chaos and disorder
of immediate experience into regularity and array, renders the
world in the various symbolic systems of language, art, science,
and religion. For our awareness of how human life at its highest
is augmented in this way beyond the ebb and flow of brute sense
experience we are, I believe, historically, indebted to Kant, but
almost every modern thinker who has attacked the question as
to wherein lies man's distinctiveness has finally turned to the
creative activity of the imagination as its primary source.

The world, said Kant, does not initially present itself to us
as an already ordered unity—nor is the mind simply a blank
tablet, as Locke had contended, upon which the world imprints
itself. The world as given, he insisted, is rather a plurality of
sensation upon which the mind works, transforming it into
an ordered whole. Kant referred to this synthetic power of mind
as "the transcendental unity of apperception," the chief element in which he considered to be the imagination, the "fundamental faculty of the human soul," which, in overcoming the
disconnectedness of our sense impressions, virtually creates the
world of things and persons that common sense assumes to be
simply *there* but that is really *there* as a product of the imagination. The imagination is, then, the very basis of practical life,
for to carry on the practical affairs of everyday we must be able
to react to a *Gestalt*, and the point is that this whole, whether
it be a dog or an automobile or a child, is a conglomerate of
sense impressions which we apprehend as a unified, isolatable
entity through the agency of an imaginative faculty that is therefore basic to perception and, as such, a universal possession of

mankind. Without it man has no *world*, for to possess a *world* is to have not merely an endless continuum of sensations but an interrelated system of wholes which are the products of an imaginative synthesis of discrete sense-data. By this imaginative labor upon the stuff of life we arrive not only at that prehension of experience which simply enables us to carry on the business of living from day to day but also at the somewhat more disinterested activity which we call "science," for both ultimately reach their fruition, as it were, in the ascertainment and manipulation to human ends of what lies outside the world of imagination.

But there is a dimension of man's imaginative life that finds expression not in fulfillment of the demands of *practical* life but in *contemplation* of "what is potentially in Nature to be seen, in life to be felt, in speculation to be thought," [4] and on this highest level man *rests* in the imagination and does not *use* it as an instrument of release to that restless, diurnal world of impulse and practical intention. Here the soul takes a brief truancy from "the world of familiarity and selfish solicitude, and brings about a magical enhancement of our apprehension of the world by a re-creation of it at a new and almost undreamed-of level." [5] The effort is made to get an "imaginative prehension" of the whole of life, and from this most strenuous level of the imaginative life issue the forms of art and the visions of religion.

It was, indeed, such a view of the imagination that Coleridge was working toward in the *Biographia Literaria*, when he distinguished between the "primary" and the "secondary" imagination. He took great care, however, to insist upon the continuity between the two dimensions, for, as he put it, the "secondary" imagination is to be considered "as an echo of the former, coexisting with the conscious will, yet still as identical with the primary in the *kind* of its agency, and differing only in *degree*, and in the *mode* of its operation." Professor Irwin Edman expresses this idea by indirection when he says:

In a broad sense the key instances of art are to be found not in the concert hall or the museum, but in the field, the pasture, and the plow. In a world full of perils and uncertainties man had to learn to live before he could learn to live beautifully or bother, as it were, to create beautiful things.[6]

Professor Edman is saying here, in effect, that the imagination operative upon the natural scene, "ingeniously affecting it toward the fulfillment of human purposes," [7] is identical in the "kind of its agency" with that which lies behind, say, Joyce's *Finnegans Wake*, Picasso's *Guernica* or Schoenberg's *Pierrot Lunaire*. The only difference is "in degree"; in the one case we have "the world of familiarity and selfish solicitude" so operated upon by the imagination as to be rendered adequate to the demands of "practical" existence, and in the other case we have such a creative transformation of the world of the "primary" imagination as makes it a satisfactory dwelling place for the soul. Or, as D. G. James would put it:

The primary imagination is the condition of our having a world of experience at all; the secondary imagination the condition of our having a world which, grasped in a fuller unity of pattern, may then yield a maximum of harmonized and vital experience.[8]

Though the principle of continuity is correctly insisted upon, it is, nevertheless, true that it is only in the fullest exercise of what, following Coleridge, we are calling the "secondary" imagination that the human spirit attains to its highest estate and finds its noblest and loveliest modes of expression. And it is in this sense that we say that the artist and the saint (who are not unique beings, since all of us pursue in greater or less degree, *because we are men*, their characteristic activity, but only those who consistently embody a superior type of imaginative life), rather than the scientist or the practical man of affairs, epitomize the highest interior creativeness of human personality. Their creations, as representative of the "secondary" imagination, may well be considered as the constitutive elements of "culture," the creations of the scientist who orders the world of nature and those of the politician who orders the world of society, as representative of the "primary" imagination, being taken as the constitutive elements of "civilization." The history of religion and art, in other words, represents the deepest and most significant aspect of our pilgrimage on earth.

Ideally, of course, these two principles—"culture" and "civilization"—would not be antithetical but would rather cohere harmoniously together in the structure of the human community, each contributing to and reinforcing the other. And this ideal state of affairs would seem to have been almost attained in that theocratic society which Europe enjoyed during the Middle Ages, in which the whole of life was so ordered in accordance with a regulative spiritual principle that man as a natural entity who comprehends his environment and subjects it to human ends was not alienated from man as a spiritual subject who transcends his environment to contemplate the meaning of his existence. That is to say, man was a *person*—"a unity of a spiritual nature endowed with freedom of choice and so forming a whole which is independent of the world. . . ." [9] The unity of his imaginative life, in other words, had not yet been sundered; "culture" and "civilization" were held together in stable relationship, and the expression of this consonance between private and public values was the Church, whose majesty and authority in temporal and spiritual affairs was unquestioned.*

The Renaissance, however, in its economic and cultural liberation of the individual from the restraints of medievalism, marked

* For suggestions as to the possible fruitfulness with which this antithesis between "culture" and "civilization" may be applied as a conceptual in-

the end of the Middle Ages and the beginning of modern history, in which the most distinctive factor was to be the cleavage between what we are calling "culture" and "civilization." With the gradual substitution of the autonomous, "reasonable" individual for the Church as the center of existence went also that medieval unity which had drawn together and overarched the values of "culture" and the values of "civilization," and the result was that the values of "culture" came more and more to be centered in the detached, isolated life of this autonomous individual who, having for the first time to assume personal responsibility for his soul, was impelled to use the resources of art to the end of self-interpretation.

D. S. Savage, in illustrating this development, has made the interesting point that the literature of pre-Elizabethan England, for instance, was essentially the domain of the artificer (by which he means that artist whose chief function it is to entertain and who is himself, considered historically, a product of periods of relative peace and stability), that "Chaucer's *Canterbury Tales* were merely stories, novels in verse," but that when we touch the uneasy restlessness of the Renaissance spirit in Shakespeare

we touch the workings of a living soul. In Chaucer we touch a man who is predominantly a social being. There is not the same intensity of impact at all. This, quite apart from the question of archaism, is why Shakespeare is still alive for us, is still read and performed, while Chaucer is left unread except by students of literature and social historians.[10]

The point is, in other words, that in Shakespeare we meet something that begins to correspond deeply with the spiritual unrest of our own time.

---

strument to problems of the order with which we are dealing here, *vide* F. R. Leavis, *Mass Civilization and Minority Culture*, and Nicolas Berdyaev, *The Meaning of History.*

When we contrast, as we are doing here, "the Renaissance" with "the Middle Ages," we are, of course, dealing with ideal types which are patently compendious elisions of the historical process; but elisions which are indispensable if historical exegesis is to be informed by concern for theoretical understanding. As almost every commentator on these matters points out, all the forces that are most characteristic of modern society were in process of formation in the medieval society of the twelfth, thirteenth, and fourteenth centuries: all the elements of the new were already contained within the old. But, as Erich Fromm has well said:

. . . while it is important to see how many modern elements existed in the late Middle Ages and how many medieval elements continue to exist in modern society, it blocks any theoretical understanding of the historical process if by emphasizing continuity one tries to minimize the fundamental differences between medieval and modern society, or to reject such concepts . . . for being unscientific constructions. Such attempts, under the guise of scientific objectivity and accuracy, actually reduce social research to the gathering of countless details, and block any understanding of the structure of society and its dynamics.[11]

What, then, it is now important for us to stress is that whatever else may be said about the Middle Ages, it is yet true that man in medieval Europe, though he did not have the kind of freedom and social mobility on which modernity has so prided itself, was not alone and isolated in the sense that he was subsequently to be in modern times. He

was rooted in a structuralized whole, and thus life had a meaning which left no place, and no need, for doubt. A person was identical with his role in society; he was a peasant, an artisan, a knight and not an individual who happened to have this or that occupation. The social order was conceived as a natural order, and being a def-

inite part of it gave man a feeling of security and of belonging. . . .
Although there was no individualism in the modern sense of the
unrestricted choice between many possible ways of life (a freedom
of choice which is largely abstract), there was a great deal of
concrete individualism in real life.

There was much suffering and pain, but there was also the Church
which made this suffering more tolerable by explaining it as a result
of the sin of Adam and the individual sins of each person. While
the Church fostered a sense of guilt, it also assured the individual
of her unconditioned love to all her children and offered a way to
acquire the conviction of being forgiven and loved by God. The
relationship to God was more one of confidence and love than of
doubt and fear. Just as a peasant and a town dweller rarely went
beyond the limits of the small geographical area which was theirs,
so the universe was limited and simple to understand. The earth
and man were its center, heaven or hell was the future place of life,
and all actions from birth to death were transparent in their causal
interrelation.[12]

It is not surprising that the three great cultural masterpieces of
the period—the philosophy of Thomas Aquinas, the Gothic
Cathedral, and the *Divine Comedy*—should be consummate expressions of this great, overarching unity of private and public
values, of a social ideology and an artistic and religious sensibility
that were the common possession of all men.

But with the coming of those social and intellectual upheavals
which we associate with the Renaissance, this synthesis was
broken, and the individual, in the truly modern sense of the word,
began to emerge for the first time. When we compare, for instance, as Paul Tillich has so penetratingly done, the humanity
in a Giotto painting—say, that of St. Francis renouncing his pos-
sessions—with that in a Rembrandt portrait, we get a graphic
measurement of the great distance that has been traveled.

If we study the portraits of *Rembrandt*, especially in his later
period, we confront personalities who are like self-enclosed worlds—

strong, lonely, tragic but unbroken, carrying the marks of their unique histories in every line of their faces, expressing the ideals of personality of a humanistic Protestantism. To compare these portraits with *Giotto's* pictures of St. Francis and his monks is to recognize the difference between two worlds. Giotto's Francis is the expression of a Divine power by which man is possessed and elevated beyond his individual character and personal experiences. So are all other figures in Giotto's paintings. Between Giotto and Rembrandt are the portraits of *Titian*—individual expressions of humanity as such, representatives of the greatness, beauty and power of man. The transcendent reality to which Giotto subjects all individuals, their actions and emotions, has disappeared. The personality which found its highest portraiture in Rembrandt's pictures is the personality of the early bourgeois spirit, still subject to absolute forces, still shaped by the Protestant conscience, but already standing by itself, independent, alike of transcendent grace and of humanity. In these three painters, the development of the ideal of personality in the modern world finds classic expression.[13]

The great new development on the world's horizon, then, was the emergence of that autonomous personality whose unrestrained pursuit of his individual economic interests was somehow to serve the welfare of all, whose political judgments were somehow to cohere with his neighbor's to form a right collective judgment, and whose essential rationality, when freely expressed, was to serve as the sufficient foundation of the human community and the final canon of criticism in all matters of religious knowledge. Whereas St. Francis had declared that "man's worth is what he is in the sight of God, no more no less," Pico della Mirandola wonderfully sums up man's new feeling about himself in his speech on the dignity of man, when he represents God as speaking to Adam in the following manner:

I have set thee in the midst of the world, that thou mayst the more easily behold and see all that is therein. I have created thee a thing neither heavenly nor earthly, neither mortal nor immortal only, that thou mightest be free to shape and to overcome thyself. Thou mayst sink to a beast, and be born anew to the divine likeness. The brutes bring from their mother's body what they will carry with them as long as they live; the higher spirits are from the beginning or soon after, what they will be forever. To thee alone is given growth and a development depending on thine own free will.[14]

The most distinctive feature of this new personality, then, was that he had assumed personal responsibility for his soul, taking it out of the keeping of the Church and its tradition: this was the ultimate meaning of Renaissance cultural autonomy. Spiritual values thus ceased to be resident in an objective religious community and came rather to reside in the detached existence of the autonomous individual, the formal expression of this development being the extreme laicism of radical Protestantism.

There is little question, however, but that Western man's emancipation from the particular religious orientation that we associate with medieval culture issued in a new creativity—especially in respect to his dealings with nature, for the new humanism, in focusing his attention away from the promise of transhistorical fulfillment and the sacramental realities of the Church to the glories of this world, provided the impulse to revolutionary investigations of nature and society. And man's capacity for controlling the natural environment consequently advanced to hitherto undreamed-of levels. But it also proved to be the case that, not only religion having been so thoroughly desocialized but all cultural expressions of the "secondary" imagination as well, there were no longer sufficient spiritual resources operative in the human order to render conducive to the maintenance of human dignity those instrumentalities through which bourgeois society was achieving its distinctive gains. The result was the rise to ascendancy of what Paul Tillich has called "technical reason" [15]—the bearer of which was that distinctly modern antithesis of everything spiritual, the bourgeois man, whose special contribution to modern history was to be the detachment of the art of living from the business of living. Through the exercise of his newly acquired "technical reason" he

became increasingly able to control physical nature. Through the tools placed at his disposal by technical reason, he created a worldwide mechanism of large-scale production and competitive economy which began to take shape as a kind of "second nature," a Frankenstein, above physical nature and subjecting man to itself. While he was increasingly able to control and manipulate physical nature, man became less and less able to control this "second nature." He was swallowed up by his own creation. Step by step the whole of human life was subordinated to the demands of the new world-wide economy.[16]

Hence, as a result of the displacement of the transcendental dualism of the Middle Ages by the modern dualism *within* the empirical order between "goods" convertible to media of exchange and non-convertible "goods," such as art and literature, there arose a sharp division

between profit and poetry, money and immortality, matter and spirit. In this sense Cartesian dualism well represents the birth of modernism. The esthetic and philosophical protest precipitated the themes of alienation on the part of modern writers from Cervantes' Don Quixote, Shakespeare's Hamlet and Macbeth, to Goethe's Werther, Tasso, and Faust.[17]

The classic parable of this disruption of the unity of man's imaginative life, which has been so distinctive a feature of the whole evolution of bourgeois society, was given as early as the mid-seventeenth century in the case of Rembrandt which Herbert Read has told so well in his book *Art and Society*. Rembrandt agreed in 1642

to paint a group-portrait of a body of special constables under the leadership of a certain Captain Franz Banning Cocq, for which he was to be paid 1,600 gulden, each member of the corps contributing an equal share to this total sum. Rembrandt had reached the full command of his technique and invention, and in due course produced the painting we know as the *Night Watch*. But this was very different from the conventional group-portraits to which his patrons were accustomed, and which they might reasonably expect Rembrandt to paint. For in the past he had supplied the standard article to complete satisfaction, he had painted—for example, in *The Anatomy Lesson of Professor Tulp*, a work of ten years earlier—a group-portrait in which each member of the group was painted with equal care and on the same relative scale. But the result, for Rembrandt, had been dull and uninspired. Now, under the stress of his inspiration, he made a composition which is all liveliness and variety, an active play of light and shade, of animated mass and riotous colour. As a composition it is a triumph of the painter's art. But though Captain Cocq and his chief lieutenant are sufficiently in the limelight, the fifteen other officers who had paid their share of the cost were not slow to point out that their countenances had been obscured, their dignity destroyed, their very bodies cut in half to satisfy the exigencies of the artist's composition. And there was no hesitation about the verdict. Rembrandt was dismissed as a bad bungler and from that moment his fame as a painter declined, until he died poor and neglected twenty-six years later.[18]

And such, Mr. Read goes on to say by way of drawing the moral, has been the fate of the artist in modern times who has insisted "on maintaining his artistic standards in the face of bourgeois vanity and ignorance." [19]

Thus did the case of Rembrandt prefigure and foreshadow that deep cleft between "culture" and "civilization," between the "secondary" and the "primary" imagination, which was to be the characteristic feature of modern history and which was in a few short years to receive more public acknowledgment in the advent of the Romantic movement (Romanticism here being understood not primarily as a metaphysical doctrine, as in de Rougemont's view, but as a type of relation between the artist and the social order that first came sharply to be defined by the generations of Wordsworth and Shelley, Lamartine and Vigny, Baudelaire and Mallarmé). Indeed, the deepest significance of the Romantic movement in modern European literature must be defined in terms of the rift which, in its initial phases, it announced between social tendency and the private sensibility. Though it is true that the earlier Romantics identified themselves with the politics of the French Revolution, it is also true, as D. S. Savage reminds us, that many of them subsequently repudiated these political connections, for

what was the Revolution, after its first fervour, but a bourgeois revolution, its values the anti-cultural values of civilization, of the "enlightened reason"? Revolutions never initiate a new centrality, but always follow up a tendency already in being, taking in a sense the line of least resistance. They are symptoms of a deteriorative process, a release not of conscious creative forces but of unconscious and destructive ones. We must recognize the historical necessity of the revolution, but must also be able to stand over and above it in order to make a judgment of value. And from this viewpoint the French Revolution marks . . . a further stage in the de-socialization of culture. With the French Revolution the democratic principle, hand in hand with the principle of civilization, gains vast tracts of new territory. But democracy is still not completely triumphant, culture is still not completely annihilated. It is left for a second revolution, the world-totalitarian revolution which achieved its first victory in twentieth-century Russia, to implement this movement of democratic herd values allied with the values of civilization, and to enthrone the values of the herd over the individual while simultaneously harnessing "art" and "literature," for the first time, to the service of the ideals of the triumphant collectivist State.[20]

The modern world, in other words, considered from the standpoint of its outlawed creative minority, has been an inevitably and irretrievably romantic world, and it was probably the recognition of this fact which impelled T. S. Eliot, in a moment of reconsideration of his "classicist" program, to admit that the classic is an ideal which in our day can be realized only "in tendency." Indeed, Eliot's nostalgia for the classical is, as Professor Tindall has suggested,

perhaps the best evidence of our romanticism. In a classical period, a man does not have to go about proclaiming his classicism; nor, supposing him capable of such a proclamation, does he proceed, with Stephen Leacock's romantic hero, to dash madly off in all directions. Self-labelled classicists, ambiguously existing in our time, cannot escape its consequences, and their ideal is but another romantic retreat little different from the private religions they deplore.[21]

Romanticism has, in other words, been the destiny, the fate, of the modern artist, simply because he has been an exile: in no significant instance has he been able to bring himself to any full and unqualified acceptance of the world in which he has lived. Thus it is that "the great tradition" of modern literature—which is constituted for us by that long procession of homeless spirits that includes such figures as Leopardi, Vigny, Baudelaire, Rimbaud, Joyce, Hart Crane, and André Gide—has been primarily a romantic tradition, based upon the writer's alienation from bourgeois society. And his alienation has been so anticipatory of the ultimate tendency of modern man toward estrangement from his integral human nature that the deeper aspect of the human situation in our time can itself be deduced from the main body of our recent literature in which a central and controlling image has been that of the homeless wanderer, the deracinated "isolato." [22]

But it is also true that in spite of the anomalous position of the artist in bourgeois society, art itself has enjoyed an enormous importance—perhaps more so than ever before in the history of the West. For that remnant of the community that has remained at once aloof from the vulgarities of popular culture and yet sensitive to the spiritual issues postulated by the more problematic levels of modern experience, being unable to lay hold of a regulative and unitive principle in theological Protestantism (which has, until quite recently, been more a part of our problem than a possible answer), has turned to Art for its *rendezvous avec Dieu*. And the possibility of a restoration of cultural order being more immediately plausible through the agency of literature, since language as its medium is more pre-eminently social than the media of any of the other arts, it has come about that literature, as Ludwig Lewisohn remarked some years ago, has become "scripture" and "scripture" literature.[23]

This peculiarly modern faith that Art projects the historical program by which man's salvation is to be accomplished had many representatives in the nineteenth century and continues on into the present day to have many advocates. Matthew Arnold, for instance, in his essay on "The Study of Poetry," expressed the belief that more and more "mankind will discover that we have to turn to poetry to interpret life for us, to console us, to sustain us. Without poetry," he declared, "our science will appear incomplete; and most of what now passes with us for religion and philosophy will be replaced by poetry." And in our own day William Butler Yeats, in his essay on Blake, left no doubt but that finally Art must become a surrogate for traditional religion, when he remarked: "In our time we are agreed that we 'make our souls' out of some one of the great poets of ancient times, or out of Shelley or Wordsworth, or Goethe or Balzac, or Flaubert, or Count Tolstoy, in the books he wrote before he became a prophet and fell into a lesser order, or out of Mr. Whistler's pictures, while we amuse ourselves or, at best, make a poorer sort of soul, by listening to sermons or by doing or by not doing certain things." And I. A. Richards has assured us that poetry is something "capable of saving us." This whole modern attitude was admirably summed up some years ago by the French critic Jacques Rivière, when he observed that

if in the seventeenth century anyone had taken it into his head to ask Molière or Racine why they wrote, they would probably only have been able to answer: To amuse decent people. It was only with the advent of romanticism that literature came to be regarded as an attack on the absolute and its result a revelation.[24]

And, of course, Rivière's observation has an even more striking relevance to the neo-romanticism of our own time, which is, as T. E. Hulme aptly said, "spilt religion."

The plain fact is that for the last one hundred years, at least, Art has been valued not so much for what it is (for the representative works of modern art, in the fields of literature, painting, and music, have, as works of art, been generally abused and misunderstood by the rank and file of intelligent men) but for the extent to which it may function as a substitute for something else. The modern artist, and especially the poet and the novelist, has been for us priest and metaphysician: our poets have, in Shelley's phrase, been the "unacknowledged legislators of the world," the illumined conscience of our period. And the prototype of these artists, which we immediately recognize in the visages of Joyce, Proust, Kafka, Lawrence, and many others, is distinguished by nothing so much as by the dislocation, the isolation, which defines the ultimate position of the artist himself. His "revelation" has thus been a revelation of loneliness and its consequent spiritual disquiet.

We have considered here three examples of this sensibility in the work of Kafka, Silone, and Lawrence, in each of which it gains, in one of its aspects, a clear and representative expression. But beyond this, we are struck in these men by that which T. S. Eliot once observed in Henry James and Hawthorne— "their indifference to religious dogma at the same time as their exceptional awareness of spiritual reality." This is, of course, not uniformly true of all three in the same degree: we find Silone, for example, at every crucial point in dependence on the Catholicism that is so deeply embedded in his national heritage, though his manner of formulating it sometimes leaves one in doubt as to the degree to which he is prepared to accept its dogma as classically expounded—his inversion of traditional Christology being an instance in point. And at the other extreme is, of course, Lawrence, whose interest in dogma extended only to his predilection for a dogmatic form of utterance of an essentially private religion. Though Kafka in many ways stood near to the center of the tradition of Hebraic prophetism, he was yet sufficiently modern in his skepticism to have created, along with Lawrence, a mythical apparatus so individual and so thoroughly private as to make us feel impelled to speak constantly of Kafka's "world," a term which occurs many times in an anthology of Kafka-criticism edited by Angel Flores. So each of our writers—whose significance we have defined primarily in terms of their typicality —in greater or less degree projects a statement of isolation in terms of "exceptional awareness of spiritual reality" and, at the same time, indifference to any tradition of orthodoxy or dogma: their capability is that "negative capability" of Keats—"that is, when a man is capable of being in uncertainties, mysteries, doubts, without any irritable reaching after fact and reason." In this respect they are children of their age. It is, therefore, fitting that we consider in conclusion the relation that a writer whose imagination draws its main support from a tradition of Christian orthodoxy may bear to the spiritual problem that has been the subject of this book.

It is right too that in this connection we should consider the position of T. S. Eliot, for there are few, if indeed any other, Christian writers in the present day who strike us as being so thoroughly aware of the deeper resonances of contemporary life. And here we touch upon what has undoubtedly been the major difficulty of Christian writing in the last century or so. The Christian poet, being situated in a world that has, on the whole, been unsympathetic to the claims of the Christian system, has inevitably been compelled to adopt a posture of being over against the life that has surrounded him; and to be, in this sense, *against* one's environment, if one is a poet, is to have excluded a large part of it from one's poetry. It is for this reason, as Martin Turnell has said, that "nearly all Christian religious poetry written since Milton is minor poetry. . . ." [25] Indeed, it is probably true, as Brother George Every suggests, that

One of the last people who was able to assume an agreement among his readers about really serious and important matters was Crabbe, who was in some ways an exceedingly satisfactory poet. He could still write stories in verse at the beginning of the nineteenth century, like any other country parson talking to his own flock whom he knows and likes, and he assumes that they share with him a common belief in God and in redemption which, if not very fervent, brings with it a rather deeper insight into human weakness and strength than was common in the eighteenth century, and makes Crabbe on the whole a more interesting poet, more human and less topical, than his master Pope. And he was able to maintain throughout a poise which seems to have deserted Wordsworth when he was obliged to take up a position on the right wing in order to defend "thoughts that do often lie too deep for tears" from the onslaughts of materialism.[26]

Brother George Every goes on to characterize further Crabbe's transitional position:

Crabbe inherited from the seventeenth- and eighteenth-century poets the traditional relation of a poet or artist to an audience which shared his fundamental presuppositions. And so, perhaps, did Jane Austen, but she is a more difficult case. No doubt her adherence to good principles was sincere, but she felt deeply, and exposed with a regulated and concealed irony, the hollowness and conventionalism of most people's adherence to the very same principles of conduct. It is the concealment which marks her knowledge of the decay of common standards, the substitution of manners for beliefs. In an earlier age she would have been an open satirist. Swift had already come up against the same difficulty and chosen only a rather more obvious way round it. If any Victorian writer really possessed the old-fashioned kind of hold on his audience, based on a common moral attitude, it is much more likely to have been Dickens. And there we feel that the moral attitude has lost in subtlety; it has become confused with all kinds of sentimental recollections, so that the authentic note of tradition may be struck more accurately in George Eliot, who portrayed and implied a Christian attitude to the world and to moral problems in most of her novels, though she professed agnosticism.[27]

When we look at the position of the Christian writer over the past seventy-five years, we discover that he has generally either tended mistakenly to presuppose the conditions of which Brother George Every has taken Crabbe to be representative, and has consequently tried to produce the kind of literature that could only emerge naturally from a Christian society, or he has fully recognized the difficulty of maintaining a Christian position in our day and has therefore concerned himself chiefly with "the vicissitudes of the interior life." [28] Such fine poets as Charles Péguy and Paul Claudel, the little-known English writer Charles Williams and the distinguished French craftsman of the novel, Georges Bernanos, might well be taken, I think, as representative of that type of modern Christian writer whose very religious profundity has so betrayed him into miscalculation concerning the nature of his age that his vocabulary, being evolved in isolation from contemporary movements, strikes us

as being insufficiently comprehensive of this obtrusive present
in which we live. Their piety is real, their devoutness unques-
tionable, but they seem somehow, in Mr. Turnell's excellent
phrase, not to "suffer from the modern unrest," to be "outside
the tension" and insufficiently in touch with our modern difficulties of belief.

There has been, however, another kind of Christian literature,
a literature of "the vicissitudes of the interior life," which has its
modern origins in Baudelaire and Hopkins and the marks of
which we recognize, among contemporaries, in the poets W. H.
Auden and Robert Lowell and in the novelists François Mauriac
and Graham Greene. Here we come upon a line of modern writers who have been *against* the prevalent disposition of their age
in apprehending man as a creature extremely limited by moral
as well as physical handicaps and consequently in need of a
radical cure. But their imagery, though forged in the interior of
Christian faith, has been welded together with the more intimately known images of modern experience: they have, some
of them, often tended to employ a highly vitalized physical
imagery, recognizing that if the religious experience they want
to communicate is to be made real again, it must "be translated
into terms of physical sensation" for "those who are finding their
way from a belief that only the physical is real to a renewed belief in the reality of the metaphysical." [29] They are, in other
words, Christian writers who impress us with the sense of their
recognition of the difficulty of holding orthodox doctrine in a
heterodox world. And, above all, though they know that "poetry
can force the soul into the precincts of its last evasion," [30] they
do not believe that poetry will save the world; hence they speak
to the modern situation and are yet, in an important sense, not
themselves a part of it.

But when we turn to the writer whose work is most suggestive
of the measure of flexibility and relevance to contemporary

spiritual problems that continues to inhere in an orthodox outlook, the selection of Eliot is, of course, inevitable, for of all
present-day writers his grasp of the Christian tradition is perhaps
most complete and yet he strikes us as being a consummate
expression of "the modern temper." It is his affiliation with contemporaneity that R. P. Blackmur has in mind when he remarks:

Mr. Eliot's mind, let us say, is a mind of contrasts which sharpen
rather than soften the longer they are weighed. It is the last mind
which, in this century, one would have expected to enter the Church
in a lay capacity. The worldliness of its prose weapons, its security
of posture, its wit, its ability for penetrating doubt and destructive
definition, its eye for startling fact and talent for nailing it down
in flight, hardly go with what we think of to-day as English or
American religious feeling.[31]

But his modernity does not qualify his orthodoxy, the complete-
ness of which is indicated in his reply to Sister Mary James
Power's query concerning the nature of his spiritual persuasions:

Dear Sister:
    In reply to your letter of December 1st, perhaps the simplest
account that I can give is to say that I was brought up as a Unitarian
of the New England variety; that for many years I was without any
definite religious faith, or without any at all; that in 1927 I was baptized and confirmed into the Church of England; and that I am
associated with what is called the Catholic movement in that
Church, as represented by Viscount Halifax and the English Church
Union. I accordingly believe in the Creeds, the invocation of the
Blessed Virgin and the Saints, the Sacrament of Penance, etc.
                                        Yours faithfully,
                                        [Signed] T. S. Eliot
6 December 1932 [32]

    Eliot has faced "unflinchingly," in other words, as he him-
self once said of Pascal, "the demon of doubt which is insepara-

ble from the spirit of belief"; he has "the knowledge of worldliness and the passion of asceticism, and in him the two are fused
in an individual whole." [33] He is consequently, then, as Cleanth
Brooks has said, "so much a man of his own age that he can
indicate his attitude towards the Christian tradition without
falsity only in terms of the difficulties of a rehabilitation." [34] This
is at once his modernity and his orthodoxy, and is what makes
him so eminently suitable a subject on which to bring our discussion here to a close.

One hesitates to remark again the "unity" and the "intrica-
tion" of Mr. Eliot's poetry, for thus has almost every essay on
his work begun in the last fifteen years. But since it is true that
there is in his poetry, taken as a whole, a remarkable continuity
of intention, we must, instead of laboring the point, simply begin by assuming it. And if it is also true, as R. P. Blackmur has
said, that "Christianity is . . . the emphatic form his sensibility
fills," that "there has hardly been a poet of similar magnitude in
English whose work, not devotional in character, shows the
operative, dramatic presence of Christianity," [35] it would then
seem to follow very simply that, given the "unity" to which his
critics so constantly refer, the indispensable clue to the whole
of his work is contained in the structure of classical Christian
thought. But though this is in large measure the case, its recognition does not solve all our problems, for the apprehension of
the logic of the Christian faith demands what is perhaps the
most difficult process of imaginative recovery for modern men.
The extent of the difficulty is, indeed, revealed in the theological
confusion of one of Eliot's most formidable critics, Professor
Yvor Winters, who contends that Eliot's understanding of the
Christian doctrine of man is actually "related to the Marxist
and Fascist view that the individual lacks the private and personal power to achieve goodness in a corrupt society; it is a

utopian point of view, not a Christian one. Christianity rests upon the assumption that man can, with God's grace, save himself in a corrupt world. . . ." [36] Thus does Professor Winters reveal his own misunderstanding of Christianity, by which he is led on to a wrongheaded assessment of Eliot, for, following St. Paul, Christian thought has consistently discouraged the "assumption that men are as good as the ideals of justice and love which they entertain," [37] precisely because its estimate of evil has been so serious. Eliot's preoccupation with Original Sin and the related Christian ideas of atonement and redemption places him, in other words, in the very center of the Christian tradition, and it is, in fact, Professor Winters who, in spite of the fact that he makes mention of "grace," because of his emphasis upon the possibility of a *human* redemption of a corrupt world order, deserves the epithet "utopian."

I quote Professor Winters's strictures on Eliot's Christianity not, however, to quarrel with him about theology but only to indicate the extreme exertion of the imagination required of modern men in the recovery of the true nature of Christian wisdom and to suggest that the recognition of Eliot's dependence on Christian thought by no means solves all the critical problems. But it is nevertheless true that at the present time the reassessment of the meaning of his work can proceed from no other starting point, whether we deal with the phase which falls prior to *Ash Wednesday* or with the emphatically Christian writing of his later period.

The possible fruitfulness of this method of approach is perhaps best indicated when we come again to *The Waste Land,* which continues, I believe, to be the focal center of Eliot's poetry and at which the large and rounded estimate of the poet himself inevitably begins. D. S. Savage has suggested that "from *The Waste Land* (1922) and *The Hollow Men* (1925) it is something of a jump to the contemplative tones of *Ash Wednes-day* (1930) and the succeeding poems," [38] but is this really the case? I should rather like to propose the view that, if there is a real continuity between Eliot's earlier period (which gains its consummate expression in *The Waste Land*) and the ostensibly Christian poetry of the later period, we will find significant and crucial adumbrations of the later phase in the earlier work, without having to "jump" from it to *Ash Wednesday* or the plays or the *Quartets*.

We have too long taken *The Waste Land*, as Eliot himself has suggested with some irritation, as being simply a modern statement of pure despair, of pure revulsion from the tragic declensions of modern society, as the "poem of a generation." The poem was, to be sure, an abstract for a contemporary Inferno, but it involved considerably more than the mere articulation of the disquiet that followed upon the first World War. And one way of discovering precisely what it was beyond this is to consider the method by which it was written.

The sources of the scaffolding on which Eliot erected his verse are by this time familiar: they include Frazer's *Golden Bough*, Jessie Weston's *From Ritual to Romance*, *The Divine Comedy*, the *Upanishads*, a half-dozen Elizabethans, Shakespeare's *Antony and Cleopatra* and *The Tempest*, the English Metaphysicals, Baudelaire's *Les Fleurs du Mal*, the Symbolist poets (Laforgue, Corbière, and Mallarmé), and Wagner's *Götterdämmerung*, to mention only a few. Thus, as Stephen Spender was impelled to say, the poem, in its allusions, "is very slightly tainted by the learning of the Cambridge don." [39] But of course the point has hardly to be made now that the whole is not merely a *pastiche* of the poet's experiences in the library but is rather an immeasurably intricate condensation of modern experience in terms of the "heap of broken images" which constitutes our condition.

The late F. O. Matthiessen defined the problem that Eliot faced and explicated in the most illuminating way the method which he employed for handling it, and perhaps the quickest way of getting at the relevant issues here is to put ourselves in mind of the light which Matthiessen cast upon our subject. The "problem" (which was not only Eliot's but that of the modern poet generally) he puts in the following manner: "The modern educated man possesses a knowledge of the past to a degree hardly glimpsed a century ago, not only of one segment of the past, but, increasingly, of all pasts." But

The difficulty with our knowledge to-day consists in the fact that instead of giving the individual's mind release and freedom, the piling up of so many disparate and seemingly unrelated details can merely oppress him with their bewildering variety . . . with the futility of any certainty. . . . The problem for the artist is to discover some unified pattern in this variety; and yet, if he believes as Eliot does that poetry should embody a man's reaction to his whole experience, also to present the full sense of its complexity.

How, though, may he do this?

Faced with so great a range of knowledge as a part of the modern consciousness, he can bring it to satisfactory expression in one of two ways, either by expansion or compression. It can hardly be a coincidence that each of these ways was carried to its full development at almost the same time, in the years directly following the War. Joyce chose the first alternative for *Ulysses* and devoted more than a quarter of a million words to revealing the complexity involved in the passage of a single ordinary day. In the following year Eliot concentrated an interpretation of a whole condition of society into slightly over four hundred lines.

But, beyond the necessity of the poet's choice as to whether he shall "expand" or "condense,"

He can accomplish this double task of accurately recording what he has felt and perceived, and at the same time interpreting it, only if he grasps the similarity that often lies beneath contrasting appearances, and can thus emphasize the essential equivalence of seemingly different experiences. Such understanding and resultant emphasis constitute Eliot's chief reason for introducing so many reminiscences of other poets into the texture of his own verse.[40]

And so the numerous quotations from European and non-European literatures [41] which have mystified so many of Eliot's readers actually reinforce a quite basic logic of the poem. They at once symbolize the character of the modern poet's vision, which is a vision of "the apparent irrelevance and unrelatedness of things" (a vision that issues in a constant inspection of experience), and, at the same time, they are evocative of that whole literary order from Homer to Joyce, which has, as Eliot has reminded us, "a simultaneous existence" and which itself proceeds from a spiritual unity that once had actual vitality and may yet function creatively again if properly rehabilitated.

The presiding symbol in the organization of the poem is, of course, that of a "waste land," a symbol acquired by Eliot through his reading of Jessie Weston's From Ritual to Romance, which appeared only two years before Eliot's transmutation of its basic idea into poetry. Miss Weston had been concerned to examine the element of constancy and recurrence in the history of mythology, and takes up in her book such myths as those of the vegetative genesis of the seasons, the rebirth of human fertility, the Grail legend of purification, and the Christian myth of Resurrection. She finds that in all of them, despite surface differences, there is implied a profound concern with the genesis of life, a concern which she regards as being related to man's perennial fascination with the mystery of death and rebirth. She finds also the racial imagination tending to express this primal concern in the form of a myth, toward which all kindred myths move, of a land reduced to utter ruin by a curse that has not only blighted the soil and sterilized the reproductive processes of animal life but has even left its tragic mark upon the lord of the land, the Fisher King. And this illness can be cured only through the redemptive activity of a knight who, taking upon himself the misery of the land, assumes "the task . . . of restoration." [42]

In terms of this basic symbol, then, of a blighted country reduced to waste, Eliot, through the additional device of the swift recapitulation of large segments of cultural history by the apparently obscure literary allusion, sought to comprehend not only that "Unreal City,/Under the brown fog of a winter dawn," that was post-War London but also the other waste lands of man's spiritual history and the several continuities between them that somehow conspire to make them all variants on a constant theme. And this transcension of the merely contemporary for the structurally constant in the history of human personality which is so characteristic of Eliot's unique apprehension of the alienated modern consciousness is revealed, it is being suggested, not only in the *content* of the poem but also in the *formal* devices upon which it is reared. It is, indeed, probable that this particular strategy of intellection was a consequence of his already crystallizing theological orientation which was only to be fully discernible, however, in the later work. When he tells us in the opening lines of *Burnt Norton* that

> Time present and time past
> Are both perhaps present in time future,
> And time future contained in time past.

and when he tells us in *The Family Reunion* that

> . . . all past is present, all degradation
> Is unredeemable. As for what happens—
> Of the past you can only see what is past,
> Not what is always present. That is what matters.

we feel the accent of the poet's speech to be familiar; we feel
that we have heard it before, and we have, for the idea that is
involved in the very warp and woof of the poem of 1922 gains
the most explicit statement farther on in *Burnt Norton:*
". . . and all is always now." But "Your ordinary murderer,"
says Harry in *The Family Reunion,*

> cannot realize
> That everything is irrevocable,
> The past unredeemable.

Here we have it, then—the eternal presence of all time, and its
unredeemability. Its unredeemability, that is, by human con-
trivance. This is the unformulated presupposition of *The Waste
Land,* a presupposition that has its authentic roots in the Christian view of human destiny.

The prevailing disconcertion of those who live in the "waste
land" is defined in the opening section of the poem, "The Burial
of the Dead." "April," says the narrator, the month of rebirth,
the period of the "disturbance of the quiet seasons," [43] "is the
cruellest month, breeding/Lilacs out of the dead land, mix-
ing/Memory and desire, stirring/Dull roots with spring rain."

April is, of course, the cruellest of seasons because the disen-
gagement of the self from death into life which April symbolizes
is painful—painful because death (that is, spiritual lassitude)
is easier than life. April postulates Rilke's question:

> Earth, isn't this what you want: an invisible
>   rearising in us?
> . . . What is your urgent command, if not transformation?

And we do not want to be transformed, we shun the clarity of
day: we prefer the long dark months of Winter which "kept us
warm, covering/Earth in forgetful snow, feeding/A little life
with dried tubers." "We do not wish anything to happen," says

the chorus in *Murder in the Cathedral*, echoing these opening
lines of *The Waste Land*, for

> Seven years we have lived quietly,
> Succeeded in avoiding notice,
> Living and partly living.

Yet April insistently comes again to this lost country and its
lonely inhabitant, whose listless, solitary, international wander-
ings are suddenly suggested by the snatch of conversation the
poet recalls, that took place in the Hofgarten, just as summer
was surprising him and his companion with a shower of rain.

And as the protagonist contemplates remorsefully the "dull
roots" of his life for which the "stirring" of the "spring rain" is
so disquieting, he adopts for a moment what he supposes to be
the perspective of the "Son of man," who, as he looks upon this
land of waste, must surely be unable to see anything other than

> A heap of broken images, where the sun beats,
> And the dead tree gives no shelter, the cricket
>   no relief,
> And the dry stone no sound of water.

Yet, in the apparently irreparable ruin of his soul's integrity—
as it is thus stated here by obscure allusion to the picture of the
world's apostasy in the second chapter of the Book of Ezekiel
and the vision of Ecclesiastes, as recorded in the twelfth chapter of his Book—it is significant that the accent of Old Testament rigorism into which his speech suddenly falls somehow
encourages him to go on to perceive the newer covenant whereby

> There is shadow under this red rock,
> (Come in under the shadow of this red rock) . . .

Thus the tension is for a moment relaxed, and, in the protagonist's brief glimpse of the possibility of renewal "somewhere
on the other side of despair" [44] we sense relief. But whatever this

dimly glimpsed refuge be, it is not an evasion of suffering, for immediately there follow the lines:

> And I will show you something different from either
> Your shadow at morning striding behind you
> Or your shadow at evening rising to meet you;
> I will show you fear in a handful of dust.

"Shadow under this red rock"—but "fear in a handful of dust," or, as St. John of the Cross would phrase it, "the quiet Desert of the Godhead" at which we arrive by way of "the Divine Darkness. . . . This Abyss is our salvation." In other words, Eliot is adumbrating Dante's *"l'abisso dell' eterno consiglio,"* the abyss of the eternal counsel, wherein the pilgrim must serve a willing apprenticeship, taking up the attitude, later to be formulated in *East Coker,* that enables a man to say to his

> soul, be still, and wait without hope
> For hope would be hope of the wrong thing; wait
>   without love
> For love would be love of the wrong thing; there is
>   yet faith
> But the faith and the love and the hope are all in
>   the waiting.
> Wait without thought, for you are not ready for
>   thought;
> So the darkness shall be the light, and the stillness
>   the dancing.[45]

Then come the lines—

> *Frisch weht der Wind*
> *Der Heimat zu*
> *Mein Irisch Kind,*
> *Wo weilest du?*

—from the song in Wagner's *Tristan* that is sung by the young sailor who is on board the ship that is bringing Isolde to Cornwall and who sings out of the exuberance of his youth and the fullness of his love. And from this the protagonist's reverie moves on to a personal experience of love, long-forgotten and, one feels, almost deliberately pressed down beneath consciousness: he recalls a garden and a girl and hyacinths, figures which echo similar scenic images from the waiter's sad reminiscences in *Dans le Restaurant,* from *The Love Song of J. Alfred Prufrock,* and from *Portrait of a Lady.*

We shall encounter this image of a "garden" again and again in Eliot's poetry, and we are all indebted to Leonard Unger for having made us aware of the meaning of the symbol.[46] He has explained that the figure of the "garden" which constantly recurs throughout Eliot's work represents for the poet a rare moment of contact with reality, of "sudden illumination," that interrupts the conventional immediacies of a man's social and biological existence as the most completely meaningful moment of that life. If we were to employ the discriminations of classical Greek to denote the quality of temporal experience Eliot has in mind, we would perhaps not use the term *chronos,* which signifies "formal time" or mere duration, but *kairos,* "the right time," the fulfilled moment, the moment which is fulfilled because in it the eternal breaks into the temporal.*

Here we find our narrator, then, recalling a garden and a girl in that garden who gave him hyacinths, but recalling also that

> my eyes failed, I was neither
> Living nor dead, and I knew nothing
> Looking into the heart of light, the silence.

* *Vide* Paul Tillich, *The Protestant Era,* Chs. II and III, where Professor Tillich, though presenting a systematic exposition of a theological and historical problem in terms of his doctrine of *kairos,* yet casts a good deal of light on Eliot's conception of the dialectical relation between time and eternity (which is, of course, most fully explored not in *The Waste Land* but in *The Quartets*), between which and Tillich's own theory there is a considerable equivalence.

Thus his emphasis, as Mr. Unger has reminded us, is not really on the experience itself, but on "his removal from it, his failure to see its meaning." [47] It is significant too, in this connection, that the line which follows this passage, *"Oed' und leer das Meer"* ("Empty and wide the sea"), is the guard's reply, in the third act of Wagner's opera, to Tristan that the ship bringing Isolde to Cornwall is nowhere to be seen. Thus does Mr. Eliot, in the subtlest manner, suggest the failure of love in the waste land, while at the same time stating the more general truth of man's estrangement from the "garden" of grace.

With the passage in which Madame Sosostris figures centrally, we come upon the first explicit treatment of the religious problem. Its tone is predominantly negative and critical, for its focus is on apostasy and irreligion. But no explicit references are made to the apostasies of modern Christendom which are approached indirectly through materials drawn from Miss Weston's *From Ritual to Romance.* Miss Weston deals with the Tarot cards in connection with the ancient fertility rites of the East in which they were originally used to foretell the seasonal rising of the water which was, of course, the most important event in the people's lives. The clairvoyante Madame Sosostris thus has noble ancestors, against the background of whom her essential vulgarity ("If you see dear Mrs. Equitone,/Tell her I bring the horoscope myself:/One must be so careful these days") stands out all the more prominently. We find her telling the fortune of our protagonist, whose destiny she discovers to be identical with that of the drowned Phoenician Sailor ("Here, said she,/Is your card, the drowned Phoenician Sailor"). That her wisdom is counterfeit is revealed in her advice to her client: "Fear death by water." Thus she fails to realize, as Cleanth Brooks has searchingly observed, along with "the other inhabitants of the modern waste land that the way into life may be by death itself." [48] Nor is she able to "find the Hanged Man," whom Eliot tells us in the appended "Notes" to the poem he has associated with the Hanged God of Frazer, a generic type which includes the figure of Christ. Madame Sosostris can see only "crowds of people, walking round in a ring," and is thus a perfect embodiment of the moral and spiritual obliquity to which the vocation of religious prophetism has sunk in the modern world.

The last dozen and a half lines of "The Burial of the Dead," which are so evocative of the *fourmillante cité* of Baudelaire's *Tableaux Parisiens*, are perhaps the most moving lines in the entire poem, for they project with greater intensity than perhaps any other single passage a public world wherein we, *les hypocrites lecteurs*, have wandered through *le noir illimité*:

> Unreal City,
> Under the brown fog of a winter dawn,
> A crowd flowed over London Bridge, so many,
> I had not thought death had undone so many.
> Sighs, short and infrequent, were exhaled,
> And each man fixed his eyes before his feet.
> Flowed up the hill and down King William Street
> To where Saint Mary Woolnoth kept the hours
> With a dead sound on the final stroke of nine.

In directing our attention to the third canto of the *Inferno* here ("I had not thought death had undone so many . . .") Eliot would have us know, of course, that he has in mind those forlorn spirits in Dante's Limbo "who spent/Life without infamy and without praise . . . who rebelled not, yet avowed/To God no loyalty, on themselves intent." [49] But the density of the poet's reference is clarified even more when we realize that he has in mind also Baudelaire's *Au Lecteur* and the Baudelairean *ennui*, as is conclusively indicated by the final line of "The Burial of the Dead." We must remember that *ennui*, the spiritual lassitude which issues in the listless desire of desire, creates the principal circle in Baudelaire's Inferno: it is for him

> a state of abstraction, of removal from the paradox which gives tension and significance to our life . . . from the world of good and evil to an *abstract* world of moral and spiritual unconsciousness, where we are not troubled by the asymmetry of the principal paradoxical problems of life. Ennui convinces us that the Devil does not exist; that he is a childish or a medieval superstition, fantastic and impossible. So rid of the Devil, the person possessed by ennui does evil, not knowing that it is evil.[50]

Baudelaire states the matter in a tone of banter that is yet profoundly grave:

> Mais parmi les chacals, les panthères, les lices,
> Les singes, les scorpions, les vautours, les serpents,
> Les monstres glapissants, hurlants, grognants, rampants,
> Dans la ménagerie infâme de nos vices,
>
> Il en est un plus laid, plus méchant, plus immonde!
> Quoiqu'il ne pousse ni grands gestes ni grands cris,
> Il ferait volontiers de la terre un débris
> Et dans un bâillement avalerait le monde;
>
> C'est l'Ennui!—l'œil chargé d'un pleur involontaire,
> Il rêve d'échafauds en fumant son houka.
> Tu le connais, lecteur, ce monstre délicat,
> —Hypocrite lecteur,—mon semblable,—mon frère!

The man who goes in quest of all desires—who "ferait volontiers de la terre un débris"—only ends in the torment of the failure of desire, with the old king in *Spleen*, of whom Eliot's Fisher King in "The Fire Sermon" is strangely reminiscent (though we are told in the "Notes" that the Fisher King is drawn from Miss Weston's Grail legends), who is, says Baudelaire,

> Riche, mais impuissant, jeune et pourtant très-vieux. . . .
> Rien ne peut l'égayer . . .

Ennui, then, is our state of mind apart from the consciousness of sin, and it is the dwelling place of Satan, for the bored man, having no longer any knowledge of evil, has no defense against the Devil's wiles and is thus bereft of dignity. This is, indeed, the meaning of that apparently cryptic passage in Eliot's essay on Baudelaire, in which he says:

. . . so far as we do evil or good, we are human; and it is better, in a paradoxical way, to do evil than to do nothing: at least, we exist. It is true to say that the glory of man is his capacity for salvation; it is also true to say that his glory is his capacity for damnation. The worst that can be said of most of our malefactors, from statesmen to thieves, is that they are not men enough to be damned.[51]

This is also the meaning of those four lines in the last passage of "The Burial of the Dead" (into which a devastating analysis, of incredible intricacy, is packed of the secularism which prevails in modern society) that tell of the crowd, swarming listlessly over London Bridge, from whom were exhaled:

> Sighs, short and infrequent . . .
> And each man fixed his eyes before his feet.

The "short and infrequent" sigh is the only vocal gesture of which those whose wills have been overcome by ennui and whose minds have been enervated by unbelief are capable.

But then the protagonist sees one he knows in the crowd and stops him, crying:

> "Stetson!
> "You who were with me in the ships at Mylae!
> "That corpse you planted last year in your garden,
> "Has it begun to sprout? Will it bloom this year?
> "Or has the sudden frost disturbed its bed?
> "Oh keep the Dog far hence, that's friend to men,
> "Or with his nails he'll dig it up again!
> "You! hypocrite lecteur!—mon semblable,—mon frère!"

Professor Matthiessen's spadework is helpful and illuminating at this point, for he points out that the "name of the battle where Stetson fought is that of one in which the Carthaginians were defeated. . . ." [52] Thus Eliot, by having his protagonist recognize a friend who was with him not at Château-Thierry but at Mylae, suggests that there is a constant element in all human conflict which makes all of its specific occasions essentially similar.

And Stetson's corpse? "Will it bloom this year?" Not if "the Dog" is kept "far hence." Here we must recall that the time is April, "the cruellest month, breeding/Lilacs out of the dead land," the season during which "dull roots" are stirred with spring rain. And consequently, in terms of the symbolism of the poem, it is logical that Stetson should be asked if, in this season of rebirth, his "corpse," the dull clod of his unredeemed soul, will soon begin to sprout and bloom. But his interrogator, fully aware of his reluctance to submit to the process of redemption, without allowing him to reply, rushes on to say, with a tinge of irony: "Oh keep the Dog far hence, that's friend to men,/Or with his nails he'll dig it up again!" Now it is curious that the figure of the Dog should have puzzled so many readers of Eliot. He has himself sought to give us help in unraveling its meaning by referring us to the passage from the Dirge in Webster's *White Devil* that goes:

> O keep the wolf far hence, that's foe to men,
> Or with his nails he'll dig it up again.

And Cleanth Brooks, taking Eliot's reference perhaps too trustingly, has asked:

Why does Eliot turn the wolf into a dog? And why does he reverse the point of importance from the animal's normal hostility to men to its friendliness? If, as some critics have suggested, he is merely interested in making a reference to Webster's darkest play, why alter the line? I am inclined to take the Dog as Humanitarianism and the related philosophies which in their concern for man extirpate the supernatural—dig up the corpse of the buried god and thus prevent the rebirth of life.[53]

But had it occurred to Mr. Brooks to take the figure of "the Dog" as referring at once to Webster's "wolf" and possibly also to Francis Thompson's "Hound of Heaven," he might have avoided what here seems to me to be extremely dubious exegesis and concluded that Eliot turns the wolf into a dog in order to draw indirectly upon the strength of both Webster's and Thompson's images (though it is, indeed, rare to find him making use of a Victorian). He does not *altogether* "reverse the point of importance from the animal's normal hostility to men to its friendliness." In allowing his lines to evoke Webster's, he suggests antithesis between the Dog and man, but in calling up Thompson's Hound, whose "love's uplifted stroke" we await and yet from whom we flee "down the arches of the years . . . down the labyrinthine ways," he suggests that the very antithesis is the basis of the friendliness. We shun, in other words, Christ's constant and abiding love for us, which is so different from our love of each other and of Him; we try not to hear His knocking at the door of our lives, for we know that if we would remain in winter's warm and forgetful snow, He must be kept "far hence." We do not want to be saved, and this is our tragedy: it is the tragedy of Pascalian *acedia*, of the indolent will and the slothful imagination, that is slothful because it is evil.

Now as we look back over this first section of the poem, surely at least one of our initial assertions about Eliot's work is borne out: it has, in its structural aspect, an almost immeasurable density. We have devoted several pages of exegesis to a brief seventy-six lines, and if we were aiming at a closer reading of the text, several pages more would be fully in order. His method, as Professor Matthiessen has already told us, is one of compression; his speech is not that of the public prosecutor, nor are his conclusions those of the attorney for the defense—but there is, nevertheless, a conclusion, from which we must draw our own.

Beyond the employment of compression, however, there is something else we must notice here, and that is what Mr. Brooks has termed "the application of the principle of complexity": it is especially on the complexity of the poet's historical references that I want briefly to remark. For it is instructive, I think, to call to mind the large inclusiveness of Eliot's waste land. It is at once the waste land of Miss Weston's medieval legends, of Dante's Limbo, of Elizabethan England, of Baudelaire's Paris, and of contemporary London; and the stress is on the "unrealness" of them all. Thus we see how completely wrong was the view of the poem expressed by Malcolm Cowley some years ago in *Exile's Return:*

Beneath the rich symbolism of *The Waste Land,* the wide learning expressed in seven languages, the actions conducted on three planes, the musical episodes, the geometrical structure—beneath and by means of all this, the poet is saying that the present is inferior to the past.[54]

This is, of course, precisely the opposite of what Eliot is saying: at no point has his basic tendency been towards any simple pejorative juxtaposition of contemporary history against the past. He has rather sought, as he himself once said of Joyce, to "manipulate a continuous parallel between contemporaneity and antiquity." And though his manner of handling history may make for ambiguity, we must recognize the ambiguity for what it is—namely, a mode of communication and a consequence of fidelity to the labyrinthic nature of experience.*

* In fairness to Mr. Cowley it should be noted that in preparing the revised edition of *Exile's Return* (Viking, 1951), he apparently sensed the

What is most important, though, is that the category of alienation—which is, of course, for Eliot, as it is for the other writers with whom we have been dealing, the definitive category for the description of contemporary man's spiritual situation, in both its individual and collective aspects—is here given formulation in terms which, from our present perspective upon Eliot's career, appear to look forward to his return to Christianity. The poem is, in other words, something radically other than "the poetry of drouth," which has for too long been the easy and fashionable way of talking about it. The traditional vocabulary of Christianity is rarely resorted to, to be sure (and though this may confuse the literal-minded, for them there can be no help), but is it not precisely at this point that the relevance of Eliot's rehabilitation of Christian wisdom is most clearly visible? He is deeply aware of the process of banalization that has overtaken the traditional language of religion in our time and of the consequent necessity of discovering a new language through which the transcendent meaning of reality may appear today as it once did in ages past. And so he sought in *The Waste Land* not to state a new system of belief, as would seem to be indicated by Stephen Spender's suggestion that

Instead of a basis of accepted belief, the whole structure of Eliot's poem is based on certain primitive rituals and myths. . . . The authority behind *The Waste Land* is not the Catholic Church, nor romantic lore, but anthropology from the volumes of Sir James Frazer's *The Golden Bough*.[55]

He sought rather to restate a traditional system of belief through a system of terminological conventions that might enable us to by-pass the language generally used for doctrinal exposition

---

inadequacy of this assessment and sought to alter it in so far as is permitted by the restricted freedom allowed an author in the revision of a work, the original spirit of which has to be retained. He now says: ". . . beneath and by means of all this, *we felt* [italics mine] the poet was saying that the present is inferior to the past."

which, however true we may feel it to be, has lost much of its vitality and persuasiveness. But the vision of life around which the poem is organized is, nevertheless, an authentically Christian one. It emerges at no point, however, either in the form of didacticism or generalizations about the nature of religious experience, for the poet realizes that "the gap between modern secular experience and traditional religious forms is not of the kind that a true artist can bridge by mere assertion," that "the attempt to do so can only lead to . . . rhetoric and abstraction." [56] And so, though the motif of resurrection makes its appearance in terms of symbols drawn from ancient fertility rites and though, in the final section of the poem, the benediction is pronounced by the Thunder in Sanskrit, the Christian inspiration is, nevertheless, from first to last, the basic and presiding element. The logic which we encounter is thus a logic of the Christian imagination rather than a logic of Christian concepts.

The decisive element in the poem for the validation of this perspective is the view of man to which the poet holds. We have said that the category of alienation is central for Eliot, but it is not an alienation that is centered in a private physiologic disturbance (which is what one feels at times with Lawrence), nor does it consist essentially in the problematic nature of the individual's relation to modern society (which is Silone's basic focus). It is rather with the moral isolationism of modern man —whose velleity is the consequence of his inordinately voluptuous propensities—that Eliot is chiefly concerned, and also with the ethical neutrality of the social order which he has created. The archetypal modern figure with whom Eliot is dealing is

> an easy tool,
> Deferential, glad to be of use,
> Politic, cautious, and meticulous;

> Full of high sentence, but a bit obtuse;
> At times, indeed, almost ridiculous—
> Almost, at times, the Fool.[57]

The questions that occupy his days bespeak his inner sterility:
"Shall I part my hair behind? . . . Do I dare to eat a peach?"
And the deepest riddle to which he gives his rational faculties is
the lifeless abstraction of the chess game. He simply "sprawls
at the window-sill and gapes," measuring out his life "with coffee spoons." Thus our modern world ends "not with a bang
but a whimper," for its inhabitants are "hollow men . . . stuffed
men/Leaning together/Headpiece filled with straw." [58] Neither
Prufrock nor Madame Sosostris nor "the one-eyed merchant"
can find the Hanged Man, for there is "an overwhelming question" which they evade with lesser questions:

> "What shall we ever do?"
>   The hot water at ten.
> And if it rains, a closed car at four.
> And we shall play a game of chess,
> Pressing lidless eyes and waiting for a knock
>   upon the door.

And so theirs is an "Unreal City," only "A heap of broken
images, where the sun beats,/And the dead trees give no shelter,
the cricket no relief,/And the dry stone no sound of water," for
"the Dog," who might dig up again their corpses, is kept "far
hence."

We have here, then, a picture of despair, but the despair is
not the poet's despair; and though it is recorded subjectively,
it is not subjectively held by the poet himself. That is to say,
the spiritual extremities which he portrays are not measured
against the background of Bertrand Russell's hostile country
of *A Free Man's Worship* or any "trampling march of unconscious power" but against "the Life we have lost in living,"
"the wisdom we have lost in knowledge," against the Incar-

nation. And so the melancholy of *The Waste Land* is something radically different from that which we associate with the heroes of Gertrude Stein's "lost generation"—with Hart Crane and Scott Fitzgerald and all the other sad young men of their time. Indeed, it was not, as has so often been said, "the poem of this generation" but *the* poem *about* this generation, composed from a vantage point which they could not understand, that vantage point being a profound understanding of the Church's doctrine of Original Sin. The poetry, in other words, was, in Wilfred Owen's phrase, "in the pity." And the pity was the more profound because it comprehended the "alienation" of modern men, finally, not in terms of their victimization by Society or by ontological disability, but in terms of their having perpetrated their own condition. That is to say, Eliot simply began at the beginning, where the decay of faith had left them; and our "estrangement" became for him, basically, not from Society or even from ourselves, but from God.

But, of course, to comprehend the human situation in such terms, if one is an artist, means that one cannot simply begin with abstract assertion and declamation but that one must rather adopt a concrete starting point, for the artist knows that "if you start somewhere you may end everywhere, but if you start nowhere that is also where you end." [59] And Eliot's starting point is contemporary London and "the terrible dreariness of the great modern cities." [60] To terminate, as we have done, our analysis of *The Waste Land* with "The Burial of the Dead" is to omit, indeed, much of the richness and variety that inhere in the definition Eliot gives to our theme in terms of contemporary experience: it is to pass over many of the unforgettable sketches of this "dreariness" that he gives us in later sections of the poem. For though "The Burial of the Dead" may rightfully be said to anticipate and contain the whole of the poem in its seventy-six lines, there are amplifications of its statements in succeeding sections that unquestionably contribute to the enrichment of the whole. There are, for instance, the several portraits in "A Game of Chess": the woman, in the opening lines, for whom the sumptuous appointments of the room in which we find her, with their rich evocations of a great cultural past, have no meaning at all, who is stirred only by the odors of her perfume. There is the snatch of middle-class conversation between a nameless man and woman ("My nerves are bad to-night. Yes, bad. Stay with me./"Speak to me. Why do you never speak. Speak./"What are you thinking of? . . . /"Are you alive, or not? Is there nothing in your head?"). And there are the Cockney women in a London pub with their talk of Lil, whose husband Albert, after four years in the army is coming home; one says to the other that she has chided Lil for looking "so antique" and warned her to "make herself a bit smart," for if Lil "don't give it him, there's others will"—but Lil, "pulling a long face," apparently has excused herself by saying:

> I can't help it . . .
> It's them pills I took, to bring it off . . .
> (She's had five already, and nearly died of young
>   George.)
> The chemist said it would be all right, but I've
>   never been the same.
> You *are* a proper fool, I said. . . .
> What you get married for if you don't want children?

The saddest of all these scenic compositions is that of the little typist and the carbuncular young man whose quick, jerky movements on their sordid bed of love are the spastic motions of the depraved and the damned. Their love requires no preliminary kiss or caress, but only the practical assault: the young man's

> Exploring hands encounter no defence;
> His vanity requires no response,
> And makes a welcome of indifference.

And after their evening's climax is achieved, he

> Bestows one final patronising kiss,
> And gropes his way, finding the stairs unlit . . .

> She turns and looks a moment in the glass,
> Hardly aware of her departed lover;
> Her brain allows one half-formed thought to pass:
> "Well now that's done: and I'm glad it's over."
> When lovely woman stoops to folly and
> Paces about her room again, alone,
> She smoothes her hair with automatic hand,
> And puts a record on the gramophone.

All of this culminates in the tremendous crescendo of the
final section:

> Here is no water but only rock
> Rock and no water and the sandy road
> The road winding above among the mountains
> Which are mountains of rock without water
> If there were water we should stop and drink
> Amongst the rock one cannot stop or think
> Sweat is dry and feet are in the sand
> If there were only water amongst the rock . . .
> There is not even silence in the mountains
> But dry sterile thunder without rain
> There is not even solitude in the mountains
> But red sullen faces sneer and snarl
> From doors of mudcracked houses
> > If there were water

> > And no rock
> > If there were rock
> > And also water

> And water
> A spring
> A pool among the rock
> If there were the sound of water only . . .
> But there is no water

Thus the staccato-like insistence upon the fact of drouth leads us to a sense of delirium. But the deeper suggestion conveyed by the intensity of the repetition in these lines is that we must accept the fact of drouth, the absence of health in our condition, and that though this acceptance may culminate in an ecstatic hysteria, this ecstasy may itself issue in a vision of "the third who walks always beside you," who is Christ. Significantly, there soon follows "a flash of lightning. Then a damp gust/ Bringing rain." And the poem concludes with the Thunder urging us to "Give" (*Datta*), "Sympathize" (*Dayadhvam*), and "Control" (*Damyata*), and pronouncing the benediction —"Shantih shantih shantih": "The Peace which passeth understanding."

These, then, are the fragments and the broken images;

> Ora conosce quanto caro costa
> Non seguir Cristo . . .*

But how may this strange disherison be repaired?—"after such knowledge, what forgiveness?" Eliot's answer is that though we have—to paraphrase a line from the ninth chorus from *The Rock*—been mourning "in a private chamber, learning the way of penitence," we must now also "learn the joyful communion of saints," for

> What life have you if you have not life together?
> There is no life that is not in community,

---

* Dante, *The Divine Comedy*, "Paradiso," Canto XX, 46–47: "He knoweth now how dearly costeth it/Not to be Christ's liege . . ."

> And no community not lived in praise of God.
> Even the anchorite who meditates alone,
> For whom the days and nights repeat the praise of God,
> Prays for the Church, the Body of Christ incarnate.[61]

And down this pathway, Eliot maintains, lies renascence and reconciliation. But he, following T. E. Hulme, has "none of the feelings of nostalgia . . . the desire to recapture the sentiment of Fra Angelico, which seems to animate most modern defenders of religion. All that seems . . . to be bosh." [62] As Eliot has himself said, "we must treat Christianity with a great deal more *intellectual* respect than is our wont; we must treat it as being for the individual a matter primarily of thought and not of feeling." [63] His meaning is that "it is not enthusiasm, but dogma, that differentiates a Christian from a pagan society." [64] And so he is not interested in the Jesus-intoxicated, hallelujah-shouting, hymn-singing, testifying associations of "saved" men that have been too representative of non-liturgical Protestantism in modern times. His focus is rather on that solid structure of faith and grace which is, in our time, and in every time, the real extension of the Incarnation: it is within its fold that we come to know ourselves and each other and that Stranger who, when He is encountered here, ceases to be a stranger and becomes known as Lord and Saviour. "We can lean on a rock," says a priest in *Murder in the Cathedral,*

> we can feel a firm foothold
> Against the perpetual wash of tides of balance of
>   forces of barons and landholders,
> The rock of God is beneath our feet. . . .

And this rock is the Church of Christ, within which there is mourning for His Passion and rejoicing for the salvation which He accomplished, but a mourning and rejoicing which the world cannot understand. In this fellowship, between which and

the world there can be no permanent *modus vivendi,* we gain
release from the prison of our solitary identities into the glorious
liberty of the children of God. *Ubi Christus ibi Ecclesia,* for,
as Professor J. S. Whale has said,

Christ's work of reconciliation re-establishes not only our filial relation to God, but also our fraternal relation to one another. These
are not two different facts requiring co-ordination: they are correlative: indeed they are one and the same fact. Christ is the head
of a new humanity. To be saved by him is to be incorporated into
the new community, his Church, of which he is not so much
Founder as Foundation.[65]

Eliot does not give us, in any systematic way, an ecclesio-
logical theory. He simply assumes the pre-eminence of the
Church as God's agency for accomplishing man's redemption,
and one feels that he is deeply steeped in the traditions of
Catholic churchmanship. It would, I think, be fair to say that
Eliot's chief concern is not with the close examination of the
Church, the *corpus Christi,* but rather of the process by which
it is reached: his presiding focus rests not on the nature of the
precincts within which beatitude is enjoyed but upon its *expense,* its *cost,* upon the *discipline* of redemption whereby the
soul attains its highest blessedness. And since redemption, for
the Christian mind, involves not simply a readjustment within
temporal experience but of the temporal itself to its Ground,
the consequence of this stress upon the expense of beatitude in
Eliot's thought is the further preoccupation with the relation
of time to eternity. It is this interrelation of themes which increasingly dominates Eliot's poetry from *Ash Wednesday* on
and which is raised into highest relief in *The Family Reunion*
and the *Quartets.* This is, then, a poetry of purgation, and
though F. O. Matthiessen warned us against the glibness of
taking *The Waste Land* and "The Hollow Men" as Eliot's
Inferno and the subsequent poetry as his *Purgatorio,*[66] he was

himself yet forced to concede the inevitability of this analogy of structure between Eliot and Dante.[67]

In setting forth the way by which the soul makes itself ready for "the completion of its partial ecstasy./The resolution of its partial horror," in the House of God, Eliot's use of the sixteenth-century Spanish mystic, St. John of the Cross, is, one feels, as decisive for his poetry as his earlier use of Jessie Weston's *From Ritual to Romance*. St. John is perhaps the most famous of those post-Reformation doctors of the negative way who, living in the tradition of Christian Neo-Platonism, elaborated a doctrine of ascent and descent, by way of stating the method whereby the soul arrives at experience of and union with the Ground of Being. He was a zealous follower of St. Teresa. His two major works are, *The Ascent of Mt. Carmel* and *The Obscure Night*, the pervading thought of each being expressed in a single sentence from the first: "The journey of the soul to the Divine union is called *night* for three reasons: the point of departure is privation of all desire, and complete detachment from the world; the road is by faith, which is like night to the intellect; the goal, which is God, is incomprehensible while we are in this life."

Now it is this *via negativa* around which much of Eliot's later work is organized. It begins to be adumbrated in the speaker's expressed recognition in the opening lines of *Ash Wednesday* of the debility and impotence that must be endured without complaint, and it gains explicit statement in the lines from *Burnt Norton*:

> Descend lower, descend only
> Into the world of perpetual solitude,
> World not world, but that which is not world,
> Internal darkness, deprivation
> And destitution of all property,
> Desiccation of the world of sense,

Evacuation of the world of fancy,
Inoperancy of the world of spirit;
This is the one way, and the other
Is the same, not in movement
But abstention from movement; while the world moves
In appetency, on its metalled ways
Of time past and time future.

The speaker in the first section of *Ash Wednesday* who acknowledges that "time is always time" and who then declares, "I rejoice that things are as they are and/I renounce the blessed
face/And renounce the voice," follows the counsel of *The
Ascent* to take the way of solitary evacuation which is the active way of the proficients. "This is the one way"—but what
of "the other"? This too is the same, yet not the same, for it
is "not in movement/But abstention from movement": it is
the passive way of the *Dark Night*, in accordance with which
the soul simply waits in stillness for its purgation.

Eliot, in speaking of Bishop Andrewes's sermons, has said:

Andrewes' emotion is purely contemplative; it is not personal, it
is wholly evoked by the object of contemplation, to which it is
adequate; his emotions wholly contained in and explained by its
object.[68]

Thus he has unintentionally suggested, as he so frequently does
in his criticism, the genius of his own work, for the matter of his
later poems, as distinct from the earlier, is a purely contemplative emotion. And those who have criticized him for having lifted the later verse "from the graphic presentment of ac-
tuality" [69] are those who have failed to appreciate the validity
of contemplative emotion as poetic subject matter. This is, at
any rate, what Eliot is trying to express in *Ash Wednesday*, the
plays, and the *Quartets*.

Now I have suggested that the interests that stir Eliot's later
poetry into movement are closely affiliated with the purgatorial

system of St. John of the Cross—the doctrine of the soul's descent, the stress upon the *via negativa*, the insistence upon the wisdom of ignorance, the appropriateness of humility—and these interests receive their fullest statement, I believe, among the plays, in *The Family Reunion*. As a venture into poetic drama, *The Family Reunion* is far from successful: its technical weaknesses are bald and distracting. At no point does Eliot lay hold of and clarify a social situation of significance, which is, for the dramatist, to be fatally deficient in an essential of modern drama. The aunts and uncles of Harry Lord Monchensy who are intended to provide moral contrasts with the hero, their nephew, are so trivial as to be frequently ridiculous, and though Eliot himself dismisses them, we hardly feel he has the right to do so "without ever having created them." [70] His poetry is, to be sure, frequently excellent, but it "suffers from the lack of a dramatic context to give it precision and receive its impact." [71] The flirtation with the ghosts and Furies of Greek tragedy is disastrous, as has been amply demonstrated on the occasions of the play's performance. And above all, there is Eliot's failure to probe the social and ethical implications of his hero's ruthless conduct which represents a shockingly premature situation of Harry's despair above social restraints. With all this and much more Mr. C. L. Barber has concerned himself in his excellent essay, and with a great deal that he says I find myself in fundamental agreement. But I cannot agree with him in his contention that the play is finally unintelligible apart from psychoanalytic interpretation of its ambiguities, for however vexatious they may be in the secular atmosphere of the modern theatre, they are yet intelligible in the light of the logic of Eliot's Christian symbolism and the consistencies of his total work.

Eliot attempted in *The Family Reunion*, as he has more recently done in *The Cocktail Party*,[72] something that he does only rarely in his later poetry—the dramatization of the religious problem without visibly relying on a structure of dogma, a strategy obviously intended to disarm the modern theatre audience of its usual secular defenses and thus make impossible any facile acceptance or rejection of the supernatural. This is done within the *genre* of the drawing-room comedy of manners. And into this setting he thrusts not only a chorus but the ancient Eumenides in modern evening dress who are, presumably, intended to function as the long arm of God from which the human delinquent cannot escape. With these archaic stage properties the poet proposes to bring off a contemporary drama of guilt and expiation.

The hero, Harry Lord Monchensy, returns home to an English country house, Wishwood, after several years abroad, in a state of inner discontent and unhappiness, pursued by the Furies. We learn that seven years earlier his brief and loveless marriage had been brought to an end on board an ocean liner, and he is not certain whether he pushed his wife over or whether he simply watched her slip overboard and drown. But ever since, Harry has felt himself unremittingly pursued by ghosts whom he sees only darkly and whom we see on two occasions in the embrasure of a window, once when he converses with his cousin Mary and again when he talks with his aunt Agatha. And so he has returned home, to the point of departure, hoping to "escape from one life to another," but he finds that this place where he had thought "life was substantial and simplified" was a "simplification" that had taken place in his memory: from none of the shadows of the past can he escape, and even "other memories,/Earlier, forgotten, begin to return. . . ." So there is no peace for him in terms of illusory childhood satisfactions, for, as Agatha says early in the play, "everything is irrevocable . . . the past is irremediable,/Because the future can only be built/Upon the real past." And Harry, numbed by "the sudden extinction of every alternative," has been seeking a past that never existed. In his disappointment, he turns to Mary and asks if "the instinct to return to the point of departure" is not, after all, only folly. She replies:

> But surely, what you say
> Only proves that you expected Wishwood
> To be your real self, to do something for you
> That you can only do for yourself.
> What you need to alter is something inside you
> Which you can change anywhere—here, as well as
>   elsewhere.

Stung by the searching penetration of Mary's insight, Harry petulantly denies her capacity to understand him. But Mary, quietly, insistently, reminds him that

> The cold spring now is the time
> For the cold ache in the moving root
> The agony in the dark. . . .

thus echoing those opening lines from *The Waste Land* where the poet tells us that April is the cruelest month. Harry senses the quality of spiritual rebirth she is hinting at and, recognizing its difficulty, declares remorsefully: "Spring is an issue of blood/ A season of sacrifice. . . ." Then Mary, suspecting that Harry's conviction of the painfulness of rebirth may reinforce his reluctance to submit to the process of redemption, responds with the deeper insight:

> Pain is the opposite of joy
> But joy is a kind of pain
> I believe the moment of birth
> Is when we have knowledge of death
> I believe the season of birth
> Is the season of sacrifice. . . .

And now Harry, profoundly affected by the girl's simple wisdom, cries out:

> You bring me news
> Of a door that opens at the end of a corridor,
> Sunlight and singing; when I had felt sure
> That every corridor only led to another,
> Or to a blank wall . . .

Now at this point we should put ourselves in mind of a certain indebtedness of Eliot to Lewis Carroll's *Alice in Wonderland* which Louis L. Martz was the first to discover. Mr. Martz recalls that at the beginning of her adventures Alice wanders about "in a long, low hall" in which she comes upon a "golden key" that will unlock "a little door." And he quotes the following passage:

Alice opened the door and found that it led into a small passage. . . . She knelt down and looked along the passage into the loveliest garden you ever saw. How she longed to get out of that dark hall, and wander about among those beds of bright flowers and those cool fountains, but she could not even get her head through the doorway.[73]

"From then on," he reminds us,

despite her adventures, Alice never forgets "the little door into that lovely garden"; "I've got back to my right size: the next thing is, to get into that beautiful garden—how is that to be done, I wonder?" It is not until well past the middle of her story that she finally walks "down the little passage: and *then*—she found herself at last in the beautiful garden, among the bright flower-beds and the cool fountains." [74]

Now Mr. Martz rightfully, I think, takes Harry's memory of "a corridor" as an instance of Eliot's appropriation of Alice's experience as "a symbol of the search for spiritual refreshment, for a change of heart, a change of vision. . . ." [75]

The brief conversation between Harry and Mary comes to an end, and the parlor comedy of manners resumes, with Harry being confronted by Uncle Gerald, the retired servant of the Empire in India, the maiden Aunts Ivy and Violet, Uncle Charles, the London clubman, Dr. Warburton, the family physician, and Denman, the parlourmaid—all of whom, with the exception of Agatha and Mary, offer him undiscriminating ears and unperceptive hearts. They "don't understand what it is to be awake,/To be living on several planes at once . . ."; seeing nothing, they "can always show the suitable emotions. . . ." Finally Harry, in his exasperation at their failure to comprehend his new seriousness, says to them:

> What you call the normal
> Is merely the unreal and the unimportant.
> I was like that in a way, so long as I could think
> Even of my own life as an isolated ruin,
> A casual bit of waste in an orderly universe.
> But it begins to seem just part of some huge disaster,
> Some monstrous mistake and aberration
> Of all men, of the world, which I cannot put in order.

The development of the action, then, leads us to the discovery that, in terms of the logic of the play, Harry's real problem is not one of simple moral default, for the realm toward which he is moving is one in which the ethical is teleologically suspended, in which the issue of whether or not he murdered his wife is of secondary importance. His real situation is finally brought home to him in the climactic scene of the play, when Agatha leads him into the obscure background of his past, telling him of the vacancy and lovelessness into which his parents' marriage had fallen at the time of his birth. She tells him of her own love for his dead father whom, she says, she at one time prevented from taking his mother's life, and of her own maternal love for Harry. "What we have written," she says,

> is not a story of detection,
> Of crime and punishment, but of sin and expiation.
> It is possible that you have not known what sin
> You shall expiate, or whose, or why. It is certain
> That the knowledge of it must precede the expiation.
> It is possible that sin may strain and struggle
> In its dark instinctive birth, to come to consciousness
> And so find expurgation. It is possible
> You are the consciousness of your unhappy family,
> Its bird sent flying through the purgatorial flame.
> Indeed it is possible. . . .

Now, Harry has been granted the grace of clarification, has been given the knowledge of his origins for which he has been inarticulately yearning, and in the joy of self-discovery, he exclaims:

> Look, I do not know why,
> I feel happy for a moment, as if I had come home.
> It is quite irrational, but now
> I feel quite happy, as if happiness
> Did not consist in getting what one wanted
> Or in getting rid of what can't be got rid of
> But in a different vision. This is like an end.

This is indeed "a different vision" and "an end"—but "an end," as Agatha reminds him, which may be "a beginning," for out of this acceptance of the cross of conditions comes that "uninterrupted news that grows out of silence" of which Rilke speaks in one of his Orphic songs. And one recalls Meister Eckhart's word: ". . . none shall ever taste eternal bliss but those who stand with Christ in depths of bitterness."

Harry accepts, then, his past, with humility and without complaint, in a moment of granted clarity, in the realization that he is "still befouled" but that "there is only one way out of defilement—/Which leads in the end to reconciliation." He

realizes now that he "must go," must follow the "bright angels"
—but where?

> Where does one go from a world of insanity?
> Somewhere on the other side of despair.
> To the worship in the desert, the thirst and deprivation,
> A stony sanctuary and a primitive altar,
> The heat of the sun and the icy vigil
> A care over lives of humble people,
> The lesson of ignorance, of incurable diseases.
> Such things are possible. It is love and terror
> Of what waits and wants me, and will not let me fall.

One here recalls the words of Porphyry the Neo-Platonist:
". . . the fallen soul must embrace fatigue." And we recall
Luther's assurance that "cheerfully despairing . . . you will
find peace": we sense the poet's invocation again of St. John's
purgatorial way of the *Dark Night* which he began in *Ash
Wednesday* and which he continues in the *Quartets*.

Need we accept now C. L. Barber's assertion that we have
here "non-communicative, asocial psychic products" which
"cannot be otherwise understood" except in psychoanalytic
terms? Let us quickly grant that much of Eliot's symbolism may
"draw support from unconscious impulses which many psy-
chologists classify as sexual," but let us admit also, as Mr.
Barber himself does before he apparently decides to retract,
that to point to this support need not compromise the objective validity of the symbolism itself. Let us further admit that
the play, considered from the standpoint of its usability in the
modern theatre, must remain something special and limited
in appeal, for the necessities of that medium have come to demand, above all things, that a significant social context be established and interpreted, and this Eliot has failed to do. It
may also be argued in this connection that because our contemporary theatre has as its central *raison d'être* the explication

of *social* ambiguity, it is impossible successfully to use its resources for the projection of a theme the force of which depends on the transcension of such ambiguity in the interests of a religious enterprise. But can it be argued, as Mr. Barber does, that the nature of Eliot's meaning is essentially obscure? That meaning seems clearly to be a Christian meaning, invoking the orthodox Christian conception of the dialectical relation of the "old life" to the "new life" which is born out of the former's demise. The despair, in other words, which Harry chooses has, as Kierkegaard said of the despair which he discovered to be basic to the Christian experience of grace, "something of the eternal in its dialectic." In "the awful daring of a moment's surrender," Harry chooses the "sickness unto death," and this "awful evacuation" cleanses and purifies.

It has been suggested that Eliot sets forth his understanding of the Christian experience of reconciliation primarily not in terms of the consolations to be enjoyed by the baptized communicant of the Church (though he does this too in his presentation of Becket in *Murder in the Cathedral*) but rather in terms of the *cost* of the spiritual life—as seen, however, retrospectively from within the Church—and that this preoccupation with the *expense* of beatitude conditions him to the acceptance of such a delineation of the Christian pilgrimage as one gets in a thinker like St. John of the Cross, with his emphasis upon the rigors of the Christian life and the *via negativa*. Nowhere in the later poetry does one get a fuller sense of this characteristic bent of Eliot's than in those poems which he brought together under the title *Four Quartets*, where the religious dialectic that we have been tracing is exhibited with consummate intellectual and artistic clarity.

Of these four poems that which is, I believe, most important for our present argument is the war-born poem "East Coker," for it contains the poet's clearest statement of the response that

is to be made to experience. And we have by now grasped Eliot's
rendering of that experience: it is the essentially human experience, as formulated by Harry in *The Family Reunion*, of dereliction, of

> separation,
> Of isolation unredeemable, irrevocable—
> It's eternal, or gives a knowledge of eternity,
> Because it feels eternal while it lasts.

It is the experience of the "degradation of being parted from
my self," of being "not a person, in a world not of persons/But
only of contaminating presences." And what is the response
that the poet proposes? Only the acceptance of such separation
and isolation as the essential solitude of every soul which
would dare "another intensity/For a further union, a deeper
communion," which would, "by relating itself to its own self
and by willing to be itself" ground itself "transparently in the
Power which constituted it." [76] It is thus again the choice of
solitude, the choice of "the dark cold and the empty desola-
tion," which the poet urges, for this we are told in the concluding lines of the second section of the poem is the way of
humility, and

> The only wisdom we can hope to acquire
> Is the wisdom of humility: humility is endless.

In his remarkable essay on "East Coker," James Johnson
Sweeney has pointed by implication to the level of political belief in the poem that rests upon the religious ideas. And when
one relates, as he does, Eliot's constant manipulation of the
motto that was embroidered on the chair of state of Mary
Queen of Scots ("In my beginning is my end; in my end is my
beginning") to his preoccupation in the first sections of the
poem with the ironic differences between our present age—
"the late November"—and that early spring of the English

Renaissance, it is impossible to avoid the realization that Eliot takes seriously the Johannine doctrine of purgation not only as a spiritual discipline but also as a relevant political program.[77] So F. O. Matthiessen was altogether right in saying that the opening line of the poem—"In my beginning is my end"—announces, on Eliot's part, an extension into history of the speculative meditation on time of "Burnt Norton" (the first of the *Quartets*).[78]

Mr. Sweeney is responsible for the brilliant discovery that the title of the poem, taken together with Eliot's own name, provides the clue to the meaning of the first two sections. East Coker is a Somersetshire village from which Eliot's Puritan ancestors emigrated in the seventeenth century to America. But it is also the reputed birthplace of that sixteenth-century essayist and theorist, Sir Thomas Elyot, whose characteristically Renaissance utopian conceptions were set forth in his *Boke named the Gouvernour*. And Mr. Sweeney has shown how those concluding lines from the first section of "East Coker," in which Eliot's imagination takes him back to the East Coker of the earlier Elyot and his Renaissance vision of the ultimate peace which awaits the human community—

> The association of man and woman
> In daunsinge, signifying matrimonie—
> A dignified and commodious sacrament.
> Two and two, necessarye coniunction,
> Holding eche other by the hand or the arm
> Whiche betokeneth concorde. . . .

—derive from this sixteenth-century manual of humanist politics. Mr. Sweeney argues that Eliot, as he writes shortly after the outbreak of the second World War and contemplates the general disorder and calamity of our time, is impelled to recall Sir Thomas Elyot and the high confidence with which his generation (Pico della Mirandola, Erasmus, Sir Thomas More) faced the future—a confidence which yielded, however, not progress, but the mechanistic secularism out of which developed the contemporary catastrophe. So the line which keeps insisting itself throughout the introductory movement of the poem— "In my beginning is my end"—announces the poet's recognition that the beginning of modern history, in the autonomous anthropocentrism of the Renaissance, contained the seeds out of which was to come the retrogressive barbarism of our own age, that "the quiet-voiced elders" of that earlier time bequeathed us "merely a receipt for deceit." He does not want, therefore, to

> hear
> Of the wisdom of old men, but rather of their folly,
> Their fear of fear and frenzy, their fear of possession,
> Of belonging to another, or to others, or to God.
> The only wisdom we can hope to acquire
> Is the wisdom of humility: humility is endless.
>
> The houses are all gone under the sea.
>
> The dancers are all gone under the hill.

What, then, is there left to us? Only a twilight hour of impotence and confusion of spirit; and in "this meadow of calamity,/This uncongenial place, this human life" [79]

> all go into the dark,
> The vacant interstellar spaces, the vacant into the vacant,
> The captains, merchant bankers, eminent men of letters,
> The generous patrons of art, the statesmen and the rulers,
> Distinguished civil servants, chairmen of many committees,
> Industrial lords and petty contractors, all go into the dark,
> And dark the Sun and Moon, and the Almanach de Gotha
> And the Stock Exchange Gazette, the Directory of Directors,
> And cold the sense and lost the motive of action.

This is the radical extremity of the contemporary human condition. And our response to it, says Eliot, must be the acceptance of it, the acknowledgment of it in humility, for the patient cannot be cured unless he acknowledges that he is ill. The soul must be told to "be still," that the darkness may come upon it—"Which shall be the darkness of God."

Reinhold Niebuhr has said:

All birth in the realm of man's historic institutions is rebirth. The old self must die in order that the new self may be born. The new self is a truer self, precisely because it is more intimately and organically bound to, and involved in, the life of its partners in the human enterprise. But the new self, whether in men or in nations, can not be born if the old self evades the death of repentance, seeking rather to establish itself in its old security and old isolation.[80]

And it is along these same lines that Eliot is thinking, for he is in fact proposing the Christian conception of death-into-life, the doctrine of regeneration, as a doctrine of profound cultural and political relevance. What we must understand in this traditional Christian view which Eliot has reclaimed is that the crises and distempers of history are apprehended as having not only a negative but an affirmative aspect, as being in some way a violent reconstitution of a divided spiritual unity, containing, as they do, the irruption of a transcendent reality into our immanence. The degradation and despair that periodically cover the human scene in spiritual eclipse, when humbly and penitently borne by man as the consequence of his sin, are thus understood as being not utterly spendthrift of life but as being actually restorative of health and order. It was indeed this vision of the *askésis* by which the natural order is redeemed by grace that impelled Kierkegaard to declare: ". . . had I not died I should have died indeed"; it was this "cosmic mystery play" that Rilke had in mind when he declared in one of the Orphic songs:

Out of destruction soared your constituent song.

> Only because hostility cruelly divided
>> have we become hearers at last and a mouth for the world.

And it is this redemptive pattern of being wrought out of alienation and despair which, I think, Eliot has in mind when he
urges the soul to "let the darkness come upon you":

>> be still, and wait without hope
> For hope would be hope for the wrong thing; wait without
>> love
> For love would be love of the wrong thing; there is yet
>> faith
> But the faith and the love and the hope are all in the
>> waiting. . . .

The "agony/Of death and birth" must be borne in humility and
patience and in solitariness, for

>> In order to arrive there,
> To arrive where you are, to get from where you are not,
>> You must go by a way wherein there is no ecstasy.
> In order to arrive at what you do not know
>> You must go by a way which is the way of ignorance.
> In order to possess what you do not possess
>> You must go by the way of dispossession.
> In order to arrive at what you are not
>> You must go through the way in which you are not.

This is clearly the "strait way" of St. John's "dark night of
the spirit" which, when entered upon by the pilgrim who confesses that "Our only health is the disease. . . . And that, to
be restored, our sickness must grow worse," leads to fellowship
with Christ the Redeemer, the "wounded surgeon," who

>> plies the steel
> That questions the distempered part;
> Beneath the bleeding hands we feel
> The sharp compassion of the healer's art
> Resolving the enigma of the fever chart.

And though we persist in thinking "That we are sound, substantial flesh and blood," we yet have a deep and abiding knowledge that we have erred and are lost sheep, that we have followed too much the devices and desires of our own hearts, that there is no health in us. So consequently, as we contemplate each year what was accomplished in our behalf outside the city walls on a lonely hill long years ago, we are constrained to "call this Friday good."

Thus we have now come full circle from the Stygian depths of *The Waste Land* to the lambent center of Eliot's horizon: the "hint half guessed, the gift half understood," [81] which is the Incarnation and the Atonement.

> Here the impossible union
> Of spheres of existence is actual,
> Here the past and future
> Are conquered, and reconciled. . . .[82]

And we have seen that this reconciliation lies somewhere on the other side of agony and mortification:

> The dove descending breaks the air
> With flame of incandescent terror
> Of which the tongues declare
> The one discharge from sin and error.
> The only hope or else despair
>   Lies in the choice of pyre or pyre—
>   To be redeemed from fire by fire.
>
> Who then devised the torment? Love.
> Love is the unfamiliar Name
> Behind the hands that wove
> The intolerable shirt of flame
> Which human power cannot remove
>   We only live, only suspire
>   Consumed by either fire or fire.[83]

Professor James Muilenburg of Union Seminary once expressed to me in private conversation dissatisfaction with what
he considered to be the incompleteness of Eliot's appropriation
of the Christian faith: steeped as he is in the Biblical-prophetic
tradition, it was his feeling that Eliot's deep immersion in
classical mysticism propels him toward a kind of Catholic
Gnosticism which, though not heretical, is yet insufficiently in
touch with the prophetic tradition to satisfy the requirements
of a responsibly Biblical faith. His main citation was the
Quartets which, he contended, exhibit, primarily, not the
Hebraic-prophetic-Biblical feeling about the concrete stuff of
history but, rather, essentially Platonist speculations about the
metaphysical problem of the relation of time to eternity—speculations reaching back perhaps to Plotinus and the Pseudo-
Dionysius, to Clement and Origen, to St. John of the Cross and
Boehme, but not to Isaiah and Jeremiah and Amos.

This feeling has, I think, been shared by many Christian interpreters of Eliot and was voiced a few years ago by Robert W.
Flint in an article ("The Four Quartets Reconsidered") in
The Sewanee Review.[84] And it is a point of view which I do
not think can be summarily denied, for there is a certain un-
avoidable ambiguity in Eliot in this regard that grows out of
his strong attraction to the tradition of Christian mysticism
which has almost always had Platonist elements in it. But, on
the other hand, it may of course be true that those who have
decisively shaped a major strain of modern Christian sensibility
—Kierkegaard, Barth, Brunner, Niebuhr—have, in their consistent polemic against the Platonist strains in the Christian
tradition, too narrowly defined the purity of Christian vision.
And even if this not be the case, I cannot persuade myself that
the kind of criticism of Eliot that I have just outlined is, in
the first instance, wholly justified. For, as I have indicated,
my reading of his work constantly collides with a spiritual logic

in which the stress is upon the necessity of a "leap in the dark," of sacrifice, of "despair" and travail, of the coordination of contraries, of the submission of the order of nature to that of divine grace, of Christ the Redeemer, of Resurrection—all of which belongs to that "strange world within the Bible." And always in the background there is the Church itself, for the sake of whose gifts the tremendous cost of the spiritual life is seen to be infinitely worthwhile and into the anonymous accent of whose language the poet's own speech frequently falls, as when, for instance, he declares in the fifth section of *Ash Wednesday*:

> If the lost word is lost, if the spent word is spent
> If the unheard, unspoken
> Word is unspoken, unheard;
> Still is the unspoken word, the Word unheard,
> The Word without a word, the Word within
> The world and for the world;
> And the light shone in darkness and
> Against the Word the unstilled world still whirled
> About the centre of the silent Word.

So whatever there may ultimately have to be said in criticism of Eliot's poetic practice, of his contribution to the history of the English language, his relation to the integral Christian tradition will have to be acknowledged as finally decisive and thoroughgoing, and his adequacy to the spirituality of our age will have to be defined in terms of his having brought to bear upon it the essential catharsis of the Christian religion, for his was one of the voices that led us back to the Place where it is well to be, since here a man

> vivit purius,
> Cadit rarius, surgit velocius, incedit cautius,
> Quiescit securius, moritur felicius,
> Purgatur citius, proemiatur copiosus.

CONCLUSION

The aim of relation is relation's own being, that is, contact with the *Thou*. For through contact with every *Thou* we are stirred with a breath of the *Thou*, that is, of eternal life. . . .

In the great privilege of pure relation the privileges of the world of *It* are abolished. . . . By virtue of this privilege we are not given up to alienation from the world and the loss of reality by the *I*—to domination by the ghostly. Reversal is the recognition of the Centre and the act of turning again to it. In this act of the being the buried relational power of man rises again, the wave that carries all the spheres of relation swells in living streams to give new life to our world. . . .

But the *I* that steps out of the relational event into separation and consciousness of separation, does not lose its reality. Its sharing is preserved in it in a living way. In other words, as is said of the supreme relation and may be used of all, "the seed remains in it." This is the province of subjectivity in which the *I* is aware with a single awareness of its solidarity of connexion and of its separation. Genuine subjectivity can only be dynamically understood, as the swinging of the *I* in its lonely truth. Here, too, is the place where the desire is formed and heightened for ever higher, more unconditioned relation, for the full sharing in being. In subjectivity the spiritual substance of the person matures.

—Martin Buber, *I and Thou*

WE HAVE NOW COME to the conclusion of our project—which was to survey the rehearsal of our contemporary discomposure, as it is to be found in the work of certain representative modern writers. Albert Guerard, Jr., in his recent essay on Joseph Conrad, has said: "A great novelist may be the historian of his age in several ways: by dramatizing its political and economic conflicts, by reflecting its intellectual assumptions, or by revealing the concealed sources of its moral unrest." [1] And it is, I think, to some extent on each of these levels that Kafka, Silone, Lawrence, and Eliot move. Silone, to be sure, is characteristically concerned with the public frustrations of the socially excommunicated individual, and Lawrence is chiefly preoccupied with the self-encystment of the private ego, as it is apprehended in the sexual relation; while Kafka and Eliot are primarily interested in the estrangement of modern man from the sources of religious consolation. But they are all at one in dramatizing the plight of the contemporary man or woman "upon whom life closes down inexorably, divesting him or her of the supports and illusory protection of friendship, social privilege, or love," and who, being thrown violently "out of an accepted relationship with family or society," is, in the moment of crisis, suddenly made "aware of a hostile or unknown world which must be learned anew, conquered or possibly renounced, before survival is possible." [2] Their characters inhabit a world in which, above all else, they are marked by the conditions of moral and spiritual isolation, and so they are, as they weave their art out of the myriad ambiguities of contemporary existence, in the deepest sense, spiritual historians of our period.

The Jewish philosopher and theologian, Martin Buber, has defined the boundaries of our human cosmos in the following manner:

Man's threefold living relation is, first, his relation to the world and to things, second, his relation to men—both to individuals and to the many—third, his relation to the mystery of being—which is dimly apparent through all this but infinitely transcends it—which the philosopher calls the Absolute and the believer calls God, and which cannot in fact be eliminated from the situation even by a man who rejects both designations.[3]

And it is, I think, with the second and third types of relation that our writers are primarily concerned. If the first—man's "relation to the world and to things"—be taken as designative of what we usually have in mind when we use the term *nature*, it would seem to appear that our subjects' vision neither promotes Leopardi's angry resentment over

> la natura, il brutto
> Poter che, ascoso, a commun danno impera.

> nature, the brutal
> Power that, hidden, rules to the ruin of all.[4]

nor Arnold's disenchanted recognition that

> Nature and man can never be fast friends.[5]

Neither Lawrence nor Silone, neither Kafka nor Eliot, is characteristically preoccupied with modern man's isolation from the world of nature, though one feels they are aware of it, and Eliot writes, in one connection,

> In the pleasant countryside, there it seemed
> That the country is fit only for picnics.

and asks in the same poem

> Where is the Life we have lost in living? *

---

* Ninth Chorus from *The Rock*. It should be noted here that the tendency of many of our modern poets when writing of our alienation from nature is not, in contrast to such nineteenth-century figures as Leopardi and Arnold, to censure nature for its cold indifference to the human enterprise but is

Their interest focuses rather on *the tragedy of severance* of the *human* relation and of man's "relation to the mystery of being." And when our four subjects are properly juxtaposed against each other, they may be considered as contributing to a continuous and developing discussion of the problem of alienation in these terms. That is to say, we have found Lawrence defining the human tragedy in terms of life being so constituted as to necessitate our *coexistence* with others as discrete, individual, finite entities. It is the fact of what Harry Slochower has called "man's individual boundedness," [6] the fact that men are "walled away from each other, like so many houses," [7] what I have termed *ontological solitude*—it is with this dimension of the human predicament that Lawrence is concerned. He feels, as Isabel remarks in Melville's *Pierre*, that "there can be no perfect peace in individualness." And so his men and women chafe under "the anguish of being *two*" and strain toward an effective transcendence of the particularity of selfhood by seeking to possess each other more fully than they may ever be possessed. Lawrence's drama is that of man becoming insecure in his finitude and consequently feeling lonely in the midst of the tumultuous human world. It is a drama that culminates in an act of mystical self-immolation whereby, through the ecstasy of sexual love, the individual seeks ravishment to that "desert" wherein the bifurcations of human individuality are canceled out by the fullness of mystic unanimity.

But to such an analysis of the human situation Silone, one supposes, were he to argue with Lawrence's ghost, would want to reply: Lawrence, your terror and your hysteria are out of all proportion to the actual human fact. Life is not nearly so desperate as you report it to be—or rather, ours is a different kind

---

rather to scold the modern megalopolitan, as Eliot does by implication in the quoted lines above, for his irreverent use and exploitation of nature.

of desperation. It is not the human material that we are over which we should fret, but rather what we do with it in our freedom. It is our continual crucifixion of Our Lord over which we should grieve—the fact that "He is still living His agony here on earth." And He will, of course, continue to do so until we "practice the human presence" as it was His wont to do, until we take our neighbor unto ourselves in charity and in love, as we are bidden to do by those who, living "outside the law," seek to show us "a different way of living." For, Lawrence, there are such, you know, in our midst. And they are not apostles of your blood-religion. They have, to be sure, "gone out of the temple," and we, in our blindness, hunt them down like wild beasts; but they yet "hunger and thirst after righteousness," and, as Bergson said, "The apparition of each of these souls has been like the creation of a new species composed of one unique individual." Indeed, we might well look upon them as, in a way, extensions of the Incarnation. Their contemporary likeness is that of the revolutionary figure of the Underground who combats our great modern heresy of political Totalitarianism—but in the interest not merely of political ends but rather in the interests of deeply moral and spiritual ends. They can, if we heed them, lead us out of our isolation, reconciling us with "the Man on the Cross": they can do this, because they "carry within themselves the truth of Christ." No, Lawrence, it is not true as you suggest, that the metaphysical requirements of man's fundamental human nature establish as a necessary condition of historical existence the kind of social fragmentation by which we have been so much afflicted in the modern world. Nor does the redemption proper to man involve a sloughing off of our fundamental nature, as finite human creatures, in the interests of a flight from the world of finite individuality into some mystical companionship of co-inherence. The world that is exhibited in your books has, to be sure, the grandeur of a tragic world, but it is "a world without guilt, for its tragic flaw is not a flaw in human nature, still less a flaw in an individual character but a flaw in the nature of existence." [8] But, as I say, our situation is not nearly so desperate. You take your objection to man as man, but what is really required is not an *ontological* reconstruction of human nature as such, but moral regeneration. So the human tragedy is not quite *necessary*, in the way that you suggest.

Yet, somewhat paradoxically, I am concerned, Lawrence, about the *necessary* alienation of a special class of humanity, of those who restore the rest of us to community with each other by leading us into "the novitiate" of a 'different way of living." I am interested in the spiritual drama that takes place in the lives of those whom Christ "chooses and draws after him" and who are therefore, as my Donna Maria Vincenza says on one occasion, "lost to their families"—and not only to their families but to all the conventional orders of our common life. I am interested in the isolation of those, such as Pietro Spina, whose isolation is ultimately *necessary* in a sense in which ours is not, since it is from the standpoint of that isolation, and the disinterestedness it allows, that they lure the rest of us back into the *élan* of life.

At this point, if we might broaden the terms of our dialogue by a further resurrection of the dead and such a magical operation upon space and time as would bring Kafka into the presence of our dialogists, we might well imagine him as saying: Silone, if I may recur to the symbolic language that I employed in my book *The Castle*, you are right in insisting that life in the "Village" has a more ultimate value than Lawrence ascribes to it, but you do not integrate fully enough into your representation of life in the "Village" that mysteriously threatening and ominous reality which hovers over the world and which is "wholly other"—the "Castle." While you, Lawrence, are right in insisting that the human tragedy is a tragedy of finitude, though the tragic implications of man's finitude are not fully manifest, as you seem to feel they are, in the mere necessity of our having to *coexist* with other discrete, finite beings between whom and ourselves there is consequent separateness. No, they are not fully manifest until we see the fact of our finitude as constituting the ultimately insurmountable hindrance to reconciliation with the mystery of Being. And if we are to talk of man's alienation, this is the really important dimension of it that we should consider. It is what we might call man's metaphysical loneliness that is the deepest fact of self-knowledge. That is to say, it is not merely our lack of relationship with other human individuals but our dereliction in the realm of the Absolute that is the ground of man's most abiding melancholy.

So, one imagines, might such a discussion proceed.

But now when we come to Eliot, we come upon a modern poet who knows the cosmic exile of Kafka's dry desert for what it is—namely, the exile of Hell; and thus we come full circle from the radical paganism of Lawrence to the equally radical orthodoxy of Paul and Kierkegaard, and the Catholic humanism of Dante.

Wallace Fowlie, in writing of Maritain, has said:

A novelist like Kafka and a painter like Rouault both illustrate what Maritain describes as being the defect of the modern spirit. It seems to be a form of uneasiness, a sentiment of estrangement and unfamiliarity with its environment. . . . The modern form of solitude, as we see it in the novels of Kafka and the paintings of Rouault, lacks the sense of discipline which religious solitude possesses. Maritain has pointed out many times that the notion of a Church, of religious belief, prevents sentimentality in one's inner life. The solitude which has a discipline, in the religious sense, is almost, if not exactly, a death of self in order to find God.[9]

And this is indeed the direction into which Eliot so converts the solitude of modern man that it becomes an occasion for confession and faith. The progress of his poetry, as we have seen, moves from the description, in his earlier phase, of our contemporary anguish to the demand, implicit in all of his later work, that our solitude be *accepted* and *maintained*, as a discipline, as an *askésis*, by which "a further union, a deeper communion" may be attained and the creature rehabilitated in God. His chorus in *Murder in the Cathedral* who are, as they tell us at the end of the drama, "type of the common man" suffer from their dereliction and loneliness, and they know that they suffer. Yet, as Becket tells them, "They know and do not know, what it is to act or suffer." For, "To rest in our own suffering," says Agatha in *The Family Reunion*, as does the Chorus, without *choosing* it, ". . . Is evasion of suffering. We must learn to suffer more." The soul, that is, must *choose* solitude, in order that it may go

> to the empty land
> Which is no land, only emptiness, absence, the Void,
> Where those who were men can no longer turn the mind
> To distraction, delusion, escape into dream, pretence,
> Where the soul is no longer deceived, for there are
> no objects, no tones,
> No colours, no forms to distract, to divert the soul
> From seeing itself, foully united forever, nothing
> with nothing. . . .[10]

We must go this way, in other words—"the secret way," as Meister Eckhart called it—because, as Eliot says,

The Kingdom of God is for none but the thoroughly dead.

But, in the silence and the void,

> Who shall then plead for me,
> Who intercede for me, in my most need?

The answer is given in the prayer of the *Cathedral* Chorus which follows:

> Dead upon the tree, my Saviour,
> Let not be in vain Thy labour;
> Help me, Lord, in my last fear.

> Dust I am, to dust am bending,
> From the final doom impending
> Help me, Lord, for death is near.

The "vacuum of disintegration" becomes, in other words, a "sacred void"—and, as Edna St. Vincent Millay once said, "utter/Terror and loneliness . . ./drive a man to address the Void as 'Thou.' " [11] The experience is that from which proceeded those lines from St. Augustine's *Confessions*: "Let us delight to find Thee by failing to find Thee rather than by finding Thee to fail to find Thee." Eliot's discovery, as was Augustine's, is of the Incarnation: he has found

the rehabilitation and the "dignification" of the creature not in a species of isolation, thus enclosing the creature within itself, but in an opening up of the creature to the universe of the divine and the supra-rational. . . . Such a humanism, which considers man in the integrality of his natural and supernatural being and which sets no *a priori* limits to the descent of the divine into man, could be termed the *humanism of the Incarnation.* [12]

There is, indeed, one feels, a certain quality of "sentimentality" in Lawrence and Kafka that is absent in Silone and Eliot. And here, of course, one treads on dangerous ground, when one places Lawrence and Kafka in conjunction with each other in terms of their shared "sentimentality," for what W. H. Auden has called Lawrence's "wooziness" is a quality obviously poles apart from Kafka's characteristic attitude of extreme reticence and reserve. So the term "sentimentality" is not being used here to suggest gushiness or extravagant emotion but rather that curiously perverse attitude of servile acquiescence in the self's disability that sometimes takes possession of the spiritual life, impelling the individual to apprehend the true essence of the self as located in that very disability. There is, I think, "sentimentality," in this sense, in Lawrence and Kafka—and a sentimentality which derives, basically, from their shared "Manicheism," which, though far from explicit in Lawrence, we have already traced, as it grows out of his lyrical discontent with the limitations imposed upon personal relations by the fact of human finitude. And Kafka's "Manichean" strain is not only at the surface of his work but also at its heart, inhering in the absolute antinomy that he maintains from beginning to end between Nature and Spirit, between the finite human subject and the incommensurable Divine Subject, the *Deus absconditus.* For both, the fundamental solitude of the human creature is the ultimate fact of his existence. Theirs is, in other words, the purest pessimism, and this is their "sentimentality."

But, significantly, neither Silone nor Eliot seems inclined to suppose that a posture of prostration before the disability of alienation is in any final sense necessitated by the human situation. Silone envisages the possibility of the solitude of the revolutionary having "a discipline, in the religious sense," providing the basis for a special morality—the morality of the Christian socialist, whose portrait he draws in a pattern remarkably similar to Bergson's "mystic"; and thus he goes on to what is in essence an "heroic humanism." And Eliot too does not allow his sharp sense of the existential human fact to force upon him the supposition that there is no other role for the human spirit than that of the "isolato." He would rather, as we have seen, have us apprehend our estrangement as the appropriate occasion for the practice of something approximating the purgatorial disciplines of St. John of the Cross which involve, of course, a deepening of one's solitude—but in order that the self's dissociation may yield the intuition of the presence in the self of Something which, though transcending it, is yet the constitutive Power of the self and the hidden possibility of its reconciliation. So Maritain's dictum, as paraphrased by Wallace Fowlie—that "the notion of a Church, of religious belief, prevents sentimentality in one's inner life," that the "modern form of solitude as we see it in the novels of Kafka and the paintings of Rouault lacks the sense of discipline which religious solitude possesses"—though at first it may appear to be merely the cant of official Catholicism, yet receives, at least in terms of our four subjects, a kind of verification. For, in sharp contrast to the pure pessimism in which both Lawrence and Kafka, in different ways, finally end, both Silone and Eliot are asking that the modern man *discipline* his solitude toward "a further union, a deeper communion": in the case of Silone, the demand being addressed to a special type of man, the revolutionary figure of our twentieth-century Underground, our modern hero; in the case of Eliot, the demand being addressed to all of us.

In whatever manner, though, we seek to discriminate among our four writers, the essential equivalence between them, upon which the unity of this book is based, would seem to be a substantial one. And that equivalence consists in their tendency to construe modern experience in such a way as implies the primacy for them of the category of alienation. This is the perspective from which they seem almost to insist that their work be assessed. The issue can, of course, be obscured if, for instance, we continue frivolously to take Lawrence as merely a kind of talented pornographer, interested chiefly in the sexual frolics of the human animal or Silone as merely the creator of a kind of incisive, if vaguely fictionalized, international sociology. The issue can also be obscured if the attempt is made to judge the appropriateness of my application of this category to these writers in terms of the extent of its relevance to their respective personal histories, for their works have not been considered here as essays in self-definition but rather—as literature must, finally, always be viewed—as comments on human experience, and as such, having an autonomous existence, quite apart from the personal histories of those who produced them. The issue that has been raised here, in other words, through the use of literary materials is, clearly, not a literary issue, but one of a philosophical and religious order, that pertains to the universe of discourse once designated by philosophers and theologians as "anthropology," wherein the central question concerns the nature of man, as that "essential" reality may be stated in terms of a synoptic view of the human situation.

Kant on one occasion formulated his conception of the scope of philosophical inquiry in terms of four questions:

1. What can I know? 2. What ought I to do? 3. What may I hope? 4. What is man? Metaphysics answers the first question, ethics the second, religion the third, and anthropology the fourth.[13]

It is his final question—what is man?—which is basic for Lawrence and Silone, Kafka and Eliot, though they would, I think, agree with Kant when, in an afterthought, he added: "Fundamentally all this could be reckoned as anthropology, since the first three questions are related to the last."[14] Indeed the special ambiguity in the work of these modern writers, when it is considered as an aspect of the contemporary "literature of anthropology," consists in its commingling of Kant's third and fourth questions, for they do not suppose, as do so many of our modern schoolmen, that the exploration of the final question can be pursued apart from the metaphysical-religious "presupposition of the concrete man's bond with the absolute." [15] I have, to be sure, following Maritain, distinguished the vision of solitude supported by a personal affiliation with a tradition of dogma that one gets, for example, in Silone and Eliot from the same vision unsupported by such affiliation that one gets in Kafka and Lawrence, in which there tends to be a certain morbid "sentimentality." But such a distinction should not be interpreted as a denial of the religious element that is common to them all, quite apart from their acceptance of or abdication from traditions of orthodoxy. They are all preoccupied with the question as to the ultimate "hopes" that man may entertain; Lawrence and Kafka, to be sure, seem, finally, to feel that there is very little for which man may hope, but the centrality of the religious question in their work can, nevertheless, hardly be gainsaid.

That these men should all feel impelled to define the man of their time in terms of isolation and estrangement, and the world in which he lives as a "waste land" awaiting redemption, is not at all strange. When one recalls those icily nonchalant monuments of Le Corbusier and Mies van der Rohe, the terrifying music of Stravinsky's *Pétrouchka* and Schoenberg's *Pierrot Lunaire*, those hauntingly disenchanted clowns and acrobats of Rouault and the early Picasso, the lonely urban wildernesses of Giorgio de Chirico, the cinema of Chaplin and Cocteau, and the plays of Sartre—when one takes such a running inventory of the representative art and literature of our period, it becomes clear how very much a part of their milieu our four subjects are. Their large typicality thus gives to their work an international intelligibility that transcends all parochial barriers. They are, if I may repeat, "spiritual historians of our period."

My concern in this book has been chiefly to summarize and elucidate the evidence which they have amassed, in their effort to portray something of the permanent nature of man against the background of the stresses of modern experience. And certainly there is a very searching comment on those "stresses" implicit in what one feels is their compulsion to organize their experience from the special standpoint in terms of which their work has here been interpreted; indeed, the very imperiousness of the modern writer's inclination to view the human creature as alienated and estranged probably suggests a further confirmation of the reality of his subject matter.

The question as to the adequacy of the respective resolutions offered by our four authors of the moral and spiritual problems which they enunciate raises, of course, a whole complex of issues that asks for much broader definition than is possible within the scope of the present essay. One basic question, though, that may be touched upon in conclusion emerges at the point at which Silone and Eliot raise, in emphatic form, the issue of Christianity's relevance to the problem of selfhood. And to establish the full import of their position it is perhaps required that we observe once again what has appeared to be a crucial difference between Kafka and Lawrence, on the one hand, and Silone and Eliot, on the other. We have seen that both Lawrence and Kafka regard "man's essential loneliness and seclusion . . . [as] the heritage of finitude" and feel that they can be "overcome only in the measure in which man participates actually in something infinite." [16] Both, however, insist upon the canon *finitum non est capax infiniti*. With Lawrence, the loneliness and seclusion of human individuation are overcome in a mystical experience the special quality of which depends upon the annihilation of the very individuation that is so inherently a mark of selfhood. And Kafka, failing to discover any path leading from "the Village" to "the Castle" (or vice versa), is forced to the pessimistic conclusion that if man "heads . . . for the earth, his heavenly collar throttles him, and if he heads for Heaven, his earthly one does the same." Now it is this failure of metaphysical vision in both which is, I believe, the root of the peculiar morbidity and pessimism that they share and that I have termed their "sentimentality."

But Silone and Eliot discern that what, for Lawrence and Kafka, appears to be a defect in existence itself is really "a contingent defect in the soul of each man, the defect of the sin which he commits in his freedom." [17] "In the sacred history of man on earth," says Silone, "it is still, alas, Good Friday." "The only wisdom we can hope to acquire," Eliot declares, "is the wisdom of humility." And so, they conclude, in effect, that if man

can realize that fact, if he can weep for himself, if he can repent, he can also be saved. He can be saved by hope and faith. His hope and faith will separate the character of life in its essential reality from life as it is revealed in sinful history.[18]

They discern, in other words, the ultimate possibility of a genuine reconciliation with "the mystery of Being"—but a reconciliation that does not involve an annihilation of the particular self, for their understanding of the human situation is based upon the major presupposition of Christian wisdom: namely, as Paul Tillich puts it, that of an *essentially* "undisrupted unity between man and the infinite ground and *telos* of his being—religiously speaking, God." [19]

So it appears, then, that of these four modern writers, those who succeed in marking out a strategy of reconciliation for the alienated self that does not require the abrogation of responsible, autonomous selfhood are those who have a vital relation to the Christian faith. And this suggests, in answer to the question raised above, that Christianity is deeply relevant to our modern problems of estrangement and dissociation, that, indeed, as Amos Wilder has well said, it may make its supreme contribution

to men in forcing them to accept the role of responsible selfhood in their relations to their fellows and to reality. Here all evasions into the cult of the unconscious and the irrational, however sophisticated, are forbidden. Aesthetic solution of conflict whether in the exquisite forms of Yeats' "Byzantium" or the more violent forms of Jeffers are precluded. They are all sub-personal. The artist must not win his excitement and power cheaply by abandonment of himself to the volcanic but anarchic forces of the soul. The modern instances of Baudelaire and Eliot show how adequate to extreme contemporary need is the essential katharsis of Christianity, what accesses of restorative energies are available.[20]

NOTES

PREFACE

1. These quotations, and the appended translations, are drawn from Wallace Fowlie's *Jacob's Night: the Religious Renascence in France*, pp. 95–96.

INTRODUCTION

1. *Vide* his introduction to Carl Becker's *Freedom and Responsibility in the American Way of Life*.
2. F. O. Matthiessen, *The Achievement of T. S. Eliot*, p. 5.
3. Paul Tillich, *The Protestant Era*, p. 88.
4. Martin Buber, *Between Man and Man*, p. 126.

FRANZ KAFKA

1. From the Preface to Djuna Barnes's *Nightwood* (New Directions, n.d.).
2. M. Chaning-Pearce, *The Terrible Crystal: Studies in Kierkegaard and Modern Christianity*, p. xii.
3. Paul Goodman, *Kafka's Prayer*, p. 65.
4. *Ibid.*, p. 85.
5. *Ibid.*, pp. 86–87.
6. *Ibid.*, pp. 93–94.
7. Edwin Berry Burgum, "K. and the Bankruptcy of Faith," *Accent*, Spring, 1943.
8. Harry Slochower, "Franz Kafka—Pre-Fascist Exile," *A Franz Kafka Miscellany* (a supplement to Issue V–VI of *Twice a Year*).
9. John J. Kelly, "F. K.'s *Trial* and the Theology of Crisis," *The Southern Review*, Spring, 1940.
10. Edwin Berry Burgum, *op. cit.*, p. 153.

11. Franz Kafka, " 'He': Notes from the Year 1920," *The Great Wall of China*, p. 269.

12. R. O. C. Winkler, "The Significance of K.," *Scrutiny*, December, 1938.

13. George Woodcock, "Kafka and Rex Warner," *Focus One*, 1945, p. 65.

14. Max Lerner, "F. K. and the Human Voyage," *Ideas for the Ice Age*, p. 150.

15. Julian Symons, "A Comment," *Focus One*, 1945, p. 43.

16. Charles Neider, *The Frozen Sea: a Study of Franz Kafka*, p. 9.

17. Philip Rahv, "Franz Kafka: the Hero as Lonely Man," *The Kenyon Review*, Winter, 1939, pp. 61–62.

18. Kathleen Raine, "A Comment on Kafka," *Focus One*, 1945, p. 45.

19. Philip Rahv, *op. cit.*, p. 71.

20. D. S. Savage, "Franz Kafka: Faith and Vocation," *Focus One*, 1945, p. 17.

21. Max Brod, *Franz Kafka: a Biography*, p. 24

22. *Ibid.*, p. 6.

23. *Ibid.*, p. 30.

24. *Ibid.*, p. 157.

25. Eduard Geismar, *Lectures on the Religious Thought of Sören Kierkegaard*, p. 1.

26. *Ibid.*, p. 2.

27. Max Brod, *op. cit.*, pp. 22–23.

28. Edmund Wilson, "A Dissenting Opinion on Kafka," *The New Yorker*, July 26, 1947, p. 54.

29. Herbert Read, *Form in Modern Poetry*, p. 17.

30. Max Brod, *op. cit.*, p. 48.

31. *Ibid.*, p. 24. There are many other such passages in Brod's biography.

32. Edmund Wilson, *op. cit.*, p. 55.

33. Herbert Tauber, *Franz Kafka: an Interpretation of His Works*, p. 16.

34. Max Brod, *op. cit.*, pp. 32–33.

35. Philip Rahv, *op. cit.*
36. *Ibid.*, p. 68.
37. Herbert Tauber, *op. cit.*, p. 23.
38. *Ibid.*, p. 14.
39. Claude-Edmonde Magny, "The Objective Depiction of Absurd-ity," *Quarterly Review of Literature*, II, No. 3, 213.
40. Franz Kafka, "Reflections on Sin, Pain, Hope, and the True Way," *The Great Wall of China*, pp. 293–294.
41. Franz Kafka, "Investigations of a Dog," *The Great Wall of China*, pp. 8–9.
42. *Ibid.*, pp. 27–30.
43. Sören Kierkegaard, *Fear and Trembling*, p. 115.
44. *Ibid.*, p. 52.
45. Herbert Tauber, *op. cit.*, p. 139.
46. D. S. Savage, *op. cit.*, pp. 20–22.
47. Herbert Tauber, *op. cit.*, pp. 142–143.
48. *Ibid.*, p. 118.
49. T. S. Eliot, *The Waste Land*.
50. Herbert Tauber, *op. cit.*, p. 88.
51. Albert Camus, "Hope and Absurdity," *The Kafka Problem* (ed. by Angel Flores), p. 255.
52. Eliseo Vivas, "Kafka's Distorted Mask," *The Kenyon Review*, Winter, 1948, p. 63.

IGNAZIO SILONE

1. Edmund Wilson, *The Wound and the Bow*, p. 30.
2. *Ibid.*, p. 34.
3. *Ibid.*, p. 62.
4. D. S. Savage, *The Personal Principle: Studies in Modern Poetry*, p. 29.
5. Mary M. Colum, *From These Roots: the Ideas That Have Made Modern Literature*, p. 249.
6. Alfred Kazin, *On Native Grounds*, p. 16.
7. Harry Slochower, *No Voice Is Wholly Lost*, p. 323.
8. Ignazio Silone, *Fontamara*, Foreword.

9. Ignazio Silone, *Bread and Wine*, p. 21.
10. *Ibid.*, pp. 174–175.
11. *Ibid.*, p. 176.
12. Lionel Trilling, *E. M. Forster*, p. 65.
13. F. O. Matthiessen, *American Renaissance: Art and Expression in the Age of Emerson and Whitman*, p. 367.
14. Isaac Rosenfeld, "Silone's Spiritual Journey," *The Nation*, June 22, 1946.
15. George Woodcock, "Ignazio Silone," *Focus Two*, 1946, p. 47.
16. Harry Slochower, *op. cit.*, p. 64.
17. A. G. Hebert, *Liturgy and Society*, p. 191.
18. Arnold J. Toynbee, *A Study of History* (abridgment of Vols. I–VI by D. C. Somervell), p. 217.
19. *Ibid.*
20. George Woodcock, *op. cit.*, p. 50.
21. Henri Bergson, *The Two Sources of Morality and Religion*, p. 86.

D. H. LAWRENCE

1. Elizabeth Bowen, "D. H. Lawrence: Reappraising His Literary Influence," *The New York Times Book Review*, February 9, 1947.
2. Diana Trilling, *The Portable D. H. Lawrence*, "Editor's Introduction," p. 13.
3. R. P. Blackmur, *The Double Agent: Essays in Craft and Elucidation*, p. 103.
4. *Ibid.*
5. William York Tindall, *D. H. Lawrence and Susan His Cow*, p. 193.
6. Emery Neff, *A Revolution in European Poetry: 1660–1900*, p. vii.
7. *Vide* Mario Praz, *The Romantic Agony*, Introduction.
8. *Vide* H. J. C. Grierson, "Classical and Romantic: a Point of View," *The Background of English Literature*.
9. *Ibid.*, p. 266.

10. D. S. Savage, *The Personal Principle: Studies in Modern Poetry*, pp. 17–18.
11. H. J. C. Grierson, *op. cit.*, pp. 271–272.
12. M. C. D'Arcy, *The Mind and Heart of Love*, p. 51.
13. Denis de Rougemont, *Love in the Western World*, pp. 75–76.
14. *Ibid.*, p. 80.
15. *Vide* C. S. Lewis, *The Allegory of Love*.
16. Denis de Rougemont, *op. cit.*, p. 93.
17. *Ibid.*, p. 33.
18. *Ibid.*, p. 38.
19. *Ibid.*, p. 195.
20. *Ibid.*, p. 212.
21. *Ibid.*, p. 292.
22. D. H. Lawrence, *Sons and Lovers*, p. 415.
23. Denis de Rougemont, *op. cit.*, p. 120.
24. *Ibid.*, p. 123.
25. John Middleton Murry, *Son of Woman: the Story of D. H. Lawrence*, p. 8.
26. *Ibid.*, p. 20.
27. R. P. Blackmur, *op. cit.*, pp. 114–116.
28. *The Letters of D. H. Lawrence* (ed. by Aldous Huxley), pp. 78–80.
29. Horace Gregory, *Pilgrim of the Apocalypse*, p. 37.
30. Denis de Rougemont, *op. cit.*, pp. 34–35.
31. *Ibid.*, p. 33.
32. John Middleton Murry, *Adam and Eve: an Essay toward a New and Better Society*, p. 89.
33. *Ibid.*, p. 95.
34. Denis de Rougemont, *op. cit.*, pp. 64–65.
35. *The Letters of D. H. Lawrence* (ed. by Aldous Huxley), p. 502.
36. D. H. Lawrence, *Reflections on the Death of a Porcupine*, p. 129.
37. "How can I equilibrate myself with my black cow Susan?" he asked in *Reflections on the Death of a Porcupine*. "There *is* a sort of relation between us. And this relation is part of the

mystery of love. . . . The queer cowy mystery of her is her changeless cowy desirableness."

38. Diana Trilling, *op. cit.*, p. 22.
39. W. E. Hocking, *Types of Philosophy*, p. 248.
40. John Middleton Murry, *Son of Woman: the Story of D. H. Lawrence*, p. 157.
41. John Middleton Murry, *Adam and Eve: an Essay toward a New and Better Society*, pp. 128–129.
42. *Ibid.*, p. 130.
43. John Middleton Murry, *Son of Woman*, p. 180.
44. *Ibid.*, p. 189.
45. *Ibid.*
46. *The Letters of D. H. Lawrence* (ed. by Aldous Huxley), p. 588. To Middleton Murry, October 25, 1923.
47. D. H. Lawrence, *Studies in Classic American Literature*, "Mobv Dick."
48. *Ibid.*
49. *Ibid.*, "Whitman."
50. *Ibid.*
51. *Ibid.*
52. *Ibid.*
53. William York Tindall, *op. cit.*, p. 144.
54. *The Letters of D. H. Lawrence* (ed. by Aldous Huxley), pp. 562–564.

T. S. ELIOT

1. John Hospers, *Meaning and Truth in the Arts*, Ch. VI.
2. D. G. James, *Scepticism and Poetry*, p. 63.
3. Ernst Cassirer, *An Essay on Man: an Introduction to a Philosophy of Human Culture*.
4. Irwin Edman, *Arts and the Man*, p. 32.
5. D. G. James, *op. cit.*, p. 46.
6. Irwin Edman, *op. cit.*, p. 37.
7. *Ibid.*, p. 36.
8. D. G. James, *op. cit.*, pp. 47–48.

9. Jacques Maritain, *True Humanism*, p. 2. *Vide* the whole of Ch. I on this subject.

10. D. S. Savage, *The Personal Principle: Studies in Modern Poetry*, p. 17.

11. Erich Fromm, *Escape from Freedom*, p. 40, footnote.

12. *Ibid.*, pp. 41–42.

13. Paul Tillich, "The World Situation," *The Christian Answer* (ed. by Henry P. Van Dusen), p. 10.

14. Quoted in Jacob Burckhardt's *The Civilization of the Renaissance in Italy*, pp. 215–216.

15. Paul Tillich, *op. cit.*, pp. 4–5.

16. *Ibid.*, p. 5.

17. Harry Slochower, *No Voice Is Wholly Lost*, p. xiii.

18. Herbert Read, *Art and Society*, p. 75.

19. *Ibid.*

20. D. S. Savage, *op. cit.*, p. 24.

21. William York Tindall, *D. H. Lawrence and Susan His Cow*, p. 199.

22. *Vide* the chapter entitled "Myths of Modern Poetry" in Wallace Fowlie's recent book, *Jacob's Night: The Religious Renascence in France*, for an illuminating discussion of this matter.

23. *Vide* Ludwig Lewisohn, "Introduction," *Expression in America*.

24. Martin Turnell, *Poetry and Crisis*, pp. 4–5.

25. *Ibid.*, p. 34.

26. Brother George Every, *Christian Discrimination*, p. 42.

27. *Ibid.*, pp. 42–43.

28. Martin Turnell, *op. cit.*, Ch. II.

29. Brother George Every makes this point very well in *Christian Discrimination*. *Vide* pp. 55–59.

30. Stanley Hopper, *The Crisis of Faith*, p. 126.

31. R. P. Blackmur, *The Double Agent: Essays in Craft and Elucidation*, p. 200.

32. Sister Mary James Power, *Poets at Prayer*, p. 126.

33. *Vide* Eliot's "Introduction" to the Everyman's Library edition of Pascal's *Pensées*.

34. Cleanth Brooks, *Modern Poetry and the Tradition*, p. 171.
35. *Vide* Mr. Blackmur's chapter on Eliot in *The Double Agent*, throughout the whole of which he hammers upon this central point.
36. Yvor Winters, "T. S. Eliot or the Illusion of Reaction," *In Defense of Reason*, p. 487.
37. Reinhold Niebuhr, *The Nature and Destiny of Man*, I, 279.
38. D. S. Savage, *op. cit.*, p. 92.
39. Stephen Spender, *The Destructive Element*, p. 146.
40. F. O. Matthiessen, *The Achievement of T. S. Eliot*, Ch. II: "The Problem for the Contemporary Artist."
41. Edmund Wilson counts, within the 403 lines of the poem, 35 quotations from, allusions to, or imitations of different writers, to say nothing of the passages drawn from or alluding to several popular songs and the six foreign languages, including Sanskrit, on whose literatures Eliot draws. *Vide* his *Axel's Castle*, p. 110.
42. Jessie L. Weston, *From Ritual to Romance*, p. 21.
43. T. S. Eliot, *Murder in the Cathedral*.
44. T. S. Eliot, *The Family Reunion*.
45. T. S. Eliot, *East Coker*.
46. Leonard Unger, "T. S. Eliot's Rose Garden: a Persistent Theme," *T. S. Eliot: A Selected Critique* (ed. by Leonard Unger).
47. Leonard Unger, *op. cit.*, p. 380.
48. Cleanth Brooks, *op. cit.*, p. 142.
49. Dante, *The Divine Comedy*, "Inferno," Canto III, 35–39. From the translation by Laurence Binyon.
50. Joseph D. Bennett, *Baudelaire: a Criticism*, p. 40.
51. T. S. Eliot, *Selected Essays: 1917–1932*, p. 344.
52. F. O. Matthiessen, *op. cit.*, p. 37.
53. Cleanth Brooks, *op. cit.*, pp. 145–146.
54. Malcolm Cowley, *Exile's Return*, p. 125.
55. Stephen Spender, *op. cit.*, pp. 145–146.
56. Derek Traversi, " 'The Waste Land' Revisited: a Critical Analysis of Mr. Eliot's Work," *The Dublin Review*, No. 443 (Second Quarter, 1948), p. 123.

57. T. S. Eliot, *The Love Song of J. Alfred Prufrock.*
58. T. S. Eliot, *The Hollow Men.*
59. Eric Bentley, "The Meaning of Robert Penn Warren's Novels," *The Kenyon Review*, X, No. 3 (Summer, 1948), 424.
60. Edmund Wilson, *op. cit.*, p. 106.
61. T. S. Eliot, *Choruses from "The Rock."*
62. T. E. Hulme, *Speculations*, pp. 70–71.
63. T. S. Eliot, *The Idea of a Christian Society*, pp. 4–5.
64. *Ibid.*, p. 59.
65. J. S. Whale, *Christian Doctrine*, p. 127.
66. F. O. Matthiessen, *op. cit.*, p. 11.
67. *Ibid.*, p. 178.
68. T. S. Eliot, "Lancelot Andrewes," *Selected Essays: 1917–1932*, pp. 298–299.
69. D. S. Savage, *op. cit.*, p. 94.
70. C. L. Barber, "Strange Gods at T. S. Eliot's 'Family Reunion', " *T. S. Eliot: a Selected Critique* (ed. by Leonard Unger), p. 422.
71. *Ibid.*, p. 424.
72. *Vide* Nathan A. Scott, Jr., "T. S. Eliot's *The Cocktail Party*: Of Redemption and Vocation," *Religion in Life*, XX, No. 2 (Spring, 1951), 274–285.
73. Louis L. Martz, "The Wheel and the Point: Aspects of Imagery and Theme in Eliot's Later Poetry," *T. S. Eliot: a Selected Critique* (ed. by Leonard Unger), p. 448.
74. *Ibid.*
75. *Ibid.*
76. Sören Kierkegaard, *The Sickness unto Death*, p. 216.
77. James Johnson Sweeney, "East Coker: a Reading," *The Southern Review*, Vol. VI, No. 4.
78. F. O. Matthiessen, *op. cit.*, p. 184.
79. Matthew Arnold, "Empedocles on Etna."
80. Reinhold Niebuhr, *Discerning the Signs of the Times*, p. 45.
81. "The Dry Salvages," Section V.
82. *Ibid.*
83. "Little Gidding," Section IV.

84. Robert W. Flint, "The Four Quartets Reconsidered," *The Sewanee Review*, LVI, No. 1 (1948), 69–81.

CONCLUSION

1. Albert Guerard, Jr., *Joseph Conrad*, p. 70.
2. Morton D. Zabel, "Joseph Conrad: Chance and Recognition," *The Sewanee Review*, LIII (Winter, 1945), 13.
3. Martin Buber, *Between Man and Man*, p. 177.
4. Giacomo Leopardi, "A se stesso."
5. Matthew Arnold, "To an Independent Preacher Who Preached That We Should be 'in Harmony with Nature.'"
6. Harry Slochower, *No Voice Is Wholly Lost*, p. 102.
7. *Ibid.*, p. 94. Quotation from Louis Ferdinand Céline.
8. W. H. Auden, "Editor's Introduction," *The Portable Greek Reader*, p. 20.
9. Wallace Fowlie, *Jacob's Night: the Religious Renascence in France*, pp. 73–74.
10. T. S. Eliot, *Murder in the Cathedral*, p. 69.
11. Edna St. Vincent Millay, *Conversation at Midnight*.
12. Jacques Maritain, *The Twilight of Civilization*, pp. 12–13.
13. From the *Handbook* to the lectures on logic. Quotation by Martin Buber, *Between Man and Man*, p. 119.
14. *Ibid.*
15. *Ibid.*, p. 163.
16. Paul Tillich, "Psychotherapy and a Christian Interpretation of Human Nature," *The Review of Religion*, XIII, No. 3, 265.
17. Reinhold Niebuhr, *Beyond Tragedy*, p. 168.
18. *Ibid.*
19. Paul Tillich, *op. cit.*, p. 265.
20. Amos Wilder, *The Spiritual Aspects of the New Poetry*, p. 226.

SELECTED BIBLIOGRAPHY

GENERAL

The works listed below were consulted because of their general significance for the study. Those whose scope is related to our subject-figures are again listed under the proper headings.

Berdyaev, Nicolas, The Bourgeois Mind. Trans. by Bennigsen and Attwater. New York: Sheed and Ward, 1934.

—— The End of Our Time. Trans. by D. Attwater. New York: Sheed and Ward, 1933.

—— The Fate of Man in the Modern World. Trans. by D. A. Lowrie. London: S. C. M. Press, 1935.

—— The Meaning of History. Trans. by G. Reavey. New York: Charles Scribner's Sons, 1936.

—— Solitude and Society. Trans. by G. Reavey. New York: Charles Scribner's Sons, 1938.

Blackmur, R. P., The Double Agent: Essays in Craft and Elucidation. New York: Arrow Editions, 1935.

Brooks, Cleanth, Modern Poetry and the Tradition. Chapel Hill: University of North Carolina Press, 1939.

Burckhardt, Jacob, The Civilization of the Renaissance in Italy. London: Phaidon Press Ltd., 1945.

Burgum, Edwin Berry, The Novel and the World's Dilemma. New York: Oxford University Press, 1947.

Cassirer, Ernst, An Essay on Man: an Introduction to a Philosophy of Human Culture. New Haven: Yale University Press, 1944.

Caudwell, Christopher, Illusion and Reality. New York: International Publishers, 1947.

Chaning-Pearce, M., The Terrible Crystal: Studies in Kierkegaard and Modern Christianity. New York: Oxford University Press, 1941.

Coleridge, Samuel Taylor, Biographia Literaria. London: J. M. Dent and Co., 1917.

Colum, Mary M., From These Roots: the Ideas That Have Made Modern Literature. New York: Columbia University Press, 1944.

Cowley, Malcolm, Exile's Return: a Narrative of Ideas. New York: W. W. Norton and Co., 1934.

Daiches, David, Poetry and the Modern World. Chicago: University of Chicago Press, 1944.

—— The Novel and the Modern World. Chicago: University of Chicago Press, 1939.

Dawson, Christopher, ed., Essays in Order. New York: The Macmillan Co., 1931.

Demant, V. A., The Religious Prospect. London: Frederick Muller Ltd., 1939.

Edman, Irwin, Arts and the Man. New York: W. W. Norton and Co., 1939.

Every, Brother George, Christian Discrimination. London: The Sheldon Press, 1940.

Fowlie, Wallace, Clowns and Angels: Studies in Modern French Literature. New York: Sheed and Ward, 1943.

—— Rimbaud. New York: New Directions, 1946.

—— Jacob's Night: the Religious Renascence in France. New York: Sheed and Ward, 1947.

Fox, Ralph, The Novel and the People. New York: International Publishers, 1937.

Fromm, Erich, Escape from Freedom. New York: Farrar and Rinehart, Inc., 1941.

Grierson, H. J. C., The Background of English Literature. London: Chatto, 1925.

Hebert, A. G., Liturgy and Society: the Function of the Church in the Modern World. London: Faber and Faber, 1942.

Hocking, W. E., Types of Philosophy. New York: Charles Scribner's Sons, 1939.

Hoffman, Frederick J., Freudianism and the Literary Mind. Baton Rouge: Louisiana State University Press, 1945.

Hopper, Stanley R., The Crisis of Faith. Nashville: Abingdon-Cokesbury Press, 1944.

Hospers, John, Meaning and Truth in the Arts. Chapel Hill: University of North Carolina Press, 1946.

Hulme, T. E., Speculations: Essays on Humanism and the Philosophy of Art. Ed. by Herbert Read. New York: Harcourt, Brace and Co., 1924.

Hyman, Stanley E., The Armed Vision: a Study in the Methods of Modern Literary Criticism. New York: Alfred A. Knopf, 1948.

James, D. G., Scepticism and Poetry. London: Allen and Unwin, 1937.

Kazin, Alfred, On Native Grounds: an Interpretation of Modern American Prose Literature. New York: Reynal and Hitchcock, 1942.

Leavis, F. R., New Bearings in English Poetry. London: Chatto and Windus, 1932.

Leavis, F. R., Mass Civilization and Minority Culture. Cambridge, England: Minority Press, 1930.

—— The Great Tradition. London: Chatto and Windus, 1950.

Leavis, Q. D., Fiction and the Reading Public. London: Chatto and Windus, 1932.

Lehmann, John, New Writing in Europe. London: Penguin Books, 1940.

Lewis, Wyndham, Men without Art. London: Cassell and Co. Ltd., 1934.

Lewisohn, Ludwig, Expression in America. New York: Harper and Brothers, 1932.

Mannheim, Karl, Ideology and Utopia: an Introduction to the Sociology of Knowledge. New York: Harcourt, Brace and Co., 1936.

Maritain, Jacques, True Humanism. Trans. by M. R. Adamson. London: Geoffrey Bles: The Centenary Press, 1938.

—— The Twilight of Civilization. Trans. by Lionel Landry. New York: Sheed and Ward, 1944.

—— Art and Scholasticism. New York: Charles Scribner's Sons, 1943.

Matthiessen, F. O., American Renaissance: Art and Expression in the Age of Emerson and Whitman. New York: Oxford University Press, 1941.

Mumford, Lewis, The Condition of Man. New York: Harcourt, Brace and Co., 1944.

Neff, Emery, A Revolution in European Poetry: 1660–1900. New York: Columbia University Press, 1940.

Nicholson, Norman, Man and Literature. London: S. C. M. Press, 1943.

Niebuhr, Reinhold, The Nature and Destiny of Man. 2 vols. New York: Charles Scribner's Sons, 1943.

O'Connor, William Van, Sense and Sensibility in Modern Poetry. Chicago: University of Chicago Press, 1948.

Power, Sister Mary James, Poets at Prayer. New York: Sheed and Ward, 1938.

Praz, Mario, The Romantic Agony. New York: Oxford University Press, 1933.

Ransom, John Crowe, The World's Body: Foundations for Literary Criticism. New York: Charles Scribner's Sons, 1938.

Read, Herbert, Reason and Romanticism. London: Faber and Faber, 1926.

—— Form in Modern Poetry. New York: Sheed and Ward, 1933.

—— Art and Society. London: Faber and Faber, 1945.

Reckitt, Maurice R., ed., Prospect for Christendom. London: Faber and Faber, 1945.

Roberts, Michael, The Modern Mind. London: Faber and Faber, 1937.

Savage, D. S., The Personal Principle: Studies in Modern Poetry. London: George Routledge and Sons Ltd., 1944.

Shapiro, Karl, Essay on Rime. New York: Reynal and Hitchcock, 1945.

Slochower, Harry, No Voice Is Wholly Lost: Writers and Thinkers in War and Peace. New York: Creative Age Press, Inc., 1945.

Spender, Stephen, The Destructive Element. Boston: Houghton Mifflin Co., 1936.

Tillich, Paul, The Interpretation of History. Trans. by N. A. Rasetzki and Elsa L. Talmey. New York: Charles Scribner's Sons, 1936.

—— The Religious Situation. Trans. by H. R. Niebuhr. New York: Henry Holt and Co., 1932.

—— The Protestant Era. Trans. by James Luther Adams. Chicago: University of Chicago Press, 1948.

Tindall, William York, Forces in Modern British Literature. New York: Alfred A. Knopf, 1947.

Trilling, Lionel, The Liberal Imagination: Essays on Literature and Society. New York: Viking Press, 1950.

Turnell, Martin, Poetry and Crisis. London: Sands, The Paladin Press, 1938.

Van Dusen, Henry P., ed., The Christian Answer. New York: Charles Scribner's Sons, 1945.

Wilder, Amos, The Spiritual Aspects of the New Poetry. New York: Harper and Brothers, 1940.

Wilson, Edmund, Axel's Castle: a Study in the Imaginative Literature of 1870–1930. New York: Charles Scribner's Sons, 1931.

—— The Wound and the Bow: Seven Studies in Literature. New York: Oxford University Press, 1947.

Winters, Yvor, in Defense of Reason. New York: The Swallow Press and W. Morrow and Co., 1947.

FRANZ KAFKA

I

Kafka, Franz, Gesammelte Schriften (6 vols). Ed. by Max Brod. Vols. I–IV (Erzählungen und kleine Prosa, Amerika, Der Prozess, and Das Schloss) published by Schocken Verlag, Berlin, 1935; Vols. V–VI (Beschreibung eines Kampfes; Tagebücher und Briefe) published by Verlag Heinrich Mercy Sohn, Prague, 1936.

—— Amerika. Trans. by Edwin Muir. New York: New Directions, 1946.

Kafka, Franz, The Castle. Trans. by Edwin and Willa Muir. New York: Alfred A. Knopf, 1945.
—— The Country Doctor. A Collection of Short Stories translated by Vera Leslie. Oxford: Counterpoint Publications, 1946.
—— The Diaries. 2 vols. New York: Schocken Books, 1948 and 1949.
—— The Great Wall of China: Stories and Reflections. New York: Schocken Books, 1946.
—— In the Penal Colony. New York: Schocken Books, 1948.
—— Metamorphosis. New York: Vanguard Press, Inc., 1946.
—— Parables. New York: Schocken Books, 1947.
—— The Trial. New York: Alfred A. Knopf, 1945.

II

Franz Kafka Miscellany, A. Ed. by Dorothy Norman. New York: Twice A Year Press, 1940.
The Quarterly Review of Literature, Vol. II, No. 3, 1945, "The Kafka Number," ed. by Angel Flores (guest editor).

III

Allen, Walter, "A Note on F. K.," Focus One (ed. by A. Pearse and B. Rajan). London: Dennis Dobson, 1945.
Auden, W. H., "K.'s Quest," The Kafka Problem (ed. by Angel Flores). New York: New Directions, 1946.
Belgion, Montgomery, "The Measure of K.," The Criterion, Vol. XVIII, No. 70 (October, 1938).
Brod, Max, Franz Kafka: a Biography. New York: Schocken Books, 1947.
Burgum, Edwin Berry, "K. and the Bankruptcy of Faith," Accent, Vol. III, No. 3 (Spring 1943).
Camus, Albert, "Hope and Absurdity," The Kafka Problem (ed. by Angel Flores). New York: New Directions, 1946.
Goodman, Paul, Kafka's Prayer. New York: Vanguard Press, Inc., 1947.
Hoffman, Frederick J., Freudianism and the Literary Mind ("Kafka

and Mann"). Baton Rouge: Louisiana State University Press, 1945.

Kelly, John, "F. K.'s *Trial* and the Theology of Crisis," *Southern Review*, Vol. V, No. 4 (Spring, 1940).

Lerner, Max, Ideas for the Ice Age ("F. K. and the Human Voyage"). New York: The Viking Press, 1941.

Magny, Claude-Edmonde, "The Objective Depiction of Absurdity," *Quarterly Review of Literature*, Vol. II, No. 3, (1945).

Neider, Charles, "The Cabalists," *The Kafka Problem* (ed. by Angel Flores). New York: New Directions, 1946.

—— The Frozen Sea: a Study of Franz Kafka. New York: Oxford University Press, 1948.

Nicholson, Norman, Man and Literature. London: Student Christian Movement Press, 1943.

Rahv, Philip, "The Hero as Lonely Man," *The Kenyon Review*, Vol. I, No. 1 (Winter, 1939).

—— "The Death of Ivan Ilyich and Joseph K.," *Southern Review*, Vol. V, No. 1 (Summer, 1939).

Raine, Kathleen, "A Note on K.," *Focus One* (ed. by A. Pearse and B. Rajan). London: Dennis Dobson, 1945.

Rajan, B., "K., a Comparison with Rex Warner," *Focus One* (ed. by A. Pearse and B. Rajan). London: Dennis Dobson, 1945.

Savage, D. S., "F. K.: Faith and Vocation," *Focus One* (ed. by A. Pearse and B. Rajan). London: Dennis Dobson, 1945.

Slochower, Harry, "F. K., Pre-Fascist Exile," *A Franz Kafka Miscellany*. New York: Twice A Year Press, 1940.

Spender, Stephen, The Destructive Element. Boston: Houghton, Mifflin and Co., 1936.

Symons, Julian, "A Comment," *Focus One* (ed. by A. Pearse and B. Rajan). London: Dennis Dobson, 1945.

Tauber, Herbert, Franz Kafka: an Interpretation of His Works. New Haven: Yale University Press, 1948.

Vivas, Eliseo, "Kafka's Distorted Mask," *The Kenyon Review*, Vol. X, No. 1 (Winter, 1948).

Warren, Austin, "Kosmos Kafka," *Southern Review*, Vol. VII, No. 2 (Autumn, 1941).

Wilson, Edmund, "A Dissenting Opinion on Kafka," *The New Yorker*, Vol. XXIII, No. 23 (July 26, 1947).
Winkler, R. O. C., "Significance of K.," *Scrutiny*, Vol. VII, No. 3 (December, 1938).
Woodcock, George, "K. and Rex Warner," *Focus One* (ed. by A. Pearse and B. Rajan). London: Dennis Dobson, 1945.

IV

The works listed below, though not concerned with Kafka, were found to bear upon either ideas with which he was preoccupied or critical issues arising in a consideration of his work.

Chaning-Pearce, M., The Terrible Crystal: Studies in Kierkegaard and Modern Christianity. New York: Oxford University Press, 1941.
Geismar, Eduard, Lectures on the Religious Thought of Sören Kierkegaard. Minneapolis: Augsburg Publishing House, 1938.
Kierkegaard, Sören, The Concept of Dread. Trans. by Walter Lowrie. Princeton: Princeton University Press, 1944.
—— Fear and Trembling. Trans. by Walter Lowrie. Princeton: Princeton University Press, 1941.
Read, Herbert, Form in Modern Poetry. New York: Sheed and Ward, 1933.
Swenson, David F., Something About Kierkegaard. Minneapolis: Augsburg Publishing House, 1941.

IGNAZIO SILONE

I

Silone, Ignazio, Fontamara. New York: Harrison Smith and Robert Haas, Inc., 1934.
—— Mr. Aristotle. New York: Robert M. McBride and Co., 1935.
—— Bread and Wine. New York: Harper and Brothers, 1937.
—— The School for Dictators. New York: Harper and Brothers, 1938.

—— The Seed beneath the Snow. New York: Harper and Brothers, 1942.
—— And He Hid Himself. New York: Harper and Brothers, 1946.
Silone, Ignazio, et al., The God That Failed: a Confession. Ed. by Richard Crossman. New York: Harper and Brothers, 1950.

II

Farrell, James T., "Ignazio Silone," The Southern Review, Vol. IV, No. 4 (Spring, 1939).
Rosenfeld, Isaac, "Silone's Spiritual Journey," The Nation, Vol. CLXII, No. 25 (June 22, 1946).
Slochower, Harry, No Voice Is Wholly Lost: Writers and Thinkers in War and Peace. New York: Creative Age Press, Inc., 1945.
Wilson, Edmund, "Two Survivors: Malraux and Silone," Horizon, Vol. XII, No. 70 (October, 1945).
Woodcock, George, "Ignazio Silone," Focus Two (ed. by B. Rajan and Andrew Pearse). London: Dennis Dobson, 1946.

III

The works listed below, though not concerned with Silone, were found to bear upon either ideas with which he is preoccupied or critical issues arising in a consideration of his work.

Bergson, Henri, The Two Sources of Morality and Religion. New York: Henry Holt and Co., 1935.
Caudwell, Christopher, Illusion and Reality. New York: International Publishers, 1948.
Colum, Mary, From These Roots: the Ideas That Have Made Modern Literature. New York: Columbia University Press, 1944.
Fox, Ralph, The Novel and the People. New York: International Publishers, 1937.
Hebert, A. G., Liturgy and Society. London: Faber and Faber Ltd., 1946.
Toynbee, Arnold, A Study of History (abridgment of Vols. I–VI by D. C. Somervell). New York: Oxford University Press, 1947.

D. H. LAWRENCE

I

Lawrence, D. H., Aaron's Rod. New York: Seltzer, 1922.
—— Apocalypse. New York: The Viking Press, 1932.
—— The Boy in the Bush. New York: Albert and Charles Boni, 1930.
—— Etruscan Places. New York: Viking Press, 1933.
—— Fantasia of the Unconscious. London: Secker, 1933.
—— Kangaroo. London: Heinemann, 1935.
—— Lady Chatterley's Lover. Florence: privately printed, 1928.
—— The Letters of D. H. Lawrence. Edited and with an Introduction by Aldous Huxley. New York: Viking Press, 1936.
—— Mornings in Mexico. New York: Alfred A. Knopf, 1934.
—— Phoenix, the Posthumous Papers of D. H. Lawrence. Edited and with an Introduction by Edward D. McDonald. New York: Viking Press, 1936.
—— The Plumed Serpent. London: Secker, 1932.
—— Psychoanalysis and the Unconscious. London: Secker, 1931.
—— The Rainbow. London: Methuen, 1915.
—— Reflections on the Death of a Porcupine. London: Secker, 1934.
—— Selected Poems. Edited and with an Introduction by Kenneth Rexroth. New York: New Directions, 1947.
—— Sons and Lovers. London: Duckworth, 1913.
—— Studies in Classic American Literature. New York: Seltzer, 1923.
—— The Tales of D. H. Lawrence. London: Secker, 1934.
—— The White Peacock. New York: Duffield, 1911.
—— Women in Love. New York: Seltzer, 1922.

II

Aldington, Richard, D. H. Lawrence: Portrait of a Genius But . . . New York: Duell, Sloan and Pearce, 1950.

Blackmur, R. P., The Double Agent: Essays in Craft and Elucidation. New York: Arrow Editions, 1935.

Bowen, Elizabeth, "D. H. Lawrence: Reappraising His Literary Influence," *The New York Times Book Review*, February 9, 1947.

Brett, Dorothy, Lawrence and Brett. Philadelphia: Lippincott, 1933.

Bynner, Witter, Journey with Genius. New York: Day, 1951.

Carswell, Catherine, The Savage Pilgrimage. New York: Harcourt, Brace and Co., 1932.

Eliot, T. S., After Strange Gods. New York: Harcourt, Brace and Co., 1934.

Fergusson, Francis, "D. H. Lawrence's Sensibility," *Hound and Horn*, Vol. VI, No. 3 (April–June 1933).

Gregory, Horace, Pilgrim of the Apocalypse. New York: Viking, Press, 1933.

Hoffman, Frederick J., Freudianism and the Literary Mind. Baton Rouge: Louisiana State University Press, 1945.

Lawrence, Ada, and G. Stuart Gelder, Early Life of D. H. Lawrence. London: Secker, 1932.

Lawrence, Frieda, Not I, but the Wind . . . New York: Viking Press, 1934.

Leavis, F. R., D. H. Lawrence. Cambridge, England: Minority Press, 1930.

Luhan, Mabel Dodge, Lorenzo in Taos. New York: Alfred A. Knopf, 1932.

Merrild, Knud, A Poet and Two Painters. London: Routledge, 1938.

Moore, Harry T., The Life and Works of D. H. Lawrence. New York: Twayne, 1951.

Murry, J. Middleton, Son of Woman. New York: Cape and Smith, 1931.

Reul, Paul de, L'Œuvre de D. H. Lawrence. Paris: Vrin, 1937.

Seillière, Ernest, David-Herbert Lawrence et les récentes idéologies allemandes. Paris: Boivin, 1936.

Spender, Stephen, The Destructive Element. London: Cape, 1935.

Swerdlow, Irwin, "Lawrence and the Myth." Unpublished Columbia University Master's Thesis, 1938.

T., E., D. H. Lawrence: a Personal Record. London: Cape, 1935.

Tindall, William York, D. H. Lawrence and Susan His Cow. New York: Columbia University Press, 1939.

Tiverton, Fr. William, D. H. Lawrence and Human Existence. Foreword by T. S. Eliot. London: Rockliffe, 1951.

Trilling, Diana, "Editor's Introduction," The Portable D. H. Lawrence. New York: Viking, 1947.

III

The works listed below, though not concerned with Lawrence, were found to bear upon either ideas with which he was preoccupied or critical issues arising in a consideration of his work.

D'Arcy, M. C., The Mind and Heart of Love. New York: Henry Holt and Co., 1947.

Grierson, H. J. C., The Background of English Literature. London: Chatto, 1925.

Murry, J. Middleton, Adam and Eve: an Essay toward a New and Better Society. London: Andrew Dakers Ltd., 1944.

Neff, Emery, A Revolution in European Poetry: 1660–1900. New York: Columbia University Press, 1940.

Praz, Mario, The Romantic Agony. New York: Oxford University Press, 1933.

Rougemont, Denis de, Love in the Western World. Trans. by Montgomery Belgion. New York: Harcourt, Brace and Co., 1940.

T. S. ELIOT

I

For what most nearly approaches an exhaustive check-list of Eliot's work the reader is referred to the appendix of the third number of the British monograph Focus (the Eliot number), which is cited below.

Eliot, T. S., Collected Poems: 1909–1935. New York: Harcourt, Brace and Co., 1935.

—— The Rock: a Pageant Play. New York: Harcourt, Brace and Co., 1934.

—— Murder in the Cathedral. New York: Harcourt, Brace and Co., 1935.

—— The Family Reunion. New York: Harcourt, Brace and Co., 1939.

—— Four Quartets. New York: Harcourt, Brace and Co., 1943.

—— The Cocktail Party. New York: Harcourt, Brace and Co., 1950.

—— Selected Essays: 1917–1932. New York: Harcourt, Brace and Co., 1932.

—— After Strange Gods: A Primer of Modern Heresy. New York: Harcourt, Brace and Co., 1934.

—— Essays Ancient and Modern. New York: Harcourt, Brace and Co., 1936.

—— The Idea of a Christian Society. New York: Harcourt, Brace and Co., 1940.

—— Notes towards the Definition of Culture. New York: Harcourt, Brace and Co., 1949.

—— Poetry and Drama. New York: Harcourt, Brace and Co., 1951.

II

Battenhouse, Roy W., "Eliot's 'The Family Reunion' as Christian Prophecy," Christendom, Vol. X, No. 3 (Summer, 1945).

Blackmur, R. P., The Double Agent: Essays in Craft and Elucidation. New York: Arrow Editions, 1935.

Blissett, William, "The Argument of T. S. Eliot's Four Quartets," University of Toronto Quarterly, Vol. XV, No. 2 (January, 1946).

Bradbrook, M. C., "Eliot's Critical Method," Focus Three: T. S. Eliot, a Study of His Writings by Several Hands (ed. by B. Rajan). London: Dennis Dobson, 1947.

Brooks, Cleanth, Modern Poetry and the Tradition. Chapel Hill: University of North Carolina Press, 1939.

Chaning-Pearce, M., "Little Gidding," The Nineteenth Century, Vol. CXXXIII, No. 792 (February, 1943).

Cowley, Malcolm, Exile's Return. New York: W. W. Norton and Co., 1934.

Daiches, David, Poetry and the Modern World. Chicago: University of Chicago Press, 1940.

Drew, Elizabeth A., T. S. Eliot: the Design of His Poetry. New York: Charles Scribner's Sons, 1949.

Flint, R. W., "The Four Quartets Reconsidered," The Sewanee Review, Vol. LVI, No. 1 (Winter, 1948).

Gardner, Helen L., "Four Quartets: a Commentary," Focus Three: T. S. Eliot, a Study of His Writings by Several Hands (ed. by B. Rajan). London: Dennis Dobson, 1947.

—— The Art of T. S. Eliot. London: Cresset Press, 1949.

Jones, E. E. Duncan, "Ash Wednesday," Focus Three: T. S. Eliot, a Study of His Writings by Several Hands (ed. by B. Rajan). London: Dennis Dobson, 1947.

Leavis, F. R., New Bearings in English Poetry. London: Chatto and Windus, 1932.

Martz, Louis L., "The Wheel and the Point: Aspects of Imagery and Theme in Eliot's Later Poetry," T. S. Eliot: a Selected Critique (ed. by Leonard Unger). New York: Rinehart and Co., 1948.

Matthiessen, F. O., The Achievement of T. S. Eliot: an Essay on the Nature of Poetry. Revised ed. New York: Oxford University Press, 1947.

Moore, Dom Sebastian, "East Coker: the Place and the Poem," Focus Two (ed. by B. Rajan and A. Pearse). London: Dennis Dobson, 1946.

Praz, Mario, "T. S. Eliot and Dante," The Southern Review, Vol. II, No. 3 (Winter, 1937).

Preston, Raymond, Four Quartets Rehearsed. New York: Sheed and Ward, 1946.

Savage, D. S., The Personal Principle. London: Routledge, 1944.

Schwartz, Delmore, "T. S. Eliot as the International Hero," *Partisan Review*, Vol. XII, No. 2 (Spring, 1945).

Scott, Nathan A., Jr., "T. S. Eliot's *The Cocktail Party*: Of Redemption and Vocation," *Religion in Life*, Vol. XX, No. 2 (Spring, 1951).

Spender, Stephen, The Destructive Element. New York: Houghton, Mifflin and Co., 1936.

Stephenson, E. M., T. S. Eliot and the Lay Reader. London: The Fortune Press, 1944.

Sweeney, James Johnson, "*East Coker*: a Reading," *The Southern Review*, Vol. VI, No. 4 (Spring, 1941).

Traversi, Derek, " 'The Waste Land' Revisited," *The Dublin Review*, No. 443 (Second Quarter, 1948).

Unger, Leonard, ed., T. S. Eliot: a Selected Critique. New York: Rinehart and Co., 1948.

—— "T. S. Eliot's Rose Garden: a Persistent Theme," *The Southern Review*, Vol. VII, No. 4 (Spring, 1942).

Wilder, Amos, The Spiritual Aspects of the New Poetry. New York: Harper and Brothers, 1940.

Williamson, H. Ross, The Poetry of T. S. Eliot. New York: Putnam's, 1933.

Wilson, Edmund, Axel's Castle. New York: Charles Scribner's Sons, 1931.

Winters, Yvor, In Defense of Reason. New York: The Swallow Press and W. Morrow and Co., 1947.

III

The works listed below, though not concerned with Eliot, were found to bear upon either ideas with which he is preoccupied or critical issues arising in a consideration of his work.

Bennett, Joseph, Baudelaire: a Criticism. Princeton: Princeton University Press, 1946.

Kierkegaard, Sören, The Sickness unto Death. Princeton: Princeton University Press, 1944.

Niebuhr, Reinhold, Discerning the Signs of the Times. New York: Charles Scribner's Sons, 1946.

Weston, Jessie L., From Ritual to Romance. Cambridge, England: The University Press, 1920.

Whale, J. S., Christian Doctrine. New York: The Macmillan Co., 1946.

CONCLUSION

Baillie, John, Our Knowledge of God. London: Oxford University Press, 1946.

Berdyaev, Nicolas, Solitude and Society. Trans. by G. Reavey. New York: Charles Scribner's Sons, 1938.

Buber, Martin, I and Thou. Trans. by Ronald Gregor Smith. Edinburgh: T. and T. Clark, 1942.

—— Between Man and Man. Trans. by Ronald Gregor Smith. New York: The Macmillan Co., 1948.

D'Arcy, M. C., The Mind and Heart of Love. New York: Henry Holt and Co., 1947.

Guerard, Albert, Jr., Joseph Conrad. New York: New Directions, 1947.

Hopper, Stanley R., The Crisis of Faith. Nashville: Abingdon-Cokesbury Press, 1944.

Kean, Charles Duell, The Meaning of Existence. New York: Harper and Brothers, 1947.

Nicodemus, Renascence: an Essay in Faith. London: Faber and Faber Ltd., 1943.

Tillich, Paul, The Protestant Era. Chicago: University of Chicago Press, 1948.

—— "Estrangement and Reconciliation in Modern Thought," The Review of Religion, Vol. IX, No. 1 (November, 1944).

Zabel, Morton Dauwen, "Joseph Conrad: Chance and Recognition," The Sewanee Review, Vol. LIII, No. 1 (Winter, 1945).

INDEX

Aldington, Richard, 113
Alexander, Samuel, 161
Amos, 244
Anderson, Sherwood, 7-8
Andrewes, Bishop Lancelot, 229
Andrews, Bishop C. F., 177
Aquinas, St. Thomas, 188
Arianism, 125
Aristotle, 110
Arnold, Matthew, 4, 9, 195, 248
Attic drama, 122
Aucassin et Nicolette, 122
Auden, W. H., 1, 6-7, 23, 175, 178, 200, 255; *The Age of Anxiety*, 1
Aufklärung, 122
Augustan age, 120-121
Augustine, St., 36, 74, 254; *Confessions*, 254
Augustus, reign of, 122
Austen, Jane, 67, 199

"B., Fräulein F.," 29
Balzac, Honoré de, 13, 68-69, 195
Barber, C. L., 230, 236-237
Barnes, Djuna, 1, 14; *Nightwood*, 1
Barth, Karl, 19, 244
Barzun, Jacques, 119
Baudelaire, Charles, 2, 4, 6, 13, 74, 177, 193-194, 200, 213-215, 261; *Les Fleurs du mal*, 204
Bennett, Arnold, 167
Berdyaev, Nicolas, 6, 186n
Bergson, Henri, 106, 177, 250
Berkeley, George, 67
Bernanos, Georges, 199
Blackmur, R. P., 115-117, 141, 201-202
Blake, William, 195
Blavatsky, Mme., 173
Boehme, Jacob, 44

Bogan, Louise, 11
Bohemianism, 5
Bowen, Elizabeth, 14, 70, 116
Brecht, Bertolt, 74
Brett, Dorothy, 114
Brod, Max, 16, 25-26, 28-29, 32, 36, 47, 51
Brooks, Cleanth, 202, 216-217
Brunetière, Ferdinand, 121
Brunner, Emil, 19, 244
Buber, Martin, 246-247
Buddhism, 63
Bukharin, Nicolai, 77
Burgum, Edwin Berry, 18-19

Caldwell, Erskine, 70, 73
Camus, Albert, 6, 43, 62
Carroll, Lewis, *Alice in Wonderland*, 233
Carswell, Catherine, 114
Cartesian dualism, 191
Cassirer, Ernst, 181
Catharism, 124-125, 128-129
Cavalcanti, Guido, 112
Cervantes, Miguel de, 191
Chaplin, Charles, 258
Chaucer, Geoffrey, 186
Chirico, Giorgio de, 258
Cicero, 122
Claudel, Paul, 199
Clement of Alexandria, 244
Cocteau, Jean, 177, 258
Coleridge, Samuel Taylor, 178, 183, 184; *Biographia Literaria*, 183
Conrad, Joseph, 6, 247
Cooper, James Fenimore, 168
Corbière, Tristan, 204
Corbusier, Le, 258
Cowley, Malcolm, 218
Crabbe, George, 198-199

Crane, Hart, 75, 194, 222
Crane, Stephen, 69
Crèvecœur, Hector St. John de, 168
Crisis-theology, 19
Croce, Benedetto, 42, 119; History as the Story of Liberty, 42
Crossman, Richard, 111n

Dana, Richard Henry, 168
Dante Alighieri, 74, 112, 129, 210, 213, 218, 228, 252; The Divine Comedy, 204
D'Arcy, Fr. M. C., 124
Darwin, Charles, 135
Defoe, Daniel, 67
Demant, V. A., 6
Dewey, John, 7
Dickens, Charles, 67-68, 199
Dionysius the Areopagite, 244
Dos Passos, John, 2, 70
Dostoyevsky, Fyodor, 74
Dreiser, Theodore, 69
Dryden, John, 121-122

Eastern mysticism, 123
Eckhart, Meister, 235
Edman, Irwin, 184
Eliot, George, 199
Eliot, T. S., 3, 7, 9-10, 13, 23, 117, 119, 135-136, 178-245, 247-248, 252-260, 261; After Strange Gods, 135; Ash Wednesday, 3, 203-204, 227-229, 236, 245; Burnt Norton, 207-208, 228, 239; The Cocktail Party, 3, 230; Dans le restaurant, 211; East Coker, 210, 237-241; The Family Reunion, 78, 207-208, 227, 230-238, 253; Four Quartets, 227, 229, 236-237, 244; The Hollow Men, 3, 203, 227; The Love Song of J. Alfred Prufrock, 3, 211; Murder in the Cathedral, 209, 226, 237, 253-254; Portrait of a Lady, 211; The Waste Land, 203-225, 227, 232

Elizabethan England, 5
Elyot, Sir Thomas, 239
Euripides, 122
Every, Brother George, 198-199
Existentialism, Theological, 19

Fairchild, Hoxie Neale, 119
Farrell, James T., 70, 73
Faulkner, William, 2
Fielding, Henry, 67
Fitzgerald, F. Scott, 222
Flaubert, Gustave, 51, 63, 68-69, 195
Flint, Robert W., 244
Flores, Angel, 197
Forster, E. M., 11, 117
Fowlie, Wallace, 252, 256
Francis of Assisi, St., 188-189
Franklin, Benjamin, 168
Frazer, Sir James, 135, 204, 213, 219; The Golden Bough, 204
Freud, Sigmund, 2, 34, 161-162, 168
Freudian account of religious belief, 34
Fromm, Erich, 187

Galsworthy, John, 167
Garnett, Edward, 141
Gascoyne, David, 66
Gide, André, 6, 176, 194; Corydon, 176; L'Immoraliste, 176
Giotto, 188-189
Gnosticism, 123-124, 129
God That Failed, The, 111n
Goethe, Johann Wolfgang von, 112, 195
Gogol, Nikolai, 68
Goodman, Paul, 15-17, 23, 25; Kafka's Prayer, 15
Gottfried of Strasbourg, 112
Greek tragedians, 5
Green, Henry, 14
Greene, Graham, 1, 14, 23, 63, 200; Brighton Rock, 1
Gregory, Horace, 112-114, 149, 175

Grierson, Sir Herbert, 119-122
Guerard, Jr., Albert, 247

Haeckel, Ernst, 135
Harrison, Jane, 135
Hawthorne, Nathaniel, 168, 197;
  The Blithedale Romance, 168
Hecht, Ben, 176
Hegel, Georg Wilhelm Friedrich,
  10, 135
Hemingway, Ernest, 2, 72-73
Hocking, William Ernest, 10, 160
Homer, 206
Hopkins, Gerard Manley, 200
Horace, 122
Hospers, John, 180
Hügel, Friedrich, Baron von, 177
Hugo, Victor, 4
Hulme, T. E., 119, 196, 226
Huxley, Aldous, 175
Huxley, Thomas H., 135

Idealism, 160; absolute, 10
Isaiah, 244
Isherwood, Christopher, 72

James, D. G., 180, 184
James, Henry, 5-7, 22, 197
James, William, 135
Jeffers, Robinson, 261
Jeremiah, 244
John of the Cross, St., 129, 210,
  228, 230, 236-237, 242, 244; The
  Ascent of Mt. Carmel, 228; The
  Obscure Night, 228
Johnson, Samuel, 121
Johnson, Willard, 176
Jonson, Ben, 5
Joyce, James, 11, 14, 22, 70, 74, 135,
  184, 194, 196, 205-206; Finne-
  gans Wake, 184; Ulysses, 205

Kafka, Franz, 1-3, 5-6, 10-65, 70,
  179-181, 196-197, 247-248, 251-
  252, 254-260; Amerika, 64-65;
  Aphorisms, 17; "Blumfeld," 64;

"The Burrow," 17, 64; The
  Castle, 1, 47-56, 62-64, 251; "The
  Great Wall of China," 64; "The
  Hunger Artist," 64; "Investiga-
  tions of a Dog," 43-44, 64; "The
  Judgment," 35-36, 39-42, 64;
  Letter to My Father, 25, 28;
  "The Married Couple," 28;
  Meditations, 25; Metamorphosis,
  37-39, 64; "Notes from the Year
  1920," 20; "The Penal Colony,"
  64; The Trial, 56-64
Kafka, George, 26
Kafka, Heinrich, 26
Kafka, Hermann, 26-27, 35
Kafka, Julie Löwy, 26-27
Kazin, Alfred, 70
Kant, Immanuel, 182, 257-258
Kardiner, Abram, 180
Keats, John, 153, 197
Kelly, John, 19
Kierkegaard, Michael, 31
Kierkegaard, Sören, 1-2, 7, 19, 23,
  31-32, 36, 45-47, 53, 237, 241,
  244, 252; Fear and Trembling,
  45, 47
Klein, Melanie, 16-17
Kleist, Heinrich von, 131
Koestler, Arthur, 72

Laforgue, Jules, 204
Lamartine, Alphonse Marie Louis
  de, 193
Lancelot and Guinevere, 122
Lawrence, D. H., 3, 5, 10, 88, 112-
  177, 179-181, 196, 220, 247-252,
  254-260; Aaron's Rod, 158, 164-
  167; Apocalypse, 176-177; Fantasia of the Unconscious, 156,
  158, 160, 162-164; Kangaroo,
  158; Lady Chatterley's Lover,
  140, 158, 175-176; The Lost Girl,
  158; The Man Who Died, 176;
  Mornings in Mexico, 174; The
  Plumed Serpent, 158, 173-175;
  Psychoanalysis and the Uncon-

Lawrence, D. H. (Continued)
scious, 154, 158, 160-162; The
Rainbow, 143-149, 154-155, 156-
157; St. Mawr, 174; Sons and
Lovers, 114, 133, 137-141, 158,
163; Studies in Classic American
Literature, 168-173; The Tres-
passer, 141; Twilight in Italy,
152; The White Peacock, 140-
141; The Woman Who Rode
Away, 174; Women in Love, 143,
156-160, 164
Lawrence, Frieda, 114
Leavis, F. R., 112, 114, 115n, 175,
186n
Leconte de Lisle, 4
Leopardi, Giacomo, 4, 194, 248
Lerner, Max, 21
Lewis, Sinclair, 5
Lewis, Wyndham, 119
Lewisohn, Ludwig, 195
Liberalism, 2
Lindsay, Vachel, 169
Locke, John, 182
Louis XIV, age of, 122
Lowell, Robert, 200
Lucretius, 112
Luhan, Mabel Dodge, 114

Mailer, Norman, 70
Mallarmé, Stéphane, 3, 193, 204
Malraux, André, 2, 72-73, 77-78, 88,
100, 181
Manicheism, 123
Mann, Klaus, 65
Mann, Thomas, 7, 27; Budden-
brooks, 27; Death in Venice, 27;
Tonio Kröger, 7, 27
Maritain, Jacques, 252, 256,
258
Marquand, John P., 70
Martz, Louis L., 233
Maspero, Gaston, 135
Matthiessen, F. O., 9, 88, 205, 216,
218, 239
Mauriac, François, 63, 200

Melville, Herman, 168, 249; Moby
Dick, 168-169; Pierre, 249
Middle Ages, 185-188
Mies van der Rohe, Ludwig, 258
Mill, John Stuart, 135
Millay, Edna St. Vincent, 254
Miller, Henry, 175
Milton, John, 198
Molière, 130, 196
Moore, Harry T., 115n
Mozart, Wolfgang Amadeus, 130
Muilenburg, James, 244
Murray, Gilbert, 135
Murry, John Middleton, 112, 114,
119, 136, 140, 148, 152, 164,
171, 175; Adam and Eve: an
Essay towards a New and Better
Society, 152; Son of Woman, 114
Mysticism, 62-63

Nationalisation de la littérature, La,
121
Naturalism, 14, 69-70
Neff, Emery, 118
Neider, Charles, 18, 22
Niebuhr, Reinhold, 6, 241, 244
Nietzsche, Friedrich Wilhelm, 7,
124, 177
Norris, Frank, 69
Novalis, 155

O'Hara, John, 70
Origen, 24
Orwell, George, 2, 72
Owen, Wilfred, 222

Pascal, Blaise, 2, 36, 201
Paul, St., 122, 203, 252
Péguy, Charles, 177, 199
Pericles, age of, 5, 122
Petrarch, 130
Picasso, Pablo, 177, 184, 258; Guer-
nica, 184
Plato, 122
Plotinus, 63, 244
Poe, Edgar Allan, 1, 4, 168

Pope, Alexander, 121, 198
Porphyry, 236
Pound, Ezra, 176; *Draft of XXX Cantos*, 176
Power, Sister Mary James, 201
Praz, Mario, 119
Priscillianism, 124
Protestantism, 190, 195
Proust, Marcel, 3, 11, 14, 22, 70, 196
Provençal poetry, 125

Racine, Jean Baptiste, 196
Rahv, Philip, 22, 37-38, 44
Read, Herbert, 32-34, 119, 191-192; *Form in Modern Poetry*, 32
Realism, 68
Rembrandt van Rijn, 188-189, 191-192
Renaissance, 6, 185-191
Reul, Paul de, 114
Revolutionary novel, 72
Richards, I. A., 196
Richardson, Samuel, 67
Rilke, Rainer Maria, 3, 235, 241
Rimbaud, Arthur, 4, 7, 112, 155, 176, 194; *Une Saison en Enfer*, 176
Rivière, Jacques, 196
Romanticism, 118-133, 192-194
Rouault, Georges, 177, 252, 256, 258
Rougemont, Denis de, 122-136, 154-155, 171, 193
Rousseau, Jean-Jacques, 67, 105, 130, 135; *La Nouvelle Héloïse*, 130
Royce, Josiah, 10
Russell, Bertrand, Lord, 221

Sabine, George, 7
Sansom, William, 14, 70
Santayana, George, 112
Sartre, Jean-Paul, 1-2, 177, 258; *No Exit*, 1

Savage, D. S., 53, 68, 115, 117, 120, 186, 193
Schoenberg, Arnold, 184, 258; *Pierrot Lunaire*, 184
Schweitzer, Albert, 177
Scott, Sir Walter, 4, 67
Secker, Martin, 155
Seillière, Ernest, 114
Shakespeare, William, 5, 153, 186; *Antony and Cleopatra*, 204; *The Tempest*, 204
Shelley, Percy Bysshe, 193, 195-196
Silone, Ignazio, 2-3, 10, 66-111, 179-181, 196-197, 220, 247-251, 254-260; *And He Hid Himself*, 89, 97, 107-110; *Bread and Wine*, 78-79, 88-99, 104, 110; *Fontamara*, 80-88; *Mr. Aristotle*, 111n; *The School for Dictators*, 111n; *The Seed beneath the Snow*, 88-89, 97, 99-107
Slochower, Harry, 2, 18, 93, 249
Smollett, Tobias George, 67
Socrates, 74
Sorokin, Pitirim, 180
Spencer, Herbert, 135
Spender, Stephen, 22, 204, 219; *The Destructive Element*, 22
Spengler, Oswald, 2
Stein, Gertrude, 14, 222
Steinbeck, John, 73
Sterne, Laurence, 67
Stirner, Max, 10
Stravinsky, Igor, 258
Sweeney, James Johnson, 238-239
Symbolism, 14
Symbolists, 4
Symons, Julian, 22

"T., E.," 114
Taine, Hippolyte Adolphe, 69
Tauber, Herbert, 16, 35, 41, 55
Tennyson, Alfred, Lord, 4, 132
Teresa, St., 129, 228
Thackeray, William, 67
Thompson, Francis, 217

Tieck, Johann Ludwig, 131
Tillich, Paul, 78n, 188, 190, 211n, 260
Tindall, William York, 112, 114, 118, 135, 194; *D. H. Lawrence and Susan His Cow*, 114
Tiutchev, 6
Tiverton, Fr. William, 115n
Tolstoy, Count Leo, 195
Toynbee, Arnold, 102, 106
Trilling, Diana, 116, 134, 175
Trilling, Lionel, 11, 87
Tristan and Iseult, 122, 125-128, 132, 150
Turnell, Martin, 198, 200
Tylor, Edward, 135

Underhill, Evelyn, 177
Unger, Leonard, 211-212
Upanishads, The, 204

Valéry, Paul, 5
Vigny, Alfred Victor, comte de, 4-5, 193-194
Villa, José García, 176
Virgil, 74, 122

Wagner, Richard, 131, 212; *Götter-dämmerung*, 204; *Tristan und Isolde*, 131

Warner, Rex, 2, 72
Warren, Robert Penn, 2, 14
Webster, John, 216-217
Wells, H. G., 167
Weston, Jessie, 204, 206, 212, 218, 228; *From Ritual to Romance*, 204, 206
Whale, J. S., 227
Wheelwright, Philip, 19n
Whistler, James Abbott McNeill, 195
Whitman, Walt, 168-173; *Cala-mus*, 171; *Children of Adam*, 169
Wilder, Amos, 261
Williams, Gharles, 199
Wilson, Edmund, 4, 14, 32-34, 67
Winters, Yvor, 202-203
Wolfe, Thomas, 1, 3
Woolf, Virginia, 70, 117
Wordsworth, William, 71, 135, 193, 195, 198
Wright, Richard, 70

Yeats, William Butler, 2, 4, 117, 195, 261

Zola, Émile, 68-69

Dat